Dedicated to My Wife

Frances

and our children

Elizabeth

Lee

David

TABLE OF CONTENTS

ANTON CHEKHOV

THE ICONOCLAST

LEE J. WILLIAMES

University of Scranton Press

PREFACE

This author would like to thank those who made this work possible through their assistance.

My appreciation is extended to those institutions that supported my work: the Ford Foundation, College Misericordia and the University of Scranton.

I acknowledge my debt to those who read and commented on this work as it progressed: Dr. Sidney Harcave, Dr. Louis Maganzin, and those who commented on portions of my work at the Middle Atlantic Historical Association of Catholic Colleges and Universities annual conferences in the 1970's and 1980's, especially Dr. Richard Stites. Thanks are extended to Dr. Daniel Field whose comments were very helpful at the beginning of my research.

Also of note is the important contribution of those who helped me prepare this manuscript: Mrs. Ellie Piltz, Mrs. Marsha Daly, and Mrs. Terri Proctor. My gratitude is extended to Dr. Richard Passon for his unique and ongoing support.

Finally, I recognize the support of Helen and Lee W. Williames as well as Rev. William T. Sweeney, CM.

INTRODUCTION

This author views Anton Chekhov as a change agent and iconoclast in a manner similar to Zola and Darwin. This is a view which stands as a revision to many popularly held views of Chekhov. This study will show that Chekhov was deeply influenced by the scientific method, that he was objective in his representations and that he carefully chose what he wrote about. It was his intention to explode stereotypes by clearly and objectively stating the problems of Russian society in his stories. He felt that his readers would be moved to accomplish change through individual initiative if they saw clearly what the problems were in Russia.

The effects of Chekhov's work can be seen in the myths and stereotypes that he destroyed. In 1897 Anton Chekhov exploded the century old myth of the Russian peasant and clearly stated the peasant question with the publication of his "The Peasants." This provoked immediate government censorship but it and his other stories helped open the eyes of the literate Russian public to the reality of the lives of the non-literate Russians in the decade prior to the 1905 revolution.

To demonstrate the above points, this study will present first an intellectual biography of Chekhov and then examine the objectivity and validity of his views on Russian society. This will be accomplished through a thorough presentation of Chekhov's views on the Peasants, their living conditions, how they related to others, what forces affected them indirectly and present a profile of the other key elements in Russian society. Chekhov's views will be juxtaposed with scholarly opinion to determine the truth of his views. The author draws from the primary sources of Chekhov's thought, his letters and his stories. His stories have been favored in this study because they clearly present Chekhov's views, they have a far broader scope than his plays and are unencumbered by the demands of staging. This study also draws from those primary critical sources of his thought, the studies of Chekhov by his contemporaries and later critics.

In the course of the study certain controversial points will be established. First, that Chekhov's image has been distorted over the years to meet the needs of ideologically motivated critics. These distortions demand a revisionist's correction which this study provides. Second, that the mature Chekhov was intellectually formed by two forces, his education in the sciences and his literary experience. Out of these two influences and his love for freedom he formed a unique method and philosophy of his art. Third, that his personal philosophy was such that he could best be described as a humanist and a liberal thinker with views similar to J. S. Mill or, in Russia, to the Zemstvo Liberals. Fourth, he believed that he could contribute to the reform of Russia by destroying lies and stereotypes through writing objectively and truthfully about the problems of Russia. In relation to these issues Chekhov had a unique perspective because he was born a Raznochintsy, a classless one. Fifth, that one of Chekhov's great contributions was his opening of the lives of the 'dark people' to the eyes of literate Russia. Also, that Chekhov was consciously an iconoclast but not an idealogue. Sixth, the question will be raised as to whether Chekhov was telling the truth. Were Chekhov's thoughts and perceptions of the reality of life in lower class society really correct?

A Brief Biographical Sketch of Anton Pavlovich Chekhov

Before beginning a study of the formation of Chekhov's thought and a critical examination of his perceptions it is appropriate to briefly review what are commonly understood as significant points in his life. Anton Chekhov, physician and author, lived a short but fascinating and productive life. During the course of his 44 years he practiced medicine, traveled the breadth of Russia, and wrote almost 500 stories and plays about his beloved Russia. These tales and plays have received worldwide acclaim over this past century.

In 1860 Anton Pavlovich was born a raznochinitz, a 'classless one', the son of a former serf. He was born in Tagonrog, a city on the Sea of Azov, where his unsuccessful father owned a grocery store. Here he experienced a repressive childhood as part of Russian traditional society.

The Chekhov family moved to Moscow in 1876 when Chekhov's father went bankrupt. Anton remained in Tagonrog to complete his education. He supported himself by working as a tutor. It was a time of poverty for both him and his family. Throughout this period he was learning the essence of life for the lower classes.

He was able to join his family in Moscow in 1879. They lived in a flat in the St. Nicholas district, a red light area. It was here that Chekhov entered Medical School. In order to support himself and his family he became a writer. He wrote stories primarily for humor magazines. These stories were rough hewn, funny, and good enough to permit him to gain entry into the more lucrative and better known journals in St. Petersburg. Chekhov's environment provided a rich source of material for his stories. His scientific education provided intellectual discipline that affected his writing and permitted it to became more carefully constructed and accurate. He was also beginning to reveal a real talent for sensitive and accurate characterization.

Chekhov graduated from Medical school in 1884 but continued to write both for the money and because he enjoyed it. Chekhov also practiced medicine off and on in the period from 1884 through into the mid-1890's among the poor and peasants, predominantly in the country south of Moscow. This provided serious grist for his literary mill. He clearly saw the humor in human circumstances but also clearly characterized the problems he saw around him. What emerged were well-written, new, humorous, tragic and satirical stories. These tales rang true to the readers and made Chekhov popular quickly, especially among the ordinary people. At the same time he was becoming a more serious writer, even dropping his pseudonym.

The second half of the 1880's saw Chekhov the maturing artist fix his method, as he described it to his brother Alexandr in May 1886. He indicated that his work should have: "an absence of lengthy verbiage of a political, social, or economic nature; total objectivity; truthful description of persons and objects; extreme brevity; audacity and originality: avoiding stereotypes; and compassion." Chekhov's more professional approach to writing brought him to the attention of Alexander Suvorin, editor of the conservative newspaper *New Times* (Novoye Vremya). Suvorin would become his close friend and periodic publisher.

It was in this more professional frame of mind, with his method crystallized, that Chekhov wrote "The Steppe" in 1888. Chekhov himself refers to it as an "encyclopedia of the steppe." It is the story of a boy's journey on the steppe. In this account Chekhov discusses every aspect of life and the environment there. As a confirmation and recognition of the maturity, excellence and originality of his work Chekhov was awarded the Pushkin Prize in 1888 from the Academy of Arts and Sciences.

The Pushkin Prize brought him to the attention of Tolstoi and others. He was recognized as a rising young star, who for a time fell under the influence of Tolstoi. However, his sense of concern and compassion drew him away from Tolstoi and his doctrine of non-resistance to evil.

This same drive coupled with his desire to complete a dissertation so that he might teach in medical school led him to make his famous journey to Sakhalin Island. Chekhov was strongly influenced by Darwin and hoped to do an objective study of the penal colony on Sakhalin and of the effect of the colony on the Islanders. Thus he hoped to generate his dissertation out of his journey as Darwin had done in earning his Masters degree. His work *The Island of Sakhalin* was an excellent ethnographic study but it was not accepted as a medical dissertation because it was so heavily sociological. During his journey he traveled the breadth of Russia and returned home by circumnavigating Asia. He returned having been exposed to the freedom of Siberian society, the wretchedness of Sakhalin, and to the contrasts of Japanese, Indian and Chinese cultures.

In the early 1890's Chekhov's stories focused even more on profiling concerns he had about the society by accurately recording reality. He became

iv

deeply involved in the famine relief effort during 1892-93 in Russia. He committed all his energy and financial resources to the effort. This was a clear example of Chekhov's belief that individual action could solve the problems facing Russia. He completed the effort physically and financially exhausted. He was frustrated with government inaction, ineptitude and ignorance. In spite of this he was pleased by the efforts of individuals from many classes to solve common problems.

Rising out of these feelings of frustration and hope was the drive which produced *The Peasants* in 1897. This was a work which provoked an immediate public and governmental reaction. Chekhov at this point clearly wanted his work to alter the consciousness of society as the work of Darwin and Zola had in different contexts. He wanted to move Russians to take individual action to solve Russia's problems. Chekhov was positive, hopeful, enthusiastic and critical as he smashed the false images which the Russian literate society had of itself and others. Aside from being a successful short story writer Chekhov was also a playwright. Chekhov's greatest plays where written during the period from 1896 to 1904. His plays *The Sea Gull, Uncle Vanya, The Three Sisters*, and *The Cherry Orchard* thrust him onto center stage (where he affected the theater) in Russia and Europe. He was an immense success as a playwright. The Moscow Art Theater played a role in Chekhov's initial theatrical success. Through the stage he met and married the actress Olga Knipper in 1901.

Ironically, just as he was thrust to the forefront of 'intelligent' society he had a health crisis. Chekhov had lived with the fear of tuberculosis throughout his adult life. In 1897 he had a convulsive hemorrhage and was diagnosed as having advanced tuberculosis. He would spend much of the remainder of his life writing in the warm climates of southern Russia and Europe. He died of tuberculosis in 1904 on the eve of the 1905 Revolution.

The Image of Chekhov

The image of Chekhov has been distorted repeatedly over the decades by commentators for political reasons. Chekhov's contemporaries were perhaps the worst commentators and their legacy has clouded the vision of subsequent generations down to today. Chekhov was not treated kindly by the utilitarian critics of his time. The critics warped his image as revenge for what they felt was his lack of involvement in the social struggle of the age because he would not write blatantly political tracts. The Populists looked at him as a mindless young giant who strolled through life picking what he wrote about without regard to the issues of the time. Some of them actively tried to destroy his career. The Reductionists, on the other hand, reduced Chekhov to being the poet of a dying order when in actuality he was quite critical of the "old order" in Russia. The Soviets, for their part, molded him to their own purposes into a pre-Marxist progressive who would have supported the revolution. However, it should be noted that some of the best criticism of Chekhov is from Soviet writers, despite the political limitations placed on them. These warped images of Chekhov all demand a corrective which this study will provide.

How could Chekhov through his stories have had such an explosive effect on society and warrant the title Iconoclast?

Daniel Field, in his work *Rebels in the Name of the Tsar*, asserts that Russian writers were part of the intelligentsia and, as such, had only a warped and abstract conception of peasant life. Abstracted from the reality of Russian life, they created an idealization of peasant life that had no relationship to reality.

Professor Field sees a cultural distinction between the *narod*, "the peasantry," and the *obschestvo*, "the educated society." He feels the cultural distinctions were so great that a vast social void separated the two classes making communication between them impossible. In essence they could not understand each other. Between the extremes of peasant and intellectual, there were only a few elements of the population that were traditionalist in their way of life but removed from the narod: the merchant estate, the parish clergy, and some petty squires. These groups were politically and intellectually passive and, while they might be literate, literacy was simply an attribute of caste and profession. They did not link the "educated society" and the "peasantry" nor report upon them for our benefit.[1]

Field believes the problem of using perceptions from across the gulf is further compounded by the fact that the upper class literate people held a kind of Rousseauian myth of the peasant. He believes this problem confounds historians even today.[2]

This author maintains that the writings of Anton Chekhov are and were an effective bridge for the gaps Field perceives. Chekhov's unique background, experience, and training permitted him to bridge the gap through his stories and explode the myths held by literate Russia about non-literate Russia. His work was and is still an accurate source of information on lower class Russia. Most interestingly his work is a source of lower class attitudes.

Although some scholars have serious reservations about the use of literature as a true reflection of objective reality, the Soviets have used Chekhov as a realistic representation of conditions. However they do maintain he had a limited political consciousness because he was not a Marxist.

Ernest Simmons in his *Through the Glass of Soviet Literature: Views of Russian Society*, states that " ... the emergence of nineteenth century realism and naturalism in literature placed great emphasis upon factual representation of life." Alluding to examples in European literature he observes that ". . . a student of Russian life of the last two decades of the nineteenth century would find that a study of the tales and plays of Chekhov would supplement historical and social material and statistical data."[3] Simmons notes, the writer has ". . . a wealth of human experience . . . at his beck and call, shaped by the powers of his imagination

vi

in the work of art but disciplined in it by artistic principles of organization and by physical and social environment."[4]

The usefulness of literature to the observer as an accurate reflection of reality is to a large degree determined by what a literary work's author believes truth is and how he believes he must express it. In addition, the amount of information about a society which the author has also affects the value of his work as a potential source of information.[5]

Any study of Chekhov as an objective observer and iconoclast must focus on Chekhov's intellectual development, his method, philosophy, experience, and finally the truth of what he presented. This then provides the outline of the following study.

NOTES

[1] Daniel Field, *Rebels in the Name of the Tsar* (Boston: Houghton Mifflin Company, 1976), p. 4.

[2] *Ibid.*, p. 213.

[3] Ernest Simmons, ed., *Through the Glass of Soviet Literature: Views of Russian Society*, p. 18.

[4] *Ibid.*, p. 18.

[5] *Ibid.*, p. 20.

CHAPTER I

INFLUENCES

*"Medicine is my lawful wife
and literature is my mistress"
and for both
"I choose freedom"*

Anton Chekhov

To provide a clear direction for the first half of this study this author has inferred from Professor Simmons' work, quoted in the introduction, that the key factors in evaluating Chekhov and his work are: the influences that affected Chekhov in developing his world view and method; Chekhov's method itself; Chekhov's exposure to society directly and indirectly; and his personal philosophy. These then are key indicators in evaluating Chekhov's development and credentials as an objective observer.[1]

In uncovering the mind of the mature Chekhov we will look at the influences which formed his world view and artistic method. Chekhov called medicine his lawful wife and literature his mistress. Both disciplines influenced his method, and in turn, both disciplines were enhanced and influenced by his belief in intellectual freedom.

Chekhov probably became interested in medicine as the result of a serious attack of peritonitis he suffered while on a swimming excursion as a youth. He was forced to stay at a wayside tavern, where the Jewish tavern keeper and his wife nursed him. His mother came for him the next day and placed him under the care of a Dr. Schrempf, the school physician.

Chekhov's respect for the conversations with the doctor were probably the first step on the way to a career in medicine.[2] It might also be suggested that the compassion shown him by the tavern keeper and his wife predisposed Chekhov to reject stereotypes of Jews.

This sense of compassion became strong in Chekhov and expressed itself in his medical career and his literature. Simmons states that Chekhov's primary motive for entering medicine was money.[3] This idea is not consistent with the rest of his

1

life. What is probable is that Chekhov's predisposition toward medicine was reinforced by the profession's earning potential.

Chekhov's medical education opened his mind and imprinted it with the scientific method. He was always fascinated by the experimental role of the discoverers who broke new paths. In addition to his medical studies, he enjoyed reading books on travel and exploration. He was especially interested in Darwin and his scientific method. Chekhov said, "I'm frightfully fond of his method," and the Soviet scholar Leonid Grossman feels that Darwin was one of the main planks in Chekhov's philosophy.[4] Chekhov was of the Darwinian school and was also influenced by the strictly materialistic principles in the method of Claude Bernard,[5] the French physiologist (1813-1878).[6]

Chekhov noted, ". . . There is no doubt in my mind that my study of medicine has had a serious impact on my literary activities." In particular, "It significantly broadened the scope of my observations and enriched me with knowledge . . . . It also served as a guiding influence; my intimacy with medicine probably helped me to avoid many mistakes."[7]

This scientific background led him to refuse to enter areas he did not understand. "My familiarity with the natural sciences and the scientific method . . .", he wrote, ". . . has always kept me on my guard; I have tried wherever possible to take scientific data into account; where it has not been possible, I have preferred not writing at all."[8] (Letter of October 11, 1899)

The effect of Chekhov's acceptance of the scientific method was recognized by Chekhov and accepted by his critics and contemporaries.[9] The scientific method permeated his own method thoroughly and guided him in formulating questions and identifying problems.

In addition, his medical training gave him deep insights into man's mind. Chekhov was fascinated by psychiatry which was at the time strongly physiological in its orientation as much neurology as anything. Chekhov felt that if he had not become a writer, he would have specialized in psychiatry.[10] He used psychiatric knowledge in his stories. In "An Attack of Nerves," (1888), for example, he boasted that "as a doctor, I feel that I correctly diagnosed the psychic ailment according to all the rules of the science of psychiatry."[11]

Chekhov's crisp, precise writing style may also have reflected some element of his medical training. The writing of laboratory reports, papers, and case studies leave a mark on any student. This tendency toward bare-bone facts and clear, concise brevity is evident in Chekhov's style of writing.[12]

Because Chekhov was a physician, he was able to draw upon a wealth of material unavailable to another writer living in the same place and the same time. This was especially true of the nonliterates that Dr. Field mentioned earlier. Chekhov realized this when he exclaimed, "The peasants and shopkeepers are in my hands; I've won out. One had a hemorrhage from the throat; another had his arm crushed by a tree; a third, a sick daughter." He believed, " . . . they would be in a desperate situation without me . . . I am friends with them and all goes well."[13]

(Letter of May 15, 1892) Chekhov knew and moved among the lower classes as a friend because he was a physician, a fact which transcended class.

Not only did Chekhov's medical background give him unusual access to experiences and perceptions not accorded to most writers, it also allowed him to travel more than most of his contemporaries. Ordinarily, low-born people from the provinces, like Chekhov, had difficulty traveling at home or abroad. Chekhov received a temporary passport solely on the basis of his medical diploma.[14] One of Chekhov's greatest values as a source of objective information about lower class Russia is the breadth of his experience coupled with a non-gentry perspective.

It is clear that Chekhov's scientific training had a pronounced and powerful influence on him and his emerging method. The second forceful influence was his "mistress," literature. His literary development contributed greatly to his method.

As the old saying goes, find a need and fill it. One of the reasons for the emergence of Anton Chekhov as a literary figure was a need in society which he helped fill. Russia was moving from a "monarchy of the landed gentry" into a "bourgeois monarchy." The literature of the established intellectual community focused on the decline of the landed gentry. During the period, Russia was undergoing increased urbanization, the city population doubled, a displaced peasantry was becoming an urban working class, and the middle class was growing. In the midst of these changes, a new group of intellectuals was forming in the raznochintsy, the classless ones. These were the plebeian intellectuals.

At the time, both the old, populist-oriented literature and the intellectual movement, previously devoted to helping the common people, became stagnant. The State which had never been known for contributing to literature, took no interest in filling the stagnant gap; it merely censored whatever was written. Ironically, the program of censorship under Pobedonostsev, the man indirectly responsible for policing thought at the time, may have aided the birth of a new literature by suppressing the old. In sum, by the 1880's, there was a need for a new kind of literature which neither the old literary establishment nor the State could fill. There was a need for a new literature to reflect the needs and aspirations of the "little people."[15]

To fill the void, a new breed of weekly papers or humor magazines sprang up which bore no resemblance to the thick journals of the established intellectuals. They grew up like dragons' teeth; pluck one and a thousand grew in its place. Moscow and St. Petersburg were rapidly infested with *Strekoza* (The Dragon Fly), *Oskolki* (Fragments), *Budilnik* (The Alarm Clock), *Razolecheniye* (Amusement), *Zritel* (The Spectator), and a host of other humorous pulps.[16]

In the early 1880's, Anton Chekhov, a financially strapped medical student, contributed tiny tales to most of these weeklies. He called them "smelts" because he received about a quarter cent a word and a whole story would just about pay for a meal of the tiny fish.[17] His motive for writing was to get enough from the "smelts" to pay for the support of himself and his family. It was not art; it was income. He wrote quickly for a quick return.

In 1882, Chekhov met and became friends with Nikolai Leiken, the publisher of *Oskolki* (Fragments). Leiken published Chekhov's stories on a regular basis. These stories were rarely over 100 lines long which put Chekhov under constant pressure for "extreme brevity."[18] This need to compress may have hampered Chekhov in his later unsuccessful attempts to write a novel.[19] This bare-boned style may have reinforced his matter-of-fact approach which had already developed as a result of Chekhov's experience writing medical papers and reports.

Trying to write and at the same time maintain his medical studies was a particularly difficult task, and he often had to write under "abominable conditions." In a letter of August, 1883, he recounted a litany of one night's horrors. While he tried to write, the thought of his uncompleted school work "pummeled his conscience;" a visiting relative's child "screamed" in the next room; in another room, his father read aloud to his mother, and in yet another room, someone turned on a music box. The cacophony of sound tempted him to flee to the country but it was already one o'clock in the morning. He would have gone to bed but it was occupied by a visiting relative who periodically interrupted his thoughts and wanted to talk. As Chekhov said, "It would be hard to think up a more abominable setting for a writer."[20]

After graduating from medical school, he continued writing mostly because he was quite limited financially and needed to turn out "smelts." However, by the late 1880's, he started to take his writing more and more seriously. This seriousness can be seen in a change in method which is dealt with in the next chapter.

During this decade, Chekhov progressed from *Oskolki* through the *Peterburgskaia Gazeta*, a widely circulated daily, and lastly to *Novoe Vremia* which was a major conservative daily newspaper. When Chekhov went with *New Times*, he was stimulated by new influences. The editor, Aleksei Suvorin, became Chekhov's close friend and literary advisor. His influence was of great importance in Chekhov's development because it opened doors to serious literary circles and helped him eventually to secure the Pushkin prize. Once on that plateau, he was noticed by members of the literary elite like Leo Tolstoi. Suvorin's advice, both personal and literary, aided Chekhov throughout his life. Although in later years great stresses were put on the relationship because of Chekhov's increasing rejection of the political stand of *New Times*,[21] Chekhov felt that Suvorin was the "first" one who had helped him and apparently Chekhov never forgot the help.[22] (February 21, 1886) Leiken helped Chekhov develop his brief, concise style, Suvorin introduced him to the best literary circles and helped him become known. These were important and lasting influences on the writer.

Chekhov's literary antecedents, from the point of view of style, lack substance according to Yermilov. He sees Chekhov as a bright spot in an emerging school of "democratic and progressive literature" that was by and for the people. Yermilov sees Chekhov's antecedents in two minor writers, Pomialovskii of the sixties, and Garshin of the eighties. Pomialovskii drank himself to death and Garshin committed suicide.[23] The only thing they shared with Chekhov was the little people.

If Chekhov has antecedents in this literature of the raznochintsy, they are Pisemskii and Leskov. This author agrees with Boris Eichenbaum who maintains that, "In what is most basic and essential, Chekhov's literary origins come from them." He was delighted by Pisemskii's work and he called Leskov his favorite writer. They showed the depth and breadth of Russia. All of the features of her national life and daily existence were revealed by them. They collected materials by studying Russia comprehensively, every profession and class.[24] In short, many of the things which the mature Chekhov valued were present in their work.

The influence of these antecedents of Chekhov, who wrote of the little people, was in the long run, of little importance. In any discussion of Chekhov's literary roots, the names of Tolstoi, Flaubert, de Maupassant, and perhaps Zola, are put forward. Tolstoi unquestionably exerted a powerful influence on the young Chekhov's writing as can be easily discerned from his writings.

When Anton Chekhov changed the focus of his literary activity, he dropped his humor magazine pen name Antosha Chekhonte as a symbol of his metamorphosis. It is at this time that Tolstoi exerts his strongest influence on Chekhov. From 1886 to 1887, Chekhov produced a series of stories which were Tolstoian in tone. Among them were: "Excellent People;" "A Misfortune;" "Sister;" "The Meeting;" "Cossack;" "The Beggar;" and "The Letter." However, as Chekhov matured, he rejected Tolstoi's theory of nonresistance to evil and came to intensely dislike Tolstoi's refusal to read background for topics which he wrote about. Tolstoi himself recognized his influence when he sent Chekhov a list of the tales by Chekhov that he liked the most. There were over thirty and they all manifested his influence in content or language.[25]

According to Chekhov's contemporary Ivan Bunin, Chekhov took particular pleasure in Tolstoi as well as Maupassant and Flaubert. Leonid Grossman, in his article "The Naturalism of Chekhov," believes that Zola, along with Flaubert and Maupassant, must be considered Chekhov's principal teachers. Grossman views Maupassant as the most significant because he reinforced Chekhov's realistic representation of everyday life with an emphasis on details to show the various aspects of that life. He said Maupassant made it "impossible to write in the old fashion any longer."[26]

Chekhov was attracted to Flaubert because of Flaubert's style as a short story writer, which may have influenced Chekhov's own short stories. On the other hand, Chekhov gravitated to Zola because of content and method, not style or structure as with Flaubert. Zola could be described as a naturalist by education, a poet by temperament, and a novelist by profession. Zola stressed scientific method, precise methods of observation and the reporting of the facts of reality. Flaubert aided Chekhov in his developing a short story form, and Zola reinforced Chekhov's own belief in the scientific method and a detailed representation of life. Some believe that Zola stimulated Chekhov to write "The Peasants" and "In the Hollow," which reflect Zola's and Chekhov's common method.[27]

Underlying both the influence of science and literature was Chekhov's life-long quest for freedom. That freedom was freedom of thought and the right to practice both art and science. This desire for freedom ultimately caused him to reject manifesting any political tendencies in literature, and to use literature in defense of science.

Chekhov recognized the benefits of freedom in a letter to Aleksei Suvorin dated January 7, 1889. This was written at the end of a difficult period for Chekhov for he had undergone a period of growth and adjustment in recognizing and developing his own talent and establishing a more objective method. Chekhov believed that both talent and material were the necessary ingredients for a writer. Maturity was important, too, but most indispensable was a sense of personal freedom. He confessed that early in his career, he had replaced personal freedom with carelessness, frivolity, and lack of respect for his work.

Chekhov, the raznochinitz, lamented that what the aristocratic writers received free, he had to buy with his youth. In one huge rushing sentence Chekhov sums up his life and struggle as a writer. "Try and write a story about a young man – the son of a serf, a former grocer, choirboy, schoolboy and a university student, raised on respect for rank, kissing the priests' hands, worshipping the ideas of others." He rushes onward detailing a cycle of abuse " . . . giving thanks for every piece of bread, receiving frequent whippings, making the rounds as a tutor without galoshes, brawling, torturing animals." He notes his sense of hollowness in "enjoying dinners at houses of rich relatives, (being) needlessly hypocritical before God and man merely to acknowledge his own insignificance." He surges on to his maturity " – write about how this young man squeezes the slave out of himself drop by drop and how, on waking up one fine morning, he finds that the blood coursing through his veins is no longer the blood of a slave, but that of a real human being."[28] (Letter of January 7, 1889)

One can see the intense feeling of a young man whose task since 1880 was to build and survive on "smelts." He had struggled to free his family from an apartment in the red light district of Moscow. The Dvoryanin got this free! He paid for his freedom with his youth and in the process, acquired a bittersweet maturity and a sense of struggle the Dvoryanin would never know.

Chekhov said, "I would like to be a free artist and nothing else . . ." He hated ignorance, stupidity, "Pharisaism," and tyranny which he saw not only in merchant homes and police stations, but also in science, literature and among young people. As a result, he favored no one over another and rejected all stereotypes. He concluded by saying, "My holy of holies is the human body, health, intelligence, talent, inspiration, love, and the most absolute freedom imaginable, freedom from violence and lies, no matter what form the latter two take. Such is the program I would adhere to if I were a major artist."[29] (Letter of October 4, 1888)

In his method, Chekhov incorporated a rejection of stereotypes, a fixation on absolute truth, and a rejection of ignorance and especially the tyranny of that ignorance. Chekhov would not tolerate violations of these principles even in his friends, Tolstoi and Suvorin.

His conflict with Suvorin over the violation of these principles was reflected in a letter of March 4, 1889. It was written in connection with Suvorin's handling of student disturbances in his paper *New Times*. Chekhov criticized Suvorin's columns as unsatisfactory because he could not see how anyone "can pass judgment in print on the disturbances when all mention of the facts is prohibited. The State forbade you to write, it forbids the truth to be told . . ." For Chekhov, this was an arbitrary rule.[30] Chekhov was furious at Suvorin for defending the rights of the State when they violated the rights of the people. Chekhov wanted freedom of the press and thought.

On the other hand, Chekhov was not willing to exchange the tyranny of the State for the tyranny of a protest group who demanded "solidarity." In a letter of May 3, 1888, he made it clear that among young writers, there could be no solidarity because they did not and should not all think the same way. "I am not in solidarity with you . . . ," he wrote, ". . . but I promise you to the grave complete freedom as a writer, that is, you may write wherever and however you please . . ."[31]

Chekhov tried to make good on his promise to protect intellectual activity from political pressure. The most celebrated example was the annulment of Maxim Gorkii's (A. M. Peshkov) election to the Academy of Sciences in February, 1902.[32] The Minister of the Interior recommended that the election be annulled on the grounds that Gorkii had been arrested for political activity. Nicholas II personally recommended the annulment over the heads of the distinguished members of the Academy. The announcement of the annulment was made over the signature of the Academy however, not the Tsar.[33]

Gorkii had been elected on the basis of his art and the award was retracted on the basis of his politics. This was contrary to all that Chekhov believed. He had fought for objectivity and intellectual honesty against political interference designed to color what was said or written. Chekhov's situation was made worse by the fact that he was an honorary member of the Academy and, therefore, had technically participated in the annulment. As a result Anton Chekhov formally resigned from the Academy in a letter of August 25, 1902.[34] Chekhov's protest was not for a political cause but against political interference in the Arts and Sciences. Chekhov's freedom was to say *what is* without fear.

Soviet critics Chukovskii and Yermilov both recognized the importance of absolute freedom to Chekhov and that this freedom for truth was a challenge to his age.[35] The Soviet commentator, Maria Semanova, mentions this letter on absolute freedom in her book, *Chekhov and Soviet Literature* (1966). In a fashion reminiscent of Suvorin, she states that Chekhov's demand to be a free artist and his defense of absolute freedom do not relate at all to freedom of the Arts.[36] The Soviet songwriter and underground poet, Aleksandr Galick, disagrees with her. He understood what Chekhov meant and included that meaning in his song, "I Choose Freedom." "I choose freedom, even if she's pockmarked and crude. And you go ahead and squeeze the slave out, drop by drop."[37] Aleksandr Galick was expelled from the Soviet Writers' Union in 1972 for writing songs which choose freedom. Chekhov's choice of freedom affected his method and underlies and colors the effect of all other influences upon him.

In summary, Chekhov's scientific training helped form his method and literary style. His literary experience continued the development of his economy of style. In addition he used the scientific method as the basis of his artistic method. Underlying both, and coloring them, was his desire and his intellectual and artistic freedom. These were the principal influences on Chekhov in the development of his unique method which is to be our next point for development.

NOTES

1   Ernest Simmons, *Through the Glass of Soviet Literature*, pp. 18, 20.

2   Ernest J. Simmons, *Chekhov: A Biography* (Chicago: University of Chicago Press, 1970), p. 32.

3   *Ibid.*, p. 33.

4   Leonid Grossman, "The Naturalism of Chekhov," in *Chekhov: A Collection of Critical Essays*, p. 37.

5   Grossman, "The Naturalism of Chekhov" in *Chekhov: A Collection of Critical Essays*, p. 33

6   For a discussion of Bernard's influence on Chekhov especially *introduction a l'etude de la medicine experimentale*. See A. Roskin's "Notes on Chekhov's Realism" in *Literaturny i Kritik* (1939), No. 7, pp. 58-77.

7   Karlinsky, *Letters of Anton Checkhov*, p. 367.

8   *Ibid.*

9   Added information on Chekhov's commitment to the biological sciences may be seen in Dr. Isaac Altscheller's rememberances may be seen in "Vospominaniya o Chekhove" in *Literaturnoe Nasledstvo*, ed. V. V. Vinogradov, et al (Moscow, 1960), 68:531-707.

10 E. V. Meve, *Meditsina v tvorchestve i zhizni A. P. Chekhov* (Kiev: GMIz, 1961), p. 44.

11 Grossman, "The Naturalism of Chekhov" in *Chekhov: A Collection of Critical Essays*, p. 33.

12 An example of his case study writing, see "Protokol sudebno-meditsinskogo vskrytiia (studentscheskaia rabota Chekhova)," A. P. Chekhov, *Sbornik dokumentov i materialov*, A. B. Derman, ed. (Moscow, 1947), pp. 20-23.

13 Simmons, *Chekhov*, p. 278.

14 *Ibid.*, No. 4, p. 309.

15 For a discussion of this period and Chekhov's emergence, see: Ernest Simmons, *Introduction to Russian Realism* (Bloomington: Indiana University Press, 1965), pp. 181-186; Ernest Simmons, *Chekhov: A Biography* (Chicago: University of Chicago Press, 1970), pp. 65-66; Vladimir Yermilov, *Anton*

Pavlovich Chekhov, trans. Ivy Litvinov (Moscow: Foreign Language Publishing House, N.D.), pp. 44, 45; Boris Eichenbaum, "Chekhov at Large," in *Chekhov: A Collection of Critical Essays*, edited by Robert L. Jackson (Englewood Cliffs: Prentice-Hall, Inc., 1967), pp. 21-23.

[16] Vladimir Yermilov, *Anton Pavlovich Chekhov*, p. 44; For an outline of the formats of these journals, see: L. Myshkovskaia, *Chekhov i iumoristicheskie Zhurnaly 80-Kh godov* (Moscow, 1929), pp. 81-82.

[17] Simmons, *Chekhov*, p. 66.

[18] Ronald Hingley, *Chekhov: A Biographical and Critical Study* (New York: Barnes and Noble, Inc., 1966), p. 52; For further discussion on the size of stories, see: A. P. Chekhov, *Polnoe Sobranie Sochinenii i Pisem*, (Moscow: Goslitizdat, 1944), Vol. XIII, pp. 41-42.

[19] Ralph A. Matlaw, "Chekhov and the Novel," *Anton Chekhov 1860-1960, Some Essays*, T. Eekman, ed. (Leiden: E. J. Brill, 1960), pp. 148-167.

[20] Karlinsky, *Letters of Anton Chekhov*, p. 41.

[21] *Ibid.*, p. 54.

[22] *Ibid.*, p. 56.

[23] Yermilov, *Anton Pavlovich Chekhov*, p. 45.

[24] Eichenbaum, "Chekhov at Large" in *Chekhov: A Collection of Critical Essays*, p. 22.

[25] Simmons, *Chekhov*, pp. 127, 595.

[26] Grossman, "The Naturalism of Chekhov" in *Chekhov: A Collection of Critical Essays*, pp. 39-40.

[27] *Ibid.*, pp. 36-45.

[28] Karlinsky, *Letters of Anton Chekhov*, p. 85; Also see Yarmolinsky, *Letters of Anton Chekhov*, p. 107.

[29] Karlinsky, *Letters of Anton Chekhov*, p. 109.

[30] *Ibid.*, p. 345.

[31] *Ibid.*, p. 99.

[32] Yarmolinsky, *Letters of Anton Chekhov*, pp. 423-424.

[33] Simmons, *Chekhov*, p. 56.

[34] Yarmolinsky, *Letters of Anton Chekhov*, pp. 423-424.

[35] Korni Chukovskii, *Chekhov*; Yermilov, *A.P. Chekhov*.

[36] Karlinsky, *Letters of Anton Chekhov*, p. 110.

[37] *Ibid.*, pp. 85-86.

CHAPTER II

METHOD

"Method is one-half of talent"

Anton Chekhov

"You would have me say, in depicting horse thieves, that stealing horses is an evil. But then, that has been known for a long while, even without me. Let jurors judge them, for my business is only to show them as they are . . . if I add a pinch of subjectivity, the images will become diffused . . . . . . I rely fully on the reader, on the assumption that he himself will add the subjective elements . . . ."

Anton Chekhov

Chekhov's method is unusual within the context of nineteenth century Russia and it is the essential statement of Chekhov's philosophy as an artist.[1] Chekhov approaches his subject with the eyes of a scientist and an artist. This fact permits him to play a unique role in his time as a bridge among different worlds within his society. The internal structure of this chapter is derived from Chekhov's own statement of method made to his brother which will be cited in full later. His key points stated briefly are:

1) no polemics; 2) total objectivity; 3) truthful description; 4) extreme brevity; 5) audacity, originality, and no stereotypes; and 6) compassion.

Chekhov says, "It's not that . . ." the author has a "definite view and convictions . . . nowadays everyone does; the important thing is that" the author "has a method." Whatever type of analysis is being pursued ". . . method constitutes one-half of talent."[2] (Letter of March 6, 1888). Chekhov's own method experienced an evolution as both he and his career developed.

This evolution can be seen in two models which Chekhov recommended to his brother. In 1883, Anton Chekhov, while still a medical student writing for the

11

humor magazines of Moscow, gave his brother, Aleksandr, some advice on how to write a story that would sell to the humor journal, *Fragments*: "1. The shorter, the better; 2. A bit of ideology and being up to date is most apropos; 3. Caricature is just fine, but ignorance of civil service ranks and of the seasons is strictly prohibited."[3] This is the facile advice of an author who, by his own admission, had no respect for his work at this point. He wrote only to support himself and his family while he attended medical school. As late as 1886, he did not remember spending more than twenty-four hours on any story.[4]

However, by May 1886 he had become more serious about his literary work and had a drastically different prescription to give his brother, Aleksandr, for a successful short story, "1. absence of lengthy verbiage of political-social-economic nature; 2. total objectivity; 3. truthful descriptions of persons and objects; 4. extreme brevity; 5. audacity and originality: avoid the stereotype; 6. compassion."[5] (Letter of May 10, 1886).

This then provides us with a general outline of the key elements of Chekhov's method. Chekhov felt so secure in his method that he boasted that his work *The Steppe* was an "encyclopedia of the steppe" which described, ". . . the plain, its lilac vistas, the sheep breeders, the Jews, the priests, the nocturnal storms, the inns, the wagon trains, the steppe birds and so on."[6] (Letter of January 12, 1888).

In spite of his claims to encyclopedic stature, Chekhov believed that there was much more to the act of writing than just a transfer from eye to paper, a mindless photographic exchange. He says, "The artist observes, selects, guesses, and synthesizes." For Chekhov this presupposed a question, which starts the guessing and directs the selection process. As a physician, he was very concerned with the workings of the mind and the developing field of psychiatry.

On the basis of his observations, he stated that the author begins his creations from questions with an intent. There is a premeditation or purpose in the author's work. It is not the result of "unthinking emotionality." Chekhov believes ". . . if any author were to boast to me that he'd written a story from pure inspiration without first having thought over his intentions, I'd call him a madman."[7] (Letter of October 27, 1888).

Chekhov could not conceive of being a "mindless giant" without a purpose. When the author "observes, selects, guesses and synthesizes" he does so with a question and purpose in mind.

Chekhov points out that he wrote only from memory, never "directly from observed life. What I need is to have the subject filtered through memory, and that there should remain on it, as on a filter, only what is important or typical."[8] (Letter of December 15, 1897). In the process of responding to his initial question, the author filtered out what is typical; that is why Chekhov did not write directly from one instance in life.

Because of the nature of this filtering process, Chekhov insisted that "It is bad for the artist to take on something he doesn't understand." The author ". . . must pass judgment only on what he understands . . ."[9] (Letter of October 27, 1888). In sum, the author must formulate his question, observe, and filter out the typical; but, this is to be done only in areas where he has knowledge which will permit him to make informed judgments.

Chekhov carefully chose his topics. He chose to write about things which he cared about and understood.

Chekhov's method and motive were substantially different from the method and motive of the Populists, Reductionists and Orthodox Soviets. The reason for this, according to Professor Simon Karlinsky in his article on "The lesser Russian Tradition," was that many people attribute to Chekhov the same motives and methods which were found in the general traditions of Russian nineteenth century literature. Then, most writers were motivated by an impulse comparable to the impulse of the "social sciences." They were observing human behavior, with an eye to developing means to improve it. Karlinsky believed that Chekhov, Nabokov and Pushkin followed the beat of a different drummer and this impulse is from the "biological sciences."[10]

Karlinsky stresses that the critics have sentimentalized Chekhov or imposed on him the traditional sociological values of the nineteenth century Russian intelligentsia. These were the values which Dr. Field saw as clouding their vision. They were the views that the Populists held also. This misperception of Chekhov's views remains with us today. A confused exchange between critic Irving Howe and novelist Ralph Ellison took place in *The New Leader* over Chekhov's *The Island of Sakhalin*. Karlinsky shows that the conflict occurred because neither understood why Chekhov wrote this book. They both projected what a member of the intelligentsia should have thought and attributed it to Chekhov. They did not know Chekhov, the scientist, who had produced a thoroughly researched ethnographic and demographic study of a colony of common criminals, not a study of political prisoners as they believed.[11]

Chekhov was of "the lesser Russian tradition" that drew its method from the biological sciences. That tradition stressed "objective and independent literary art, not subservient to ideology, nationalism or religion."[12] Chekhov said he did not write of "what can be" or "should be," he wrote "first of what exists."[13] (Letter of December 3, 1892).

Once again, the key points of Chekhov's method are: no polemics; total objectivity; truthful description; extreme brevity; audacity, originality, and no stereotypes; and compassion. This study will now shift its focus to a specific consideration of the principal parts of Chekhov's method. Chekhov passed over the question of including a particular political point of view in his work when he said that he lacked a "political, religious and philosophical world view" and if he did have one, it changed monthly, ". . . so I'll have to limit myself to descriptions of how my heroes love, marry, give birth, die, and how they speak."[14] (Letter of October 9, 1888).

Chekhov compared himself to the eternal or even just good writers of his century and found an important difference. The "eternal" writers all had an important trait in common. "They're moving toward something definite and beckon you to follow . . ." He stressed that, "you feel with your entire being, not only with your mind, that they have a certain goal . . ." Chekhov believed that "the best of them are realistic and describe life as it is, . . ." but because their work is saturated with an awareness of its goals, "you feel life as it should be in addition to life as it is, and you are captivated by it."[15] (November 25, 1892).

Chekhov continued the comparison by talking about writers like himself. "Us/ We describe life as it is and stop dead right there . . . we have neither immediate nor remote goals, and there is an emptiness in our souls. We have no politics, we don't believe in revolution, there is no God, we're not afraid of death or blindness."[16]

Chekhov would not let the social canons of Victorian society color his work any more than he would let politics. His friend, Maria Kiselyova, charged that he was wallowing in the seamier side of life. She wanted him to dig through the dung heap of life, find a pearl, and write about it. He replied in an eloquent letter which stated that to dig only for the pearl would destroy literature. For Chekhov, literature was an art because it portrayed life as it actually was. "Its aim is the truth, unconditional and honest." Limiting it to extracting "pearls" would kill it. The author is not a cosmetician or entertainer. "He is a man bound by contract to his sense of duty and to his conscience."[17] (Letter of January 14, 1887).

The author is duty bound, once he starts the job, to carry it through no matter how horrified. He must overcome his squeamishness and soil his imagination with the grime of life. "He is just like any ordinary reporter." Just like the reporter, he cannot limit his topics to "high-minded ladies" and "honest men."[18] Chekhov summed up by saying, "To a chemist, there is nothing impure on earth. The writer should be just as objective as the chemist; he should liberate himself from everyday subjectivity." And, the scientist as always, he concludes ". . . acknowledge that manure piles play a . . . respectable role in the landscape and that evil passions are every bit as much a part of life as good ones."[19] (January 14, 1887).

Chekhov clearly stressed objectivity and truth at the expense of any polemical tendency as a key element in his method. This belief in objectivity had its origin in the scientific and literary influences that molded him.

Chekhov's claims to objectivity are supported from many directions. Soviet critics generally support Chekhov's objectivity. Vladimir Yermilov in his *Anton Pavlovich Chekhov* said he "honestly described scenes from everyday life . . ." Recently the Soviet critic, A. P. Chudakov, reaffirmed the acceptance of Chekhov's objectivity. He believed Chekhov's objectivity increased as his style matured and he developed his characterizations.[20] A. B. Luncharskii once exclaimed that "Chekhov is so objective, so objective."[21] Gorkii maintained that Chekhov's objectivity and truthfulness made his work "equal with science." "He says nothing new, but what he does say comes out overwhelmingly convincing and simple, terribly simple and clear, irrefutably right."[22]

As previously mentioned, Chekhov's stress on objectivity had led to problems with his critics. Because of Chekhov's strict objectivity, the populist

Mikhailovskii called *The Steppe* the stroll of a mindless young giant who had no idea of where he was going or why. Objectivity led to frequent references to the indifference of Chekhov to his characters, his cold inhumanity which was only thinly veiled by his technical mastery. The dominant opinion of Chekhov during the 1880's and 1890's reflected this charge. The image faded only with the advent of the poet of twilight Russia concept.

One basis of the problem was, of course, the denial of Chekhov's objectivity. Another was that Chekhov's own words were at times misunderstood. Chekhov once told a young Russian writer, Ivan Bunin, that "one had to be ice cold before sitting down to write." What he intended was to warn Bunin about unsettling emotionality and uncontrollable didacticism which plagued those who tried to play critic or social historian at that time.[23]

The depth of the Populists' critical chill was increased when Chekhov added "indifference" to "coldness." Chekhov maintained that, "Nature reconciles man, that is, makes him indifferent. Only those who are unconcerned are able to see things clearly, to be just, and to work. Of course, this includes only thoughtful and noble people; egoists and empty folk are indifferent enough as it is."[24] Chekhov's "indifference" is obviously intended to mean the same as being "cold." The writer must be indifferent to emotional excess so that he can perfect and focus his involvement.[25]

Perhaps this coldness and indifference is better explained as restraint. Chekhov said it best when he criticized Gorkii for his ". . . lack of restraint. You are like a spectator in a theatre who expresses his enthusiasm so unrestrainedly that he prevents himself and others from hearing."[26] Chekhov showed how the careful use of restraint could lead to more involvement for the reader. If you ". . . want to make the reader feel pity," he wrote, "try to be somewhat colder – that seems to give a kind of background to another's grief, against which it stands out more clearly." He concluded, "Yes, be more cold."[27] (March 19, 1892). Even when Chekhov explained he was misunderstood, he tried to make it perfectly clear ". . . you have to be cold when you write teaching stories . . . you can cry over your stories . . . suffer . . . with your characters, but . . ." the reader must never know. "The more objective you are, the stronger will be the impression you make."[28] (April 29, 1892).

Chekhov went against the prevailing tradition of Russian literature; his uniqueness is tied to his scientific method. The critics of the 1880's and 1890's, for their own reasons, rejected his method and/or totally misunderstood it. They picked those words which would convey best what they wanted Chekhov to mean. Objectivity, coldness, indifference, and restraint all made Chekhov uninvolved, a mindless giant. Ironically, for Chekhov to tell the truth unemotionally permitted him to get more deeply involved. Chekhov the physician was setting up a slide for a microscope where all who chose to could observe the disease organism.

Chekhov's objectivity and lack of excess was reinforced by his extreme brevity.[29] According to Yermilov, Chekhov felt that "Brevity is the sister of talent" and "the art of writing is the art of contracting." He exhorted people "to write well, i.e., briefly," while he characterized his skill as knowing "... how to talk briefly about big things." Yermilov felt this was the essence of the skill of Chekhov and his heritage from his humor magazine days.[30]

Using Yermilov as a point of departure, the Soviet author A. B. Derman points out that Chekhov combined something of his scientific approach with the writing style that he acquired during his humor magazine days. In order to be factual and brief, Chekhov virtually eliminated the beginning and middle of his stories and focused on the ending.[31] Chekhov would agree with Derman's perceptions. As he explained in a letter to his friend Suvorin, he started out writing "calmly" at the beginning "but toward the middle" he became fearful that his story "will turn out too long." He worried, since he was paid by the line, that the paper would not be able to afford a long story. But when he came to the ending, it "is like fireworks."[32]

To achieve the utmost brevity, Chekhov held that one must write simply, and he crossed out anything that was superfluous. Chekhov's friends maintained: "It is necessary to take the manuscript away from him; otherwise, he will ..." reduce an entire life to "they were young, fell in love, and then got married and were unhappy." To this type of kidding, Chekhov replied: "... listen, after all, that's the way it is."[33]

Chekhov's rejection of polemics, his insistence on absolute objectivity, his belief in truth, and his extreme brevity, have all been presented individually, thus completing half the point of Chekhov's model. But the remaining points: audacity, originality, rejection of stereotypes, truthful description of details, and compassion must be dealt with as an interrelated whole.

Chekhov did not fit the realistic literary mold of the age. He belonged to the tradition of Realism, but he progressed beyond it. Ernest Simmons believed that Chekhov was the "unwitting victim of a generation of arrested progress ..."[34] Things had changed since Realism began with the great Pushkin, and Chekhov "understood the necessity of adapting ..." Realism to these new "conditions of life." Chekhov was so far outside the mold that he owes it little, if anything, for his development.[35]

The critics wanted and expected Chekhov to be what everyone else was, a Realist. Dmitri Chizhevsky pointed out that Chekhov's innovations could not be tolerated because they threatened to destroy "sacred Realism."[36] An entire literary age rallied to defend itself by trying to destroy Chekhov. Gorkii clearly illuminated the problem when he said in a letter to Chekhov in 1900: "Do you know what you are doing? You are killing Realism and you will soon finish it off ... This form has outlived its time – that is a fact?"[37] Chekhov's contemporary, N. Shapir, identified "Chekhov as a Realist-Innovator."[38] In reality, Chekhov was just rejecting the excesses of moral and spiritual extremism found in Dostoevskii and Tolstoi. Initially, he was moving back toward Pushkin who stressed rationality, objectivity and classical restraint.[39]

Chekhov realized early in his career that he was moving in new directions. In a letter of October 20, 1888, he said "Everything that I have written will be forgotten in five to ten years; but that which I am creating will remain safe and sound – therein lies my sole merit."[40] Chekhov's originality was immediately noticed by Tolstoi. He stated, "Chekhov created new forms of writing, completely new, in my opinion, to the entire world, the like of which I have encountered nowhere...." He indicated that "it is impossible to compare Chekhov, as an artist, with earlier Russian writers – with Turgenev, with Dostoevskii, or with me. Chekhov has his own special form, like the impressionists."[41]

Tolstoi believed Chekhov worked as though he were a man daubing on canvas, using whatever paint was around seemingly without selection. It seemed that none of it was related to the rest. However, if you stepped back a distance from the canvas and viewed it again, you would get a complete over-all impression, an unchangeable picture of the real life.[42] Chekhov's portrayal of persons and events are the patches of color and individual strokes that make up the impressionist portrait.[43]

Chekhov's impressionism did not interfere with his objectivity or the truth of his representations of life. On the contrary, it focused his attention specifically on the individual details which made up these patches and lines. Following his own warnings, Chekhov tended to use patches and lines which he knew and understood. These patches united to give an impression of the entire society which is based on fact. If it were not for his focus, he might have been tempted to tamper with incidentals because details could be viewed as window dressing. These details are essential details to be developed truthfully, but in a literary style which makes this appear to have been casually, perhaps even "mindlessly," chosen.

Details were then critical to Chekhov and he followed his own model by truthfully representing people and objects. Chekhov's critics focused on his apparent fixation with minutiae and ignored the great social issues of the day. Only the Soviets recognized the importance of detail. This is perhaps why some of Chekhov's best critics are the Soviets. Boris Eichenbaum used a medical analogy to explain Chekhov's intent. He stated that the genius of Chekhov's "diagnoses lay not only in that they were accurate, brilliant and convincing, but also in that he made them on the basis of the most imperceptible, minute symptoms." Chekhov discovered "traces and after-effects of disease in trifles of daily life . . . where another eye would find everything perfectly all right or unworthy of attention."[44] Eichenbaum showed how Chekhov tried to embrace every corner of Russian life and represent it accurately. Through this impressionistic method, he fused the public/political and the private/personal. He showed the great by using the small.

Dmitri Chizhevsky generally supported Eichenbaum's brilliant analysis,[45] while A. P. Chudakov divided Chekhov's details into two groups but maintained that all the details were truthfully presented.[46]

If there is one continuity in Chekhov, from his earliest stories through to his last, it may be in the truth of his detail. This is one of the great values of Chekhov.

Chekhov's final point in his model is compassion. On the surface, cold and objective, Chekhov really should reject the subjectivity of compassion. This was the misconception held by so many of his contemporary critics. Yet if we accept Chekhov's compassion and its potential for subjectivity, can he still be objective? Chekhov said "Subjectivity is a terrible thing. Things ... must be examined like objects, like symptoms, with perfect objectivity and without any attempt to agree with them or call them in question."[47] Chekhov was objective in that he would not permit influences to force him to change the facts or details he portrayed. He was not subjective. He wanted only the truth.

He would not be subjective in the sense of advocating a specific ideology or party to solve problems, but he did accept demands that, "an artist approach his work consciously ..." However, he warned about confusing two concepts: "the solution of a problem and the correct formulation of a problem." Only the second was required of the author. "Not a single problem is resolved ..." by Tolstoi's great works, but because the problems in them are formulated correctly, they satisfy you completely. "The judge is required to formulate the questions correctly, but the decision is left to the jurors, each according to his own task."[48] (Letter of October 27, 1888). Chekhov might have concluded by saying "I rely entirely on the reader to add for himself the subjective elements which are lacking in the story."[49] (Letter of April 1, 1890).

It is this author's contention, which will be proved in succeeding chapters, that Chekhov was objective in his details. He was correct in his use of these details to make up the patches of color and lines which make up his impressionistic picture of society. Chekhov's compassion led him to be subjective in the sense of his choosing the topics about which he wrote. Early in his writing career, he picked his topics from life around him. He was capable of writing truthfully about virtually anything.

He once asked his friend, Korolenko, if he knew how he wrote his stories. To illustrate his point, he picked up "the first thing to meet his eye," an ash tray, and said he could have a story about it the next day. This was the same Chekhov who gave those opportunistic instructions to his brother in 1883 on how to get a story in the humor rags of the period.

However, the Chekhov who presented his model for the serious short story to that same brother in 1888, and who had been to Sakhalin by 1892, had moved to a different level. It appears to this author that Chekhov chose to express his compassion and subjectivity by choosing topics on which he would write objectively, truthfully, and with restraint. His beautiful and factual treatment of the typical in Russian life would reveal life as it actually was, and the reader could identify any problems that existed.

Chekhov would only write on things he knew about. He rebuked Tolstoi on one occasion for his arrogance in remaining ignorant of the facts on a topic he had written about.[50] Chekhov had to be knowledgeable about the topics he chose. Chekhov expressed his compassion for Russians by writing about topics that needed to be exposed. Chekhov believed that by painting a true impression, using his objective details, he would show the problems of Russian life for what they were.

Once this was successfully accomplished, the reader could provide his own subjective contribution as to political, economic, or social solution through whatever means he deemed appropriate. Ernest Simmons pointed out that the later Chekhov began to portray realistically certain groups' social patterns. Groups such as peasants, workers, merchants, the intelligentsia, and the growing bourgeoisie. Significantly, the gentry are largely absent.[51]

Chekhov's choice of topics was his instrument to show his compassion, yet he was objective in his detail and general impression. The patches of paint and the impression when one stepped back were all correct and objective. The face to be represented was, however, Chekhov's own choice, and this choice could have been influenced by his personal beliefs. Chekhov's method permitted him to be much more than a mindless, young giant and yet held him back from the abyss of the polemical subjectivity of the ideologist.

Using Chekhov's own model as a guide, we have developed and analyzed point number two of our over-all model "method." This then leads us to a consideration of the third point. The following chapter will deal with the nature and quality of the experience which formed the factual base which Chekhov processed according to his method.

NOTES

[1] Simmons, *Through the Glass of Soviet Literature*, pp. 18, 20.

[2] Karlinsky, *Letters of Anton Chekhov*, p. 96.

[3] *Ibid.*, p. 87.

[4] Simon Karlinsky the editor of *Letters of Anton Chekhov* produces a composite by a comparative analysis of four important sources. The three most important of these were Russian: 1. The pre-revolutionary six-volume edition published by his sister, Maria, between 1912-1916. This was a period of relative freedom after the 1905 Revolution. M. P. Chekhova ed., *Pisma A. P. Chekhova* 6 vols. (Moscow, 1912-1916); 2. Volumes XIII-XX of the twenty-volume edition of Chekhov's complete works published between 1944-1951 to commemorate the fiftieth anniversary of his death. They were censored on the basis of Stalin's views. S. D. Balukhatyi, et al ed., *Polnoe sobranie sochinenii i pisem* 20 vols. (Moscow: Goslitizdat, 1944-1951); 3. Volumes XI and XII of the twelve-volume edition of *Sobranie sochinenii*, (Moscow: Goslitizdat, 1963-1964) unfortunately the letters on personal freedom were censored in this edition; 4. The fourth source were letters from Volume sixty-eight of *Literaturnoe Nasledstvo* (Moscow: Goslitizdat, 1968), a regularly appearing miscellany specializing in literary document and documentary series.

5   *Ibid.*, p. 87.

6   *Ibid.*, pp. 91, 92.

7   *Ibid.*, pp. 116-117.

8   Yarmolinsky, *Letters of Anton Chekhov*, p. 300, also see Simmons, *Chekhov*, p. 409.

9   Karlinsky, *Letters of Anton Chekhov*, p. 116.

10 Simon Karlinsky, "Nabokov and Chekhov: the lesser Russian tradition," *Tri Quarterly* (Winter, 1970), p. 11.

11 *Ibid.*, p. 12.

12 *Ibid.*, p. 15.

13 Idem, *Letters of Anton Chekhov*, p. 246.

14 *Ibid.*, p. 115.

15 *Ibid.*, p. 243.

16 *Ibid.*

17 *Ibid.*, p. 243.

18 *Ibid.*, p. 62.

19 *Ibid.*

20 A. P. Chudakov, *Poetika Chekhova*, (Moscow, 1971), p. 43.   A useful monograph which relies on original research helpful in discussions of periodization, narration, objectivity and use of detail.

21 Robert L. Jackson, "Introduction: Perspectives on Chekhov," in *Chekhov: A Collection of Critical Essays*, p. 12.

22 Boris Eichenbaum, "Chekhov at Large," in *Chekhov: A Collection of Critical Essays*, p. 25.

23 Robert L. Jackson, "Introduction: Perspectives on Chekhov," in *Chekhov: A Collection of Critical Essays*, p. 4.

24 Louis S. Friedland, *Letters on the Short Story and Other Literary Topics by Anton Chekhov*, (New York: Dover Publications, Inc., 1966), p. 62.

25 For a treatment of Chekhov's meaning of indifference, see Jerome H. Katsell, *The Potential for Growth and Change Chekhov's Mature Prose: 1888-1903.* Ph.D. dissertation, Univ. of Calif., L.A. (Ann Arbor: Univ. Microfilms International, 1972), p. 184.

26 Ralph Matlaw, *Anton Chekhov's Short Stories*, (New York: W. W. Norton and Co., Inc., 1979), p. 275.

27 Ralph Matlaw, *Chekhov's Short Stories*, p. 273.

28 *Ibid.*

29 For a brief but interesting discussion of Chekhov's brevity by Rufus W. Mathewson, see *Ward Six* (New York: Signet Classics, 1965).

30 Yermilov, *Chekhov*, p. 54.

31 A. B. Derman, *O Masterstve Chekhova* (Moscow, 1959).

32 Ralph E. Matlaw ed., *Anton Chekhov's Short Stories*, pp. 272, 273.

33 Boris Eichenbaum, "Chekhov at Large" in *Chekhov: A Collection of Critical Essays*, p. 28.

34 Simmons *Introduction to Russian Realism*, p. 182.

35 *Ibid.*, p. 183.

36 Dmitri Chizhevsky "Chekhov in the Development of Russian Literature" in *Chekhov: A Collection of Critical Essays*, p. 49.

37 *Ibid.*

38 N. Shapir, "Chekhov kak realist-novator," *Voprosy filosofii i psikhologii* (1904-1905), Vol. 79-80.

39 Robert Louis Jackson, "Introduction: Perspectives on Chekhov," in *Chekhov: A Collection of Critical Essays*, p. 6.

40 Dmitri Chizhevsky, "Chekhov in the Development of Russian Literature" in *Chekhov: A Collection of Critical Essays*, p. 51.

41 Sergeenko, *Tolstoi i ego sovremeniki* (St. Petersburg, 1911), pp. 226-228. Quoted in Boris Eichenbaum, "Chekhov at Large," in *Chekhov: A Collection of Critical Essays*, p. 27.

42 Ilya Ehrenburg, *Chekhov, Stendhal, and other Essays*, edited by Harrison E. Salisbury (New York: Knopf, 1963) p. 58.

43 Dmitri Chizhevsky, "Chekhov in the Development of Russian Literature," in *Chekhov: A Collection of Critical Essays*, p. 59.

44 Boris Eichenbaum, "Chekhov at Large," in *Chekhov: A Collection of Critical Essays*, p. 27.

45 Dmitri Chizhevsky, "Chekhov in the Development of Russian Literature" in *Chekhov: A Collection of Critical Essays*, ed. Robert Louis Jackson (Englewood Cliffs: Prentice-Hall, Inc., 1967).

46 A. P. Chudakov, *Poetika Chekhova* (Moscow, 1971); see also Ernest Simmons, *Chekhov*, p. 55.

47 Karlinsky, *Letters of Anton Chekhov*, p. 150.

48 Ralph Matlaw, *Chekhov: Short Stories*, p. 272.

49 Louis S. Friedland, ed. *Anton Chekhov Letters on the Short Story* (New York: Dover Publications, Inc., 1966), p. 64.

50 Yarmolinsky, *Letters of Anton Chekhov*, p. 267. (Letter of February 15, 1890).

51 Ernest Simmons, *Introduction to Russian Realism*, p. 206.

CHAPTER III

EXPERIENCE

*"It is bad for the artist to take on something
he doesn't understand."*
Anton Chekhov

*"Of things Russian, I love now most of all the Russian childlike
quality of Pushkin and Chekhov, their shy lack of concern over such
momentous matters as the ultimate aims of mankind and their own
salvation. They understood all that very well, but they were far too
modest and considered such things beyond their rank and position.
. . . those two were to the end distracted by the current private
interests of their artistic calling and in this preoccupation lived out
their lives also as a private matter of no concern to anyone else. And
now, this private matter turns out to be of general concern and, like
apples removed from the tree to ripen, keeps filling of itself in
positivity with ever greater sweetness and meaning."*

Boris Pasternak through
Dr. Zhivago

Chekhov, unlike most of the writers of his time, was not from the upper classes
of Russian society. He was a 'classless one,' raznochintsy, who had grown up as
part of the lower strata of Russian society. He had a different world view than most
of the writers of his time because of his birth, experience, artistic impressionism
and scientific background. This experiential base was essential to Chekhov both
for bridging the gaps between the classes in Russian society and for smashing the
false images about the lower depths of Russian society held by educated Russians.
This profile of his life experience and travels in this chapter has been drawn from
his personal correspondence.

Chekhov agreed that knowledge gained from experience was essential for any
writer. He realized that an author "observes, selects, guesses and synthesizes."
This process involved the "filtering" of many individual instances to arrive at

23

what was "typical." Since Chekhov's experience is an essential element in his role as an impressionistic, objective observer, it is necessary to catalog his various types of experience. This will establish his "knowledge" base and explain how these experiences help to form him intellectually.

Chekhov was born into a family that rested on the dividing line between the lower and middle class in Russian traditional society. Chekhov's father was obsessed with the idea of becoming a financial success as a storekeeper in Taganrog. Unfortunately, the business failed and his father moved to Moscow. The experience provided the young Chekhov with first-hand knowledge of middle class society deteriorating in a provincial town.

Chekhov also learned from his family's oral tradition. On both sides, his family had been serfs for generations. Chekhov's grandfather worked himself up to the position of foreman, amassed 3500 rubles, a fortune for a serf, and was able to buy the freedom of all but his only daughter. His owner, Count A. D. Chertkov, generously threw into the bargain Chekhov's aunt. So in 1841 the family of Yegor Mikhailovich Chekhov was legally free of bondage. Chekhov gained a very personal knowledge of serfdom from stories told by his grandfather and others in the family. He also learned of life on the great estates in this way.

Chekhov's mother, also from a former serf family, was similarly freed from bondage. She often told her children of travels with her merchant father through Russia in the time of serfdom and of the conditions in the villages. Often these stories were followed by their nurse telling them of the old days or telling the old fairy tales of Russian folklore.[1]

The process of learning from the experiences of others, especially from his family, continued throughout Chekhov's life. From Alexander, an older brother, he gleaned knowledge of what it was like to be a customs official, a journalist, and a drunken failure with various common law wives. Ivan, a younger brother, became a successful teacher in a parish school in a small town and provided Chekhov with valuable impressions regarding Russian education. Nikolai, his other older brother, an artist with limited talent, physical strength and character, died in his youth of consumption. Chekhov was introduced to the rougher levels of the artistic world through Nikolai. Chekhov learned of the life of the lower middle class in various roles from his family.

From his family's experience he had first-hand knowledge of the touch of death. Chekhov's brother Nikolai and his uncle both died of consumption. Consumption lurked as a very real threat to Chekhov. It was perhaps fear that made Chekhov refuse to recognize his own very obvious symptoms of consumption. This experience helped Chekhov, the writer, add depth to his treatment of illness, death and the fear of both.[2]

Chekhov's own early experiences were tied to Taganrog. Chekhov's grandfather, through his great shrewdness and energy, eventually became the steward of a great estate near Taganrog. Chekhov's grandfather believed that education was important for success so he made sure his children were literate. Chekhov's own father inherited a strong belief in education and sent his children to school. A classic case of a middle-class ethic in operation can be seen here.

Chekhov attended several schools in Taganrog and for one year attended a Greek school operated by an ex-pirate, Nicholas Voutsina.[3] This experience had mixed results and Chekhov learned little in the Greek school. In addition Chekhov's father was not too sure of the value of a liberal arts education; so when he turned thirteen, Chekhov was sent to tailoring classes at the district industrial school. Besides his schooling, Chekhov had to tend his father's newly opened store. His father organized a church choir in which he was forced to sing and then attend church services. Such a regime occupied most of Chekhov's waking hours.[4] Taganrog's many facets each made a distinct impression on Chekhov. Although the city had been a thriving trade center, Chekhov witnessed its decline because of changes in the Russian economy. In reality, there were two towns. One the traditional Russian town of the poor laborers and equally poor Russian shop-keepers; the other a town of Western Europeans, Greeks, Italians, Germans and even a few English, who owned the export-import firms that dominated the town's economy. Foreign millionaires supported a symphony, an opera, a local theater, and imported Italian prima donnas. The cosmopolitan environment of the city exposed Chekhov to some aspects of Western culture. Thus, the young boy experienced the contrast of Russian poverty and Western affluence.[5]

Chekhov's family moved to Moscow leaving him to fend for himself in Taganrog. Chekhov spent several years on his own at school, reading insatiably at the library and undergoing a general transformation. Chekhov developed from the sixteen year old Anton, who was still locked in by the mentality of a traditional environment, to a nineteen year old Anton Chekhov, who began to view life through the eyes of a maturing young thinker.[6] He was rejecting the values of his father's class and time but it was not a violent rebellion. It would not end until Chekhov had "squeezed the slave out" of himself by becoming a mature, intellectually free artist, years later. In the process, Chekhov was on his way toward bridging the Russian cultural gulf.

In sum, from an early age, Chekhov acquired a picture of Russian peasant life and serfdom, became aware of the quality of life of the merchant class, learned about the workings of the lower range bureaucracy, the teaching profession and the Bohemian artist community, and became familiar with life on the great estates, in the small villages, and in a provincial Russian city. He even had a passing glance at Western culture as it existed in Taganrog.

Although these general experiences and impressions were important, his own direct experiences were to provide him with his greatest amount of source material. His own experiences as a child included: periodic visits to the great estate where his grandfather was steward, living as the son of a clerk and then storekeeper, playing with peasant boys and just growing up in Taganrog. All these gave him a broad base of experience.

His personal experiences were intensified when his father went bankrupt in 1876 and he had to cope with poverty. To alleviate his financial need, Chekhov became a tutor for a wealthy man's nephew. As a tutor, he was exposed to and associated with the upper middle-class and occasionally the lower edge of the upper-class, despite his delicate economic circumstances. Chekhov knew what it was like to defer to others because you had no money and they did; a valuable insight for a writer.

His tutoring position helped him survive the bankruptcy. When he joined his family in Moscow, he started medical school and also assumed a good deal of responsibility for the family. His father's job paid little and required him to live at his place of employment. Anton Chekhov was driven to write out of financial need and thus he wrote his "smelts." The family was happy but existed only by a good deal of effort and ingenuity on Anton's part.

In Moscow the Chekhov family lived in a basement apartment of the St. Nicholas district, a red light district filled with rundown apartments and shabby shops peopled by the indigent or corrupt.[7] Chekhov tended to socialize with his brother Nikolai, an alcoholic, and his friends. He accompanied them to the Salon des Variétés a true fleshpot filled with carnal delights. Chekhov was familiar with the rough side of Moscow which proved essential to him as a writer.[8]

Chekhov was able to gradually improve his family's housing and he experienced many strata of Muscovite life. He could at various times move among students, journalists, lower class workers, middle class merchants, professionals, and finally members of the literary elite. Chekhov had seen all that there was to see in Moscow.

Chekhov loved and hated Moscow. He spent most of his adult life in the city or in the countryside around it. The effect of his experiences is revealed in many of his works.

In one of the Moscow apartments where the Chekhovs lived the floor above them was rented for weddings. The Chekhovs would hold mock weddings themselves and dance to the music from upstairs.[9] Blending such experiences with several other stories he had written while in Moscow, he created a one act light comedy, "The Wedding."

Chekhov knew about the life of merchant families in Moscow. He also wrote a detailed descriptions of Moscow life. Chekhov drew on his own early experiences and those of his cousins, who were warehousemen, salesmen, seamstresses, and of his father's working in Moscow, to write "Three Years."

Chekhov frequently observed life among his friends and often drew his stories from such real life experiences. Having Chekhov as a friend could, however, be hazardous, as a physician and his wife were to find out. Chekhov frequently attended parties given by his doctor friend and the doctor's dilettante artist wife. The wife retained Chekhov's good friend, an artist, as a tutor. During the course of the classes, the artist suggested that long trips down the Volga in the summertime would facilitate the educational process. Apparently the educational process took on a dimension that went far beyond art. Chekhov observed what was going on and in later years based his story, "The Grasshopper," so realistically that the principals recognized each other in the story and were more than a little furious at him.[10]

Chekhov did not even spare himself. His engagement to Dunya Efros was stormy at best, and served as the model for the relationship between the hero and Sarah in Chekhov's play, "Ivanov."[11]

Chekhov took every opportunity to observe life in great detail and used the observation as the basis for many of his stories. Chekhov began to observe country life after he graduated from medical school in 1884. Initially he went to visit his brother Ivan, who was a teacher in a parish school at Voskresensk (now Istra). Chekhov began to spend his summers at a house rented on the Kiselyov's estate, Babkino. Chekhov loved it in the country and learned a great deal which he would use in his stories.

In the summer of 1884 while at Voskresensk Chekhov began to acquire clinical experience as the assistant to a Zemstvo physician in the hospital at Chikino, a few miles away, sometimes helping the doctor's assistant (Feldscher) with their patients. He spent several months replacing the Zemstvo doctor at Zvenigorod about twelve miles away. The young doctor attended some Zemstvo meetings and gained knowledge of conditions in the whole region. This gave Chekhov his initial exposure to the operation of local government and social services.[2]

In the winter of 1891-1892 there was a serious famine in many parts of Russia resulting from crop failure. Chekhov thrust himself into the thick of a national crisis working on the local level to ease peasant misery. Chekhov worked hard, especially in a district of Nizhegorod Province west of Moscow, where a friend of his was a land captain. In February 1892, he visited one of the hardest hit districts of Voronezh Province. Chekhov in each case thrust himself into individually backed efforts to aid the poor. He and his friend entered into a scheme to buy horses from the farmers and then gave them back later. Chekhov saw each group in the country at its best and worst under pressure. He observed the collapse of the institutions of government when they tried to cope with crisis. He learned a very great deal in the country.

This learning continued as Chekhov bought a farm at Melikhovo in the district of Serpukhov, about sixty miles south of Moscow. When the farm failed to produce a profit he decided to rent the land to peasants. Despite this failure, he gained important knowledge at Melikovo about the problems of farming and relations with the peasantry.

Chekhov also became a member of the Sanitary Council of the district and gained first-hand acquaintance with its hospitals and with medical conditions in general. Elected to the Zemstvo of the district, Chekhov continued to manifest strong interest in medical and educational problems. He was readily accepted in the district not only because of his medical service, but also because he built three schools at his own expense, and participated in district life on a very personal level by forming a family choir which sang at the village church's Easter service. During his last winter at Melikhovo he further expanded his knowledge by taking an active part in the census. Unfortunately, his deteriorating health made it necessary for him to abandon the farm and move to the South.

These years were important ones for Chekhov. He gained an intimate knowledge of the good and bad aspects of rural life. He observed the relationships between a variety of classes, and participated in the functioning of local administration in a variety of roles in several areas of Russia.

In all his posts he actively participated in efforts to improve conditions by working within the system, especially the Zemstvo, which brought him into close contact with the liberal atmosphere which permeated them. His own efforts at working as a doctor and building schools seemed to indicate a tendency toward a traditionally liberal program of action, consistent with liberal Zemstvo thinking. During much of the remaining years of his life he focused his limited energy on his craft of writing and on the theater, but the impressions had been made and would be remembered.

Chekhov's response to these experiences can be seen in the many stories he wrote about the countryside. Kiselyov's estate, Babkino, probably served as the model for the estate in the "Cherry Orchard" and contributed material to other descriptions of declining county life. His knowledge of the peasantry gained there contributed to his great tales, "The Peasants" and "In the Hollow." Even the rambling old peasant woman in " A Tedious Business" is rooted there. This knowledge contributed to many characterizations of country doctors and rural teachers. Yermilov says it was "here he developed that love for the scenery of Central Russia which made him such a brilliant describer of the Russian countryside."[13]

Probably the greatest single source of new information for Chekhov's mental reservoir were his journeys. These began with trips to the estate where his grandfather was steward on the Donets steppe, and they continued when the brother-in-law of Chekhov's landlord took him out frequently to the country and on business trips throughout the steppe. He really enjoyed his stay at the steppe farmhouse of his pupil, Peter Kravtsov, where it was wild and primitive. Chekhov described it in a letter from Ragozin Ravine, April 30, 1887.[14]

In 1887 the scope and pace of his experience increased significantly as he traveled to South Russia and the vast Donets steppe. In April and May, Anton traveled south by rail for his health, through Tula, Orel, Kursk, Byelgorod, Kharkov, Slavyansk and to his old home Taganrog. During his travels he was best man at a Cossack wedding at Novocherkassk in the Don Valley, east of Rostov, and thereafter traveled north to a remote Cossack farm on the Donetz road beyond Zvyerevo, a remote village in primitive farming territory. Chekhov returned to Taganrog by way of Slavyansk and the Svyatogorsky (Holy Mountains) Monastery and finally returned to Moscow. Such travels expanded his knowledge and perceptions of Russian life.

He gleaned further impressions in the summer of 1888 which he spent chiefly in the Ukraine at Luka on the Psyol in Kharkov Province in a lodge on the old neglected estate of the Lintvaryovs. He used the estate as a base to visit the neighboring province of Poltava, staying on an old estate with the Smagins. This further developed his concept of the estate life of the gentry and peasantry.

In July of 1888 he visited Kiev and traveled down the Dnieper, to Fedosia in the Crimea. He saw Sevastopol and Yalta.

He intended to widen his journey by going to the Caucasus all the way to Persia. To this end he went from Kerch by small steamers to the monastery New Athos, Sukhum, and Poti and then by the Georgian military road through Tiflis to Batum where he received news of the death of his companion's younger brother and had to return.

In the summer of 1889 he tired of Moscow and wished to avoid publicity associated with winning the Pushkin Prize in 1888. He went to Luka where he remained until the death of his brother Nikolai from consumption. Depressed over the loss and unable to work, he decided to go abroad. He intended to visit his friend Suvorin in the Tyrol. He went as far as Odessa but had a disagreement with him and went to Yalta instead. Such extensive travels in southern Russia obviously helped provide material for such stories as "The Steppe," "The Savage," and "At Home."

Chekhov's greatest adventure was clearly his journey to Sakhalin. The trip was one of the most influential developments in his career. The journey itself was made before the Trans-Siberian Railway and as a result involved travel by all manner of horse drawn wheel transport and boats of many sizes. It was a hard and perilous journey through a vast and wild land filled with fascinating sights and, at times, dangerous men.

Why did Chekhov go on the trip in the first place? The "why" will also give insight as to what would be expected of him.

Several erroneous views are present in the West regarding the Sakhalin journey. One way of viewing Chekhov's trip was that the sensitive and mortally ill young Chekhov, criticized for doing nothing for the cause of Russian liberation, went to Sakhalin to expose the mistreatment of tsarist political prisoners by the officers of the crown. Another approach is that he had some secret personal reason for going which leads one to all sorts of conjecture about his motives. These impressions are both false.

Chekhov was in good spirits and reasonably good health, as he points out in a letter on June 27, 1890, from Siberia. He had been outdoors for two months, day and night, and had been swimming in the Amur.[15] Chekhov appears to have had mixed motives and wanted to combine his art, his science, and his wanderlust into a single voyage to Sakhalin.[16] Chekhov always loved exploration and explorers. He felt that if Darwin could explore and write a dissertation in the biological sciences then he would use his journey and research to write his dissertation. He believed that Sakhalin was the only place where the use of convicts for colonization could be studied at that time. He said that "all of Europe is interested in it, and we don't find it of any use?"[17] This was true but the study of Sakhalin was more a sociological or ethnographic study than medical research. As he continues in a letter of March 8, 1890, "I want to write at least one or two hundred pages to pay off some of my debts to medicine . . ."[18]

Chekhov wanted to pay a debt to medicine, as well as do something positive in a social sense, thus the dual purpose leads to confusion. Chekhov had not worked on his dissertation topic "The History of Russian Medicine" since 1887. If Chekhov completed a dissertation he would have been entitled to the title *privatdocent* and been allowed to lecture in medical school.[19] Chekhov's commitment to make the trip the source of a dissertation is confirmed throughout many sources.[20] Chekhov's choice of Sakhalin for a location for his research may have been motivated by the criticism leveled at him by the Populists. He was involved in research that was principally sociological but hoped to write a medical dissertation, all of this being part of a great adventure. Chekhov's confused motives resulted in a confused product which eventually was rejected by the medical school as a dissertation. *The Island of Sakhalin* was an excellent study if not a medical dissertation.

Chekhov spent months preparing for his trip. Indeed most of the preparation was for a scholarly expedition. Chekhov researched his dissertation topic in St. Petersburg and worked up a bibliography of over sixty-five titles on Sakhalin, only a small portion of which were on penology. He was interested in the native peoples of the island, the history of colonization, and memoirs of travelers who had been there.[21] He was especially interested in the environment and resources of the island.[22] He even organized his sister's college friends into a corps of research assistants, getting material and translating from languages Chekhov did not read. By the time Chekhov left in April for Sakhalin he had a scholar's background on the Island of Sakhalin.[23]

Chekhov left Moscow for his greatest adventure from Yaroslav station at eight in the evening, the 21st of April 1890, his only companion a flask of cognac flung over his shoulder.[24] When he arrived at the city of Yaroslav it was pouring rain and spoiled his first view of the Volga River. He found the city dirty, noticed many signs misspelled and saw strange inhabitants stalking about. Chekhov observed ignorance and dirty towns along the route. Every time he opened his eyes he added new resources for future comparison and inclusion in his stories.[25]

Boarding a steamer, he headed down the Volga. The sun shone and he saw white churches, marshy meadows, and the vast expanse of the Volga. The steamer he traveled on was a mixed blessing as was all transport throughout the journey. On the steamer he passed through Kostroma, Nizhny, and Kazan, then sailed the Kama River to Perm. "The Kama . . ." he wrote, ". . . is a most tedious river. The banks are bare, the trees are bare, the ground is brown . . . and the towns are gray." He thought the wharves of each town were crowded with second-rate intelligentsia because the arrival of any steamer broke the boredom. It was no surprise that Chekhov felt it had taken him two and a half years to sail to Perm.

From Perm to Yekaterinburg he took the train, observing that all Russian towns look the same. Yekaterinburg is exactly like Perm or Tula, or like Sumy and

Gadyach. Chekhov felt the people of Yekaterinburg "inspired the new arrival with a feeling akin to horror." He thought, "They were born in the local cast-iron foundries and are brought into the world not by a midwife, but by a machinist."[26]

While in Yekaterinburg he received word that the first steamer from Tomsk toward Lake Baikal would leave on May 18. This required a breakneck race across Siberia to make connections in what Chekhov described as a "wicker basket drawn by two horses." He left Tymen in his wicker basket on May 3.

During the first step of the journey of thousands of miles across the Siberian plain, Chekhov, chilled to the bone, observed a wealth of wildlife. He reflected that the people he met along the way were generally very fine people. He observed that none of his fellow travelers remembered anything being stolen from the coaches. He was surprised by the fact that the inhabitants had land allotments large enough to be well-off by European Russian standards. He was pleased to find the people honest, friendly, clean, well-mannered, simple, and good in their ways. If there was trouble, it was because vagabonds wandered the highways and sometimes killed each other or a peasant, although they never attacked a traveler.[27] This kind of information contradicts the stereotypes of the lawlessness of Siberia.

Chekhov saw many stereotypes fall in Siberia. He noted that Jews were respected and worked like everyone else in Siberia. He learned that it was not uncommon for a Jew to be elected as a village elder. "Exploitation by the Jews ...," he wrote, "... is unheard of." The Poles he saw in Siberia, most of whom were exiles deported after 1864, he found to be rich and poor, kind, hospitable and many of them most urbane people. The only individual he really did not like was a nobleman who ran a tavern and was a "conscienceless moneygrubber" to the core. This information is again contrary to the stereotypes of Jews and Poles.

Chekhov was fascinated by the Tartars because what he saw contradicted the savage stereotypes. He observed that a police chief told him that "... in Siberia they are better than the Russians." Chekhov, swept up by his experience, exclaimed, "My God, how rich Russia is in good people! Were it not for the cold that robs Siberia of the summer, and were it not for the officials who corrupt the peasants and the exiles, Siberia would be the richest and happiest land."[28]

During the next ten days of his trip, Chekhov was almost killed in a carriage crash, crossed the Ob and the Tom in flood stages in a rowboat, was constantly cold, wet, and hungry. He was so hungry, that, when he could get it, he crammed himself with bread. He dreamed of buckwheat groats. In Tyumen, Chekhov bought sausage for the trip, but when he opened it, he likened the stink to biting a "dog's tail smeared with tar. Pfui!"

Tomsk was much like the other towns he had seen. It was boring, drunken, had no beautiful women and was Asiatic in its lawlessness. Chekhov toured the brothels with a police officer acquaintance, until two A.M. He wrote that the episode was "Disgusting."

Chekhov purchased a carriage to make the journey from Tomsk to Sretensk and then continued his journey by boat.[29] Chekhov reached Irkutsk the night of June 4,

1890. He had covered over two thousand miles by carriage from Tyumen to Irkutsk. From Tyumen to Krasnoyarsk his enemies were flood, mud, a crash, and cold. From Krasnoyarsk to Irkutsk his enemies were heat and dust.

Chekhov moved from Irkutsk to Lake Baikal along the bank of the Angara. At the lake he had trouble getting food and had to wait days for the steamer. At this point his patience was wearing thin. "I have come to loathe sleeping. Every day you make your bed on the floor by spreading your short sheepskin with the wool outside, putting a rolled-up overcoat and a small pillow at the head;" he laments "you sleep on these hillocks in pants and vest – civilization, where art thou?"[30] Enroute to Blagoveshchensk, Chekhov's steamer ran aground and stove in her hull. While it was being patched, Chekhov toured the Ameso Cossack village of Pokrovskaya. The free way of life of the people impressed him. The inhabitants did not observe the religiously based fasts and prohibitions against meat which dominated European Russia. The girls smoked cigarettes and the old women pipes. He observed that he did not have to fear what he said and was surprised to find that even fugitive political prisoners moved about freely. He sensed a general attitude of no one really caring what happened back in Russia. "Ah, what liberalism!," he was motivated to write.[31]

Chekhov arrived in Blagoveshchensk on June 26, 1890, and wrote that he found the Amur region fascinating and "devilishly original." He realized that life there was something that "Europeans haven't an inkling of." It reminded him of tales of America. He was "in love with the Amur." The lowest of prisoners on the Amur "breathes more freely than the highest-placed general in Russia."[32]

Along the Amur, Chekhov saw the Chinese for the first time. He found them "good-natured people" who "dress austerely but beautifully, eat delicious food with great ceremony." He recognized the value of the Amur and pointed out the possibility that the Chinese would take it from Russia with Western help. The people of the Amur, he noticed, could not understand how Russia could get excited about Bulgaria and not care about something like the Amur.[33] Chekhov now had a perspective that the Europeans could not appreciate. He could look in from the vastness of Siberia at the crush of Europe.

During his trip Chekhov also came into contact with the Japanese. He found Japanese women particularly interesting "petite brunettes with large, complicated hairdos, beautiful torsos, and, as I had occasion to observe, low slung hips."

Almost as an afterthought he wrote, "They dress beautifully." He also noted that one girl's room he had seen was neat, sentimental, and cluttered with bric-a-brac.[34] Chekhov may have had a liaison with this girl and that would have enhanced the experience of the unmarried writer.

Chekhov continued down the Amur from Blagoveshchensk to Nikolaevsk, from there he crossed to the Island of Sakhalin, reaching it on July 11, 1890. Chekhov spent two months in Northern Sakhalin and received the complete cooperation of the commander general Vladimir Kononovich, who let him see everything. In the second week of September he moved on the 'S. S. Baikal' through the Tatar straight to Southern Sakhalin.

Chekhov made a census of every inhabitant of Sakhalin, which he recorded on filing cards. "I was particularly successful in the children's census and I place great hopes in it."[35] He found "starving children, a thirteen year old mistress and a pregnant fifteen year old. Girls go into prostitution at twelve, sometimes before they have menstruated." He noted that, "Churches and schools existed only on paper, that children were educated by their milieu and the penal colony environment." Orphaned or unwanted children were abused. Chekhov later was instrumental in having orphanages built for these children.[36]

For two months Chekhov pushed himself in his census research from five in the morning until dark. He saw brutalities which caused him nightmares. Gradually a bitterness began to eat at his insides which was more than he could stand. Overwork, loneliness and the fear of being trapped on the island by encircling cholera tore him apart. "As a result of all this my nerves took such a beating that I resolved never to return to Sakhalin." On October 13th, Chekhov left Sakhalin by steamer, never to return.[37]

From Sakhalin Chekhov went to Vladivostok. The contrast with Siberia was striking. "The poverty, ignorance, and pettiness are enough to drive you to despair." He saw this as a problem throughout the maritime region. In answer to Russian dreams of Pacific power he replied, "What crying Poverty!" "For every honest man there are ninety-nine thieves who are a disgrace to the Russian people."

After leaving Vladivostok his first stop was at the British colony of Hong Kong. The contrast was devastating. Some of his fellow Russians were criticizing the English for exploiting their colonies, but Chekhov wrote that the English also give roads, water mains, museums, and Christianity in return. What does Russia return for her exploitation?

He stopped at the island of Ceylon and felt he went from the Hell of Sakhalin to the Heaven of Ceylon. He "had relations . . . with a black-eyed Hindu girl, and guess where? In a coconut grove, on a moonlit night!" This was one of several romantic interludes on his trip. Chekhov pointed out that he had had a few affairs but that he was ". . . about as much like Catherine the Great as a hazelnut is like a battleship."[38] These types of relationships gave Chekhov a breadth and depth of understanding which was essential for his writing and which he drew upon for years.

Chekhov sailed around Asia and the subcontinent, finally he saw the Red Sea and, found seeing Mount Sinai a moving experience.[39] He returned to Moscow via Odessa on December 9, 1890.

Chekhov believed he was right to journey to Sakhalin. He believed it had matured him. The Sakhalin experience was too great to be dealt with immediately and when he did talk about it he never felt he said the right thing.[40] He realized he had accomplished a great deal and had "enough for three dissertations." It took Chekhov several years to write his study, *The Island of Sakhalin* which was intended to be a dissertation for the Doctorate.[41] According to Dr. Grigory

Rossolimo it was turned down by the Dean of the medical school of Moscow University probably because it was more sociological than medical.[42]

This work was a study of the penal colony but also a study of the effects of the colony on Sakhalin. Chekhov found that the native peoples were systematically being wiped out and the resources of the island were plundered and mismanaged. The trip also resulted in the stories "In Exile," "Gusev" and "The Murder." Because of that wilderness trip Chekhov matured further and it altered and expanded his perspectives. Anton Chekhov would never be the same again.

During March and April of 1891 Chekhov traveled westward to Austria, Italy, and France. He was delighted with Vienna, Venice, and Florence. He took the grand tour of Rome, Naples, Pompeii, Nice, and Paris.[43] When he saw the gaming tables at Monte Carlo he wrote that, "roulette luxury" reminded him of a luxurious lavatory.[44] For the next few years he was occupied at home but in 1894 he had to spend some weeks at Yalta for his health, and in the autumn he went south again. He moved more extensively from Feodosia to Odessa by sea, and then, after a trip to Lvov, he visited Vienna and spent a week at Abbazia, returning through Trieste, Venice, Milan, Genoa, Nice, and Paris.[45]

In the spring of 1897 a sudden and serious hemorrhage in Moscow forced him to go abroad for a year. He divided his time between Biarritz, Nice and Paris. When he returned he spent most of his time in the South and ventured abroad only for the last month of his life, spent in Germany.

Through his travels Chekhov had direct personal knowledge of Moscow and its surrounding provinces, the heart of old Russia, the Ukraine, the cradle of Russian civilization and the heart of the black earth region, St. Petersburg, the symbol of the Imperial era and the hub of the western oriented intelligentsia, the south, the Crimea and even the mysterious Caucasus; and Siberia, the hope-filled frontier, and Sakhalin. He had even seen, briefly, China and Indian culture in Ceylon.[46] He had also traveled widely in key areas of Western Civilization. All told, the knowledge which Chekhov had at his disposal, through his experience, was very impressive and would add depth and balance to his work.

NOTES

[1]   Simmons, *Chekhov*, pp. 6-18.

[2]   W. H. Bruford, *Chekhov and His Russia: A Sociological Study* (Hamden, Conn.: Archon Books, 1971), pp. 1-18.

[3]   Karlinsky, *Letters of Anton Chekhov*, p. 52.

[4]   Simmons, *Chekhov*, p. 15.

[5]   Simmons, *Chekhov*, pp. 7-9, p. 27.

[6]   Karlinsky, *Letters of Anton Chekhov*, p. 33.

[7]   Simmons, *Chekhov*, p. 35.

8   Karlinsky, *Letters of Anton Chekhov*, p. 50.

9   Simmons, *Chekhov*, pp. 195-196.

10   Simmons, *Chekhov*, pp. 180-181.

11   Karlinsky, *Letters of Anton Chekhov*, p. 46.

12   Yermilov, *Chekhov*, p. 93.

13   Yermilov, *Chekhov*, p. 93.

14   Yarmolinsky, *Letters of Anton Chekhov*, p. 57.

15   Karlinsky, *Letters of Anton Chekhov*, p. 169.

16   *Ibid.*, p. 153-155.

17   George Kennan had written an expose of conditions in Siberian prisons which appeared in the *Century Illustrated Monthly Magazine* which was banned in Russia and stimulated interest in the rest of the world about Siberian prisons. Chekhov mentions this in his letter of March 9, 1890.
     See: Yarmolinsky, *Letters of Anton Chekhov*, p. 128; Karlinsky, *Letters of Anton Chekhov*, p. 161.

18   Karlinsky, *Letters of Anton Chekhov*, pp. 158, 159.

19   Simmons, *Chekhov*, p. 345.

20   The previously noted memoirs of Dr. Rossolimo, Dr. Altschuller, and also confirmed in the memoir of another doctor friend of Chekhov's, M. A. Chlenov, "A. P. Chekhov i meditsina" in *Russkie vedomosti* ("A. P. Chekhov and Medicine," in *Russian News*), 1906, No. 1; M. A. Chlenov's rememberances, Olga Knipper's Dr. Rossolimo's and others are found in N. I. Gitovich and I. V. Fedorova, eds., *A. P. Chekhov v vospominaniyakh sovremennikov*, fourth ed., (Moscow, 1960).

21   Karlinsky, *Letters of Anton Chekhov*, p. 158.

22   Yarmolinsky, *Letters of Anton Chekhov*, p. 130.

23   Karlinsky, *Letters of Anton Chekhov*, p. 158.

24   Simmons, *Chekhov*, p. 217.

25   Yarmolinsky, *Letters of Anton Chekhov*, pp. 136-139. (Letters of April 23, April 24, 1890)

26   *Ibid.*, pp. 139-141. (Letter of April 29, 1890)

27   *Ibid.*, pp. 141-143. (Letter of May 14-17, 1890)

28   *Ibid.*, pp. 146-147. (Letter of May 14-17, 1890)

29   *Ibid.*, pp. 152-153. (Letter of May 20, 1890)

30   Yarmolinsky, *Letters of Anton Chekhov*, pp. 156-157. (Letter of June 5, 1890); *Ibid.*, pp. 157-159. (Letter of June 13, 1890).

31   *Ibid.*, pp. 161-162. (Letter of June 23-26, 1890)

32   *Ibid.*, p. 163. (Letter of June 27, 1890)

33   Karlinsky, *Letters of Anton Chekhov*, p. 168. (Letter of June 27, 1890)

34   *Ibid.*, p. 168. (Letter of June 27, 1890).

35   *Ibid.*, pp. 170-171. (Letter of September 11, 1890).

36   *Ibid.*, pp. 179-180. (Letter of January 26, 1891).

37   *Ibid.*, pp. 170-173, 179-181. (Sept. 11, 1890, Dec. 9, 1890, Jan. 26, 1891).

38   *Ibid.*, p. 266.

39   *Ibid.*, p. 173. (Letter of December 9, 1890).

40   Yarmolinsky, *Letters of Anton Chekhov*, pp. 172-173. (Dec. 17, 1890, Jan. 26, 1891).

41   Simmons, *Chekhov*, p. 211.

42   Karlinsky, *Letters of Anton Chekhov*, p. 171, 272. (Letter of September 11, 1890).

43   *Ibid.*, pp. 185-200. (Letters form Western Europe, Mar. 16, 1891 to April 24, 1891).

44   *Ibid.*, p. 196. (Letter of April 15, 1891).

45   Simmons, *Chekhov*, p. 325.

46   A good general sketch of Chekhov's travels can be found in: W. H. Bruford, *Chekhov and His Russia*, pp. 1-19.

CHAPTER IV

CHEKHOV'S POLITICS AND RELIGION

*"To hell with all the great men
and their philosophies"*

Anton Chekhov

Chekhov's political and religious beliefs are among the most misunderstood of any of the great Russian writers of the late 19th century. If one is to understand Chekhov one must understand his political and religious philosophy. In addition these views are significant in that this author contends they motivated him to write on certain subjects. Chekhov's style was impressionistic and his choice of topics became his vehicle for expressing personal concerns and his compassion. Yet he was objective in his detail and the general impression he created. His choice of topics made Chekhov more than a "mindless, young giant." It made him a window through which the reader might focus his subjectivity. Chekhov's subjectivity lay in the placement of those windows. It is necessary to present those beliefs as he most clearly revealed them in his letters or as they are conveyed in the remembrances of his contemporaries.

The most abstract of Chekhov's beliefs dealt with his religious views. In his notebooks Chekhov repeatedly stated that "Between the statements 'God exists' and 'there is no God' lies a whole vast field, which a true sage crosses with difficulty."

However, Chekhov believed the Russians picked only one of these extremes. That which lay between the poles was of little or no interest to them.[1] Chekhov did not appear to be as concerned with God as he was with the ritual and lifestyle related to religion.

As a child, Chekhov received a traditional religious upbringing forced upon him in an authoritarian manner by his father. He was compelled to sing in the choir, read the epistles and psalms in church, regularly attend services, and perform altar boy and bell ringing duty. As a result of this compulsion and other factors in his youth, his early religious experience seemed quite gloomy. In the final analysis he wrote, "I have no religion now."[2]

Organized religion or idealistic words were not important to Chekhov. He believed that one should not focus on the "forgotten words of Idealism." A person's own sense of purity and the freedom of one's soul was much more important to him. If a person did not believe in God, he should fill the gap created with something other than sensationalism. For Chekhov, it was terrible, simple, and difficult, ". . . one must seek, seek on one's own, all alone with one's conscience . . . ."[3]

In regard to religion, Chekhov saw a difference between Russia in general and the intelligentsia in particular. Chekhov felt that at the turn of the century the intelligentsia played with religious movements because it had nothing to do. In general, he believed the educated segment of society appeared to be moving further and further away from religion. He declined to comment on whether this was good or bad. He believed the religious revival movement at the end of the 19th century was a toy of the bored intelligentsia, not of Russia as a whole.[4]

Chekhov saw the dynamic of his age's culture not in organized religion, but in the beginning of a humanistic effort. This effort on the part of the educated was designed to thrust society into the modern age. It would be easier to see God in this effort than in the pretentious preaching of a Dostoevskii.[5] In the act of achieving this modern world, man would see God as clearly as two and two are four. Chekhov felt modern man in his effort to create modern culture through science and individual initiative was beginning an effort which would last for thousands of years, but that the religious movement of the intelligentsia was from the past. The religious movement among the bored intelligentsia was the survival of the gloomy, old traditional religion which Chekhov thought was dead or dying.[6]

Chekhov seemed to view religion between the two poles of "God is or is not" as a cultural phenomenon. He did not reject what he saw as good or useful in the religious tradition. He was not one to dismiss concepts such as Heaven cheaply. He looked at it from the poor man's perspective which was quite different than that of the intelligentsia from a wealthy background. Chekhov saw Heaven as a needed rest after hard work and that if it was as beautiful as the earth could be then it would be a good place.[7] Nor did Chekhov reject churchmen just because they were churchmen. Chekhov spoke highly of the local priest who often had lengthy visits with Chekhov. "He's a wonderful fellow, a widower with illegitimate children."[8]

Chekhov's attitude toward religion and his humanistic perspective were on occasion misunderstood and led to confused conclusions. Chekhov refused to accept one or the other of the Russian extreme positions as to whether God did or did not exist. Chekhov, a rational man, dwelt in the great gray area between the extremes. As a humanist, he saw value in the ethical principals of Christianity but he rejected any bigotry or narrowness of thought cloaked in religious trappings.

Boris Zaitsev, a Russian emigre, believed that Chekhov was actually a believing, orthodox Christian, whether he knew it or not. This attitude was held by many emigres and was the core of Zaitsev's book, *Chekhov*.[9]

Chekhov's attitude toward religion can be seen when he wrote to his sister while he was in France for his health. It was the first time he was away from Russia at Eastertime. He was terribly lonely and experiencing a real sense of cultural alienation. He didn't hate the West, he just loved Russia and missed being home for the holidays. It was not because he believed or did not believe in the resurrection of Christ that he wrote to his sister, 'Christ has truly risen.' No, it was a traditional greeting and a lonely echo of times of family happiness on the most important holiday of the calendar. It was part of him and his culture, but it was not intellectually part of his ideology.

He condemned the religious hypocrites and pharisees but also accepted the positive aspects of religion such as the family bond it created at Easter. Whether God existed or not, Chekhov, the humanist, saw value in what the bonds of religion could bring out in the family. He also realized the motive force religion could provide for positive action, and the basis it provided for an ethical system for mankind.

Chekhov resisted political labels just as forcefully as he resisted religious ones. He particularly hated political labels and the mindless criticism hurled back and forth between political camps. Chekhov was frequently angered by the liberal press that claimed he lacked principle because he would not write obviously political tracts in favor of the Zemstvo, the new courts, freedom of the press, and freedom in general. He felt that a paper like *Russian Thought,* which criticized him for his lack of political activities, had not left any real mark on society either and should not criticize him until it did.[10]

Chekhov was afraid of political labels. He refused the labels of liberal, conservative, gradualist or indifferentist. He was none of those. Chekhov maintained that all he wanted to be was a "free artist and nothing else . . ."[11]

While refusing political labels, he believed that he had not hidden his respect for the Zemstvo system nor for such reforms as trial by jury.[12] He had also presented some important political points publicly. Chekhov was quoted as having said that a constitution would soon be proposed in Russia.[13] In a conversation with the scholar Kovalevsky, he said that he anticipated the equality of the peasantry and the eventual disappearance of the landed gentry from the Russian countryside.[14]

It is also significant that Chekhov had given up Tolstoi's teaching of nonresistance to evil.[15] Chekhov, who believed in personal action, could now accept doing something about evil as part of his ideology. He accepted these ideas but refused any liberal or conservative label.

The notions of liberalism or conservatism were never at the heart of Chekhov's works. He believed that it was his purpose as a writer to balance the truth against lies. This was what was at the heart of his work, not political labels.[16] At the same time, Chekhov believed that he had clearly stated his views and did not want to be thought of as a spineless coward afraid of being thought liberal or conservative. Those labels just did not apply. He associated with liberals, conservatives and radicals. He maintained that he had "never been secretive" about his views.[17]

One can see Chekhov, like Luther, saying 'Here I stand'. Chekhov's problem was that he stood squarely in the middle.

Even though he rejected labels, he felt that he had a clear cut "ideology." Chekhov rejected the view that his stories lacked ideology. He felt that his stories showed sympathies and antipathies but the heart of the matter was not political. His ideology had truth at the center. He believed his work protested ". . . against lying from start to finish. . . ." "Isn't that an Ideology?"[18]

Central to Chekhov's philosophy was his stress on truth. He also refused to accept the notion that political ends justify the means. He found that "repulsive means for good ends make the ends themselves repulsive." Chekhov's commitment to truth led him to promise that if he were a politician he would never disgrace his "present for the sake of his future" even if he were promised "tons of bliss for a pennyweight of base lies."[19]

He saw the same problem with stereotypes as with political labels. Chekhov believed that hypocrisy, stupidity and tyranny were present throughout the society not just in merchants' homes and police stations. Chekhov saw these qualities ". . . in science, in literature, among the younger generation." As a result, he did not favor any particular group because he looked ". . . upon tags and labels as prejudices."[20]

Chekhov's philosophy was committed to the primacy of humanity and its right to ". . . health, intelligence, talent, inspiration, love and the most absolute freedom imaginable . . ." Chekhov believed man had the right to ". . . freedom from violence and lies, no matter what form the latter two take."[21]

He strongly believed that writers and artist should be wary of political parties and movements. In fact, he wrote that ". . . major writers and artists should engage in politics only enough to protect themselves from it."[22] Chekhov refused to enter politics in the way others wanted him to. He rejected what they believed to be politics. He chose instead to reveal lies by detailing truth.

Chekhov's belief in the truth led him to the defense of freedom of the press. He believed that it was the writer's job to defend the underdog. It was not the writer's role to condemn or persecute.[23] He hated and feared the power of censors because censorship protected the ineptitude and lies that existed in society. You could not reveal lies if you could not publish.[24]

There are many examples of Chekhov exerting himself to encourage the publication of truth. On one occasion, he tried to encourage his conservative publisher friend Suvorin to take an active role in the defense of what was right in his newspaper. On another occasion, he took careful note of a piece Suvorin had written on the subject of student disturbances.[25] He was particularly delighted when Suvorin was critical of the *Moscow News* which was a reactionary paper.[26] Chekhov tried to encourage Suvorin to write what he wanted and challenge the problems in society. Unfortunately, Suvorin never rallied to his call.

Chekhov did not like ideological or political labels. He rejected stereotypes because he found them limiting and confusing. He also hated the "herd psychology" such labels and stereotypes represented. Chekhov had much more faith in individual action than the mere mouthing of political phrases.

Chekhov's belief in individual initiative was strongly connected to his understanding that "Russia was rich in good people." He believed that it was "the officials who corrupted the people." The people could be as effective as the officials.[27] In short, Chekhov's faith rested on the individual.

Chekhov viewed Russia's salvation as emerging from the actions of individuals such as peasants, intellectuals, and people drawn from all groups scattered throughout the country. In Chekhov's vision, although such individuals were few in number and widely dispersed, they nevertheless played an inconspicuous but important role in society. "They do not dominate," he wrote, "yet their work is visible."

Chekhov saw the combined efforts of individuals creating a science which was moving inexorably forward. As a result, individuals' social consciousness was increasing and moral issues were coming to the fore. All this was being accomplished without the "intelligentsia en masse," and in spite of the other pressures of Russian society. The march of progress through the efforts of a broad base of individual acts would ultimately triumph, not the isolated acts of the revered intelligentsia.[28]

Chekhov's belief in individual initiative was brought to the fore and confirmed during a series of national crises which developed in Russia. During the famine of 1891, the government, clogged by bureaucratic ineptitude, would not permit individuals to act to solve the problem. Commenting on the crisis, Chekhov reported how "Everybody discussed how to bypass the administration and go about organizing aid independently." He noted how concerned persons sent their own representatives to the famine stricken provinces "to acquaint themselves with the situation at firsthand, set up relief kitchens, and so on."[29] Obviously impressed with such individual initiative, Chekhov was appalled to learn just how hard it was for the individual to move others during the period of famine and epidemic. Working as an individual himself, Chekhov had a difficult time trying to get help from the rich. When he went to one of his neighbors, a very wealthy countess, concerning the building of a shelter for her workers, ". . . she treated me as if I had come to apply for a job. That hurt me, and I lied to her and told her I was rich." Chekhov told the same lie to the archimandrite when he refused to help Chekhov set up preparations at the monastery in anticipation of the cholera epidemic striking the hostel run by the monastery. Chekhov in rage quoted the archimandrite as saying that the guests ". . . are well-to-do. They will pay you themselves."[30] Chekhov did not want money. He needed cooperation and got none.

These types of situations led Chekhov to state that he had ". . . no faith in our intelligentsia; it is hypocritical, dishonest, hysterical, ill-bred and lazy." He did not even believe them when they suffered and complained.[31]

Chekhov was in complete sympathy with private initiative because he saw people as having free will and having the capacity to do good as they choose. In a crisis, Chekhov did not see the use of discussions about government programs, the Red Cross and other plans. As he said, "I felt that with a modicum of composure and a kind disposition, we could bypass everything fearful and ticklish . . ." He saw no reason to meet with a cabinet minister or other officials when they were not doing an adequate job in the first place. He had gone to Sakhalin without recommendation. Why could he not go to a famine stricken province?[32]

Chekhov's individual efforts and those of his friends were frustrated by the government. The ineffectiveness of the government caused it to feel threatened by individual effort. Even though individual initiative would have provided essential aid, the government ". . . refused, declaring that the right to organize aid belonged exclusively to the Department of Church Affairs and the Red Cross." Chekhov concluded bitterly, "In short, private initiative was nipped in the bud." Chekhov realized that it took courage to defy the established order but to be successful in this, it took the authority of a great figure like Tolstoi. Courage and authority were necessary to ". . . do what duty commands."[33]

Chekhov's courage and authority led him to individual action. Chekhov agreed to a project to buy livestock from the peasants during the famine of 1891-1892. He believed that he could not count on the rich because they had already given whatever they were going to give. Chekhov wrote that "now everything depends on the average citizen, the man who gives by the ruble and half ruble." The well-to-do people who advocated private initiative in September had found refuge in traditional commissions like the Red Cross by December. Given the huge burden of work which now remained to be done, in the last analysis "it follows that only the average citizen is left." Chekhov the individual, using money from individuals, was able to aid the people in crisis in spite of the government and the hypocrites of his world. During the famine, he also gained respect for charitable societies that were independent of the government.[34]

Chekhov recognized the tremendous value of charitable societies and their great financial need. He observed that many of the sickly poor were treated and healed in the hospital. When they were released, they went back to their environment of poverty. They became sick again and died. As a result, Chekhov earnestly concluded that other institutions and services had to be provided for the poor to keep them from falling prey to disease again.

Chekhov supported a traditional liberal view that individual initiative is essential to the survival of society. In order to break the cycle of poverty which threatened society, food, clothing and shelter were provided by charitable societies which were supported by a few individuals. Chekhov believed that these charitable individuals kept society alive. If they died, so would society. In Chekhov's mind, this was a mandate for individual action. It was essential that every honorable man participate. Chekhov concluded that many people spent thousands to make people into prostitutes, slaves, syphilitics, and alcoholics. How much better it would have been to support the efforts of individuals to break this cycle and save society.[35]

Chekhov's individualism did not blind him to reality nor did it allow him to romanticize reality. When he engaged in efforts against disease, he knew that the ignorance of the peasants would be a stumbling block. "The peasants," he wrote, "... are crude, unsanitary and mistrustful, but the thought that our labors will not be in vain makes it all almost unnoticeable. . ." Chekhov became exhausted in his struggle to prepare for the cholera epidemic. His lack of money and unfamiliarity with the area made his job a draining one. Spiritually, he had a great urge to leave the cholera fight and go someplace and just write. He was alone and tired but pressed on just as Tolstoi had, facing all odds with courage.[36]

Chekhov's individual efforts on behalf of his community drained him physically and financially. "I abandoned literature long ago, and I'm poor and broke ..." He refused any pay for his work as a physician.[37] When he got deeply into his work fighting the impending epidemic, he did not have time to write and was not "... earning a kopeck until October: I don't have a thing to my name."[38] Chekhov frequently repeated this practice of overextending himself in the name of his individual commitment to the community. He lived hand to mouth for months to give thousands of rubles to build a peasant school.[39]

Chekhov was willing to recognize those who helped regardless of previous opinions. During his struggle with the impending epidemic, he saw a different side of the intelligentsia. Chekhov praised them for their hard work and sacrifice of time and energy. He noted that "In Nizhny, doctors and the entire educated sector of the population have done wonders."[40]

Chekhov hoped that individual initiative, personal freedom and self-understanding would lead to progress through planned scientific achievement and broad based learning. He was not a Slavophile in the sense that he saw, "the present" in Russia was ". . . always worse than the past." Russia stood as a contrast to progress and self-understanding. Part of the reason for this was that Russian excitability too quickly turned "... into weariness." Commenting on this tendency, he observed that as soon as the Russian left school, he bit off more than he could chew so that by the age of thirty he began to feel drained and bored without knowing why. He suggested that the Russian did not "genuinely . . . understand himself . . ." When the Russian looked at his society, he found that it offered him a "sense of decency." He looks outside himself for the causes and finds nothing. When he looked inside himself, he found an undefinable sense of guilt. Chekhov said, "This is a Russian feeling." The Russian is tired, bored, guilt-ridden and lonely.[41]

Chekhov saw the salvation of Russia in the individual. Only ethical behavior and work could counteract this Russian tendency to tiredness and boredom. Chekhov believed, "If one wants to lead a good life, one must work." The Russian must "Work with love and faith."[42]

In contrast to the need for their work, Chekhov saw Russian architects doing a few good and promising things in their early careers only to spend the rest of their lives playing cards or waiting at stage doors. There is also the doctor who builds a practice and then does not keep up with his field. In the midst of this was a host of officials who sent reports to the capital with complete indifference. These documents would perhaps restrict people's lives but the officials were indifferent. Initially fighting this official tendency is the lawyer who makes his reputation in defense of truth and then makes his fortune defending property rights. He then uses his fortune to gamble "on horses, eat oysters, and pass himself off as a connoisseur of all the arts."[43] This self-destructive tendency must be fought by individuals who want to achieve good for their society. Psychologically, the Russian must change.

The same shortcoming can be seen in the arts. An actor plays a couple of parts and then considers himself a genius. Chekhov said, "Russia is a land of greedy idlers" who gorge themselves, get drunk, and sleep through the day snoring loudly. Even when they marry it is just to bring order to the house and then take a mistress for social prestige.

Regarding Russian psychological make-up, Chekhov observed rather ruefully that, "Their psychology is a dog's psychology." Beat them and they run off, tail between their legs. Pet them and they roll over on their backs.

Gorkii felt he saw a cold, sorrowful contempt under Chekhov's words of criticism even though he was by nature compassionate. Chekhov was more disappointed than disgusted. He saw progress through hard work as essential to Russia. To overcome the shortcomings, he believed a new psychology on the part of the Russian toward progress would best be developed through education. Thus, Chekhov accepted the traditional liberal view of the saving role of education.[44]

Chekhov lamented the apparent Russian inability to solve problems and believed that the lack arose because the Russians were nervous, helpless and complaining fools who more often than not gave way to their frazzled and undisciplined nerves. Such a condition, Chekhov felt, led to disappointment, apathy, and weariness which were the inevitable consequences of the excessively excitable Russian character. He particularly held that such excitability was ". . . to a great degree, characteristic of our young people."

The excessive excitability and enthusiasm of the Russian character influenced them in their choice of political philosophies as far as Chekhov was concerned. He observed that the excitement associated with Socialism rapidly lost its zeal and was reduced to criticizing the Zemstvo, one of the few institutions Chekhov thought was trying to generate change in Russia. He felt also that Liberalism too lost its initial verve because it became confused and lacked clear, concrete definitions of goals and objectives. Perturbed over the failure of the Russian enthusiasm to follow through to results, he observed: " . . . what is all this Russian enthusiasm worth?"[45]

Part of the problem, as Chekhov saw it, was the Russian propensity to see things through the restricted vision of stereotypes. But this led to disastrous results; the Russians were honest when it was unnecessary, and thus caused pain. The Russian would do anything for his cause, even blow someone up, and feel no pangs of conscience. All of this for some rule like, "The honest laborer should exterminate the powers of darkness."[46] This kind of mindless following of old tired phrases wedded with the Russian emotionality led to irrational ideologies which were inhumane in the name of humanity.

Chekhov's preference for personal action as opposed to the utilitarian ideology of the age was evidenced in the character of Michael Khrushchev from "The Wood Demon." Khrushchev was a physician who ministered unselfishly to the peasants but he was also an active conservationist who tried to protect the forests and wildlife. The other characters in the story criticized him for pursuing a dual role and failing to become a utilitarian ideologue. Khrushchev, mirroring Chekhov's own views, believed that his program of conservation and medical action was much more productive than ideology.

Chekhov's activism was not noticed by his contemporaries or by many of his critics because, like many sincere individuals, Chekhov did what he thought was right and did not seek publicity.[47] Furthermore, Chekhov's view of what was right and appropriate was based on his humanistic scientific world view. Chekhov's world view differed from the world view of the critics who were more concerned with ideology and behavioral modification. Finally, the grand gestures of some of the great literary figures such as Tolstoi and Gorkii were of greater news value than Chekhov's action in treating peasant ills in the countryside. The critics created their various Chekhovs without regard to the facts of his humanistic individual initiative.

Chekhov's belief in individual initiative and his experience in various crises led him to respect the courage of the small men who committed themselves to help people at great expense and, at times, personal risk. These common people acted in the face of indifference or possible hostility on the part of the government. His understanding of these efforts caused him to view the action of great writers and public figures with less awe. The great men were for Chekhov the small men of courage who risked so much without the protection of fame. Even though Chekhov was at times in awe of men like Tolstoi, he resented their arrogance and was led to say, "To Hell with the philosophy of the great men of this world!"[48] Chekhov felt all great wise men were as despotic, as impolite and as insensitive as generals because they were confident of that impunity. Chekhov praised Tolstoi when he stood up for the right against convention but he was critical of him because he often flaunted his ignorance of important issues. Chekhov was particularly disturbed because no one would denounce the great men.

Chekhov applauded freedom and deplored license. He was attuned to the individual initiative of ordinary men. The courage of great men was diminished in his view because unlike the ordinary people, they were not held responsible for their actions.[49]

Chekhov believed in the freedom to write the truth. He wanted to depict life truthfully and show to what degree life deviated from the common perception of the norm. Chekhov's problem was that he did not know what the norm of life was. He said, "All of us know what a dishonorable act is, but just what honor is we do not know." One solution to this problem was to stick to the generally accepted

norm. He believed that the norm was absolute freedom. Chekhov believed in "...
freedom from coercion, from prejudices, ignorance, the devil; freedom from
passions and so forth."[50]

Affirming the basic goodness of the world, Chekhov concluded that man
created problems because man's own inner weakness often interfered with his
better instincts. To him, it was a waste to love others but not respect others as
persons or treat others with dignity.[51] Chekhov's respect for the dignity of the
individual person was clearly brought out when, on one occasion, he took his
brother Alexandr to task for treating people badly. He urged his brother to treat his
common-law wife humanely and to respect his servants and women in general.
"What heavenly or earthly power ... ," he scolded his brother, "... has given you
the right to make them your slaves?"[52]

Alexandr's brutishness struck a chord in Chekhov's memory. Chekhov
remembered his own childhood experiences of hearing his father cursing his
mother in front of the children at the dinner table because the soup was too salty.
He recalled his own horror and revulsion at such despotism which ruined his
mother's life and caused his father to constantly lament his guilt in later life.
Chekhov demanded respect for human beings, from human beings, simply because
they were human beings. Chekhov was a Humanist.[53] Chekhov rejected all forms
of inhumanity throughout his life. As a schoolboy, he defended a Jewish student
who had slapped another boy for calling him a "yid." The Jewish boy was
expelled, but Chekhov led the other students in his defense, threatening to boycott
class. This show of unanimity led the administration to back down. Chekhov
began rejecting stereotypes, bigotry and ignorance early in life.[54]

Chekhov recognized "the moral law" as a higher law than the official legal
codes of the country. When we wish to act according to conscience, we follow the
moral law because we sense what is just. If people followed only the official law of
the state, there would be something missing from their decision. Man's "conscience" must be his guide.[55]

Chekhov's belief in the ordinary man and his suspicion of officials may have led
to his strong support of the jury system which he admired. Chekhov believed in the
fundamental validity of the jury system. He felt it rested on the judgment of person
by person. It involved judgment based on prevailing social mores and customs as
well as official and moral law.[56]

Chekhov, looking through the eyes of his person-centered world view, saw
serious problems in Russia. He observed that Russians did not seem to respect
each other or themselves and as a result, saw no dignity in their work or work in
general. They tended to focus on symbols instead of commitment to individual
achievement. Russians focused on something like patriotism instead of doing
something concrete for themselves or their county. Chekhov felt, "How poor is
our conception of patriotism!" He lamented that Russians boast of their love of
their great country in the newspapers, "but how is that love expressed?" Instead of
seeking knowledge, Russians stress inordinate brazenness and conceit, instead of

work. Russians are lazy and swinish. His country's concept of honor had no justice in it. Honor did not go beyond, "the honor of the uniform," a uniform which every day guarded the prisoners' dock. Russians needed to work above all else and in this work, justice must be the central principle. That was the essence of patriotism. If the Russians had this, all else would come to them.[57]

The core of life for Chekhov was the individual human's life. Chekhov emphasized the physical man, a healthy life, human intelligence, human talent, inspiration and love. This was the profile of a humanist, well-rounded and happy. In addition, he desired for man freedom from lies and violence in any form.[58] In light of this view of man, Chekhov's scientific training does not conflict with his humanism, it merely deepens it.

Like many humanists and liberals, Anton Chekhov believed in the role and power of education as a humanizing force. Throughout his life, Chekhov benefited from and contributed greatly to education in Russia. Chekhov saw many of the problems of Russia linked to ignorance. If Russia was backward, it was because education lagged.

Chekhov daydreamed about education and pictured a cottage with a sign on it: "School." He saw decently dressed and well-fed peasants gathered around the school. This was his view of the ninth century. Chekhov thought of a second picture in the nineteenth century; ". . . the same cottage, but already dilapidated and overgrown with nettles . . ." Chekhov concluded that "in the ninth century, there were schools, hospitals. In the nineteenth, there are schools, pothouses . . ."[59] Because of his belief in education, Chekhov was acutely aware of Russia's great needs in that area.

Chekhov strongly supported the role of rural teachers in Russia because he believed that education was so vital to future Russian development and progress. He once observed to Gorkii that "The Russian village needs a good, wise, educated teacher!" He was convinced that the Russian state would eventually collapse unless it dedicated itself to the immediate development of widespread public schools staffed by well-educated, highly motivated teachers who would be able to win the respect of the Russian peasants. He lamented the fact that most teachers were poor in spirit and training, were poorly paid and were often harassed by school inspectors interested in regulations rather than education. Such a system produced teachers who led cold, isolated, and ignorant lives that stifled leadership and fostered only the desire to escape the drabness of country life.[60]

Chekhov told Gorkii that he would like to build a sanatorium for aging village schoolteachers. He conceived of a beautiful building with a library where lectures were given daily – "a teacher must know everything . . . everything!"[61]

Ernest Simmons, Chekhov's biographer, believed that deep in Chekhov lay the instincts of a teacher. He had an almost naive faith in the power of education to mold and guide the moral nature of men and women.[62] He accepted a moral law. Chekhov believed in the role of education and supported it by building schools and aiding libraries. For his zeal on behalf of national education, the government awarded him the Order of Saint Stanislaw.[63]

Although Chekhov held education in very high regard, he had negative experiences with radical students when he was a student, which may have affected his attitude toward university disturbances during the 1890's. Chekhov's reaction to the university disturbances in the late 1880's and early 1890's was initially different than his reaction to the disturbances in the late 1890's. This was, perhaps, related to his previous experiences in school with radicals, whom he held in low regard. His correspondence to his friend Suvorin indicated that he viewed student demands during the disturbances of 1890 negatively.[64] However, by 1899, his comments were much more tolerant and understanding. Perhaps the change in attitude reflected his own growth and the fact that in 1899, during the student strike at St. Petersburg University, he had an opportunity to hear the student side of issues by talking to his friend Lavrov's son, Michael, who was one of the leaders of the student strike.[65]

Chekhov's belief in education and his personal support of it placed him squarely behind the tradition of the Zemstvo liberals and in the time-honored tradition of humanism. This is totally consistent with his support of personal action. He saw education as the salvation of Russia and worked for that salvation.

Chekhov believed that if humanity was to make progress in education, or anything else, it needed goals. Otherwise, life was meaningless. These goals must at times be lofty and remote. He rejected the idea that such kinds of goals cause problems. Without lofty goals man was a beast doing nothing more than eating, drinking and sleeping. Once a person has satisfied these needs, there was nothing left for him. He might as well ". . . take a flying leap and bash his head . . ."[66] Humanities higher goals justified its existence. Chekhov believed in justice, freedom, the search for truth and also progress.

Chekhov was a firm believer in progress. His peasant background demanded it. He felt he had acquired a belief in progress early because when he was a child and was beaten, he hoped for better. It was years before the floggings stopped, but they did stop, so he became a believer in progress. Chekhov was from a Raznochintsy background and hated the vulgarity of that life. He longed for the gentle life of wit, grace and intelligence. Even with this background, Chekhov was for a while hypnotized by Tolstoi's abstract schemes. Chekhov finally broke the spell and his essential belief in progress re-emerged. In the final analysis, Chekhov believed that ". . . there is more love for mankind in electricity and steam than in" Tolstoi's "idealistic schemes."[67]

Chekhov believed in remote and lofty goals but rejected just sitting around talking about abstract idealistic words or ideologies. His belief in direct action by individuals has already been established. He had said to hell with the "ideals" of the great men and thought the ideals of the men of the sixties were not worth ". . . today's poorest Zemstvo hospital."[68]

Chekhov's experience with the Zemstvo confirmed his belief in personal action and also led him to support the Zemstvo schools and hospitals. Chekhov's experience with Zemstvo staffers was that they were intelligent, efficient, and knowledgeable. He also saw the effect of Zemstvo work. He did not have to convince the peasants that the doctors did not bring disease because they had seen Zemstvo doctors before. This was an indication that the health care system was beginning to deliver service in the countryside. Were it not for the excellent work of the Zemstvo doctors, Chekhov the physician, could have been physically attacked by the ignorant peasants as others had been in the past.[69]

In fact, when asked by a friend about building a hospital, Chekhov recommended that it be a Zemstvo hospital. The Zemstvo would provide the blueprints, a doctor, "and you will end up spending considerably less if the Zemstvo take a hand in the project." Chekhov stood squarely behind the Zemstvo.[70]

Chekhov supported both Zemstvo schools and hospitals. He even considered a book on Zemstvo schools similar in intent and scope to his work on Sakhalin. By showing the day-to-day operation of some sixty schools, he hoped to help Zemstvo officials. This was consistent with Chekhov's method as established previously in this study. Unfortunately, Chekhov never carried out the study in support of the Zemstvo.[71]

Chekhov shows in several stories that he sees man's saving grace in his capacity for active good. This is man's prime meaning. In his story, "In the Hollow," he showed the violence of man but also indicated that man's saving grace was his capacity for good. This concept was further expanded when Lidiya in "The House with the Mansard" mirrored his views that the noblest task man could have was to serve his neighbor as best he could.

Chekhov's entire life was a succession of humanistic acts begun by his individual initiative involving his twin tales of science and literature. He tried to ease famine, fought epidemics, built schools, developed library collections, gave free medical care to thousands of peasants, aided many young writers and contributed his time and money to many humanistic causes. Even his trip to Sakhalin may be viewed as a humanistic act. Chekhov's humanism was also consistent with Zemstvo liberalism.

After having reviewed Chekhov's views, it is apparent that his position was consistent with liberalism, yet Soviet scholars like Yermilov refuse to admit that Chekhov could be a liberal. "Culture with all its great values," N. Berdjaev observed, "is middle of the road . . ."[72] Berdjaev sees hostility to middle-of-the-road culture as a Russian trait. Chekhov had repeatedly rejected being set in a Russian mold, instead of rejecting middle-of-the-road culture. Jackson saw Chekhov as a "radical reaffirmation of the middle of the road," the liberal position which is necessary for the life of the ordinary man in everyday society.[73]

It is apparent that if a political label were to be placed on Chekhov, it would be consistent with a middle-of-the-road position. Chekhov would be considered a liberal. His views were consistent with those of traditional western liberalism as represented by J. S. Mill. In addition, this liberal view can be seen in Russia in those groups, which after Chekhov's death, would make up the Constitutional Democratic Party. Within this party there were two dominant groups which represented the principal liberal views in Russia. These two views are personified in Maklakov, the Zemstvo liberal, and Miliukov, the radical liberal.[74]

In gauging Chekhov's politics one can say Chekhov was a rather traditional liberal in that he accepted points which traditionally are used to characterize a liberal. He believed in the individual and individual freedom. Chekhov believed in the critical and saving role of popular education. He even stressed the government's right and duty to protect people but resisted government intervention deep into society to the point that it hampered the individual's freedom.

The progress in society would come from individual initiative and the solution to societies problems would come from individual action and individually run charities. The organizations Chekhov supported most were those that delivered primary services to the people. These were generally Zemstvo hospitals and schools as well as public libraries. He would also aid individuals who were trying to get ahead, especially in the field of his greatest influence, writing.

Chekhov was also humanistic in his belief in people for their own sake. He tied his belief in humanity and individual initiative to science and stressed the resulting progress. His political beliefs reflect his liberal view and are consistent with his humanism. Anton Chekhov at various times expressed the desire for: Freedom, Freedom of the Press, Freedom of Religion, Freedom of Thought and Freedom of Assembly. He wanted justice and trial by jury.

Chekhov supported the idea of constitutional representative government. But Chekhov would not accept the type of terrorism personified by Narodnaia Volia in order to achieve these ends. The end does not justify this type of means.

Anton Chekhov was closer to the tradition of Maklakov, the Zemstvo liberal, than he was to Miliukov, yet he combines elements of both. Chekhov accepted ideas similar to Maklakov's but rejected even the moderate Slavophile position which Maklakov held. On the other hand, Chekhov rejected Miliukov's acceptance of the validity of terrorism but accepted Miliukov's positive view of the West and western progress.[75] In the final analysis, Chekhov, who hated labels, could not be clearly labelled, he was a liberal but a unique sort, close to, but not completely, a Zemstvo liberal.

Chekhov did not show his politics in his stories. They were presented objectively. He did subjectively choose to write about topics which he, as a liberal thinker, humanist, physician and writer, felt should be exposed objectively to public review. These topics were portrayed objectively, but the precision of the description permitted the reader to see the intrinsic problems that plagued Russia. Chekhov hoped that the readers would then attempt on their own initiative to resolve the problems seen in the reality he had described so clearly in his stories.

NOTES

[1] Karlinsky, *Letters of Anton Chekhov*, p. 12-13 (note books).

2   *Ibid.*, p. 217 (March 9, 1892).

3   *Ibid.*, p. 414 (Dec. 17, 1901).

4   Yarmolinsky, *Letters of Anton Chekhov*, pp. 437, 438 (Dec. 30, 1902).

5   *Ibid.*, p. 438 (December 30, 1902).

6   Yarmolinsky, *Letters of Anton Chekhov*, p. 438 (Dec. 30, 1902).

7   *Ibid.*, p. 172 (Moscow, Dec. 17, 1890).

8   Karlinsky, *Letters of Anton Chekhov*, p. 242 (August 16, 1892).

9   Karlinsky, *Letters of Anton Chekhov*, p. 400; See also Boris Zaitsev, *Chekhov*, (N.Y., 1954).

10   Karlinsky, *Letters of Anton Chekhov*, p. 165 (April 10, 1890).

11   *Ibid.*, p. 109 (October 4, 1888).

12   *Ibid.*, p. 111 (October 9, 1888).

13   Simmons, *Chekhov*, p. 563.

14   *Ibid.*, p. 519

15   *Ibid.*, p. 564

16   Karlinsky, *Letters of Anton Chekhov*, p. 111 (Oct. 9, 1888).

17   *Ibid.*, p. 110 (October 9, 1888).

18   *Ibid.*, p. 112 (October 9, 1888).

19   *Ibid.*, p. 238 (August 1, 1888).

20   *Ibid.*, p. 109 (October 4, 1888).

21   *Ibid.*

22   *Ibid.*, p. 317 (February 6, 1888).

23   *Ibid.*, p. 317 (February 6, 1888).

24   *Ibid.*, p. 112 (October 9, 1888).

25   Yarmolinsky, *Letters of Anton Chekhov*, p. 276 (Jan. 4, 1897).

26   Simmons, *Chekhov*, p. 415.

27   Yarmolinsky, *Letters of Anton Chekhov*, p. 145 (May 16, 1890).

28   Karlinsky, *Letters of Anton Chekhov*, p. 341 (Feb. 22, 1899).

29   *Ibid.*, p. 209 (December 11, 1891).

30   *Ibid.*, p. 242 (August 16, 1892).

31   *Ibid.*, p. 341 (February 22, 1899).

32   *Ibid.*, pp. 209-210 (February 22, 1899).

33   *Ibid.*, p. 209 (December 11, 1891).

34   *Ibid.*, p. 211 (December 11, 1891).

35   Yarmolinsky, *Letters of Anton Chekhov*, pp. 277-278 (Jan. 23, 1897).

36   Karlinsky, *Letters of Anton Chekhov*, p. 237 (March 23, 1895).

37   *Ibid.*, p. 237 (August 1, 1892).

38   *Ibid.*, p. 235 (July 31, 1892).

39   *Ibid.*, p. 295 (February 8, 1897).

40   *Ibid.*, p. 240 (August 16, 1892).

41   *Ibid.*, pp. 75-77 (December 30, 1888).

42   Maxim Gorkii, "On Literature," in *Anton Chekhov's Short Stories*, Edited by Ralph E. Matlaw (New York, W.W. Norton and Co., 1979), p. 283.

43   *Ibid.*, pp. 283-284.

44   Maxim Gorkii, "On Literature," in *Anton Chekhov's Short Stories*, p. 284.

45   Karlinsky, *Letters of Anton Chekhov*, p. 78 (December 30, 1888).

46   *Ibid.*, p. 79 (December 30, 1888).

47   One of the few who stress Chekhov's program of positive action is: Kornei Chukovskii, *Chekhov the Man*, translated by Pauline Ross (New York: Hutchinson and Co., 1945).

48   Karlinsky, *Letters of Anton Chekhov*, p. 203 (September 8, 1891).

49   *Ibid.*, p. 203 (September 8, 1891).

50   Yarmolinsky, *Letters of Anton Chekhov*, pp. 112-113 (April 9, 1889).

51   *Ibid.*, p. 170 (December 9, 1890).

52   Karlinsky, *Letters of Anton Chekhov*, p. 127 (Jan. 2, 1889).

53   *Ibid.*, p. 127 (January 2, 1889).

54   Simmons, *Chekhov; A Biography*, pp. 14-15.

55   Karlinsky, *Letters of Anton Chekhov*, p. 379 (Feb. 12, 1900).

56   *Ibid.*

57   Yarmolinsky, *Letters of Anton Chekhov*, p. 170 (Dec. 9, 1890).

58   Karlinsky, *Letters of Anton Chekhov*, p. 109 (Oct. 4, 1888).

59   Yarmolinsky, *Letters of Anton Chekhov*, p. 21 (March 22, 1885).

60   Maxim Gorkii, "Fragments from Reminiscences," in *On Literature* (Moscow, 1953) pp. 32-42, quoted in *Chekhov, A Collection of Critical Essays*, (Englewood Cliffs: Prentice-Hall, Inc., 1967), pp. 195-196.

61   *Ibid.*, p. 195.

62   Simmons, *Chekhov*, p. 110.

63   *Ibid.*, p. 491.

64   Karlinsky, *Letters of Anton Chekhov*, p. 160 (March 9, 1890).

65   *Ibid.*, p. 166.

66   Karlinsky, *Letters of Anton Chekhov*, p. 246 (Dec. 3, 1892).

67   *Ibid.*, p. 261 (March 27, 1894).

68   *Ibid.*, p. 176 (Dec. 20, 1890).

69   *Ibid.*, p. 176 (Dec. 24, 1890).

70   *Ibid.*, p. 403 (June 12, 1901).

71   *Ibid.*, p. 287 (Dec. 14, 1896).

72   N. Berdjaev, *Mirosozertsanie Dostoevkogo* (Prague, 1923), pp. 233-234, quoted in R.L. Jackson, "Introduction," *Chekhov: A Collection of Critical Essays*, p. 5.

73   *Ibid.*

74   Michail Karpovich, "Two Types of Russian Liberalism: Maklakov and Miliukov," in *Readings in Russian History*, Vol. II, edited by Sidney Harcave (New York: Thomas Y. Crowell Company, 1962), pp. 91-104.

75   *Ibid.*, pp. 93-100.222

CHAPTER V

RUSSIAN COMMENTARIES

"A professor's view: 'It's the commentaries on Shakespeare that matter, not Shakespeare'."

Anton Chekhov

How is Chekhov viewed by his countrymen? How have perceptions of him evolved in Russia? This section of the study will summarize and comment on the public images of Chekhov espoused by Russian critics. Each of these images was flawed in some way.

Russian analysis of Chekhov's images fall into three principal critical schools: The Populist, The Reductionist,[1] and the Orthodox Soviet. Viewing Chekhov from its own perspective, each school has created a particular Chekhov to fit its own purposes and needs. Therefore, as one reads Russian critics, many Chekhovs emerge. The Populists see him as the clown who romps through an age of apathy into oblivion. The Reductionists see him as the sad bard of the end of a World. The Soviets see him as an almost-Marxist who lacked the consciousness to enter the bright new Bolshevik World but they were still able to see the beauty of the "little man."

Such views reflect how Chekhov was initially seen by the contemporary literary establishment. In addition many of the views of him expressed after his death were rooted in these earlier views. Still others have developed since the Russian Revolution. Each of these images of Chekhov is flawed, colored by the politics of the time.

The Populists have particularly distorted Chekhov. They were disappointed when he refused to accede to their demands that he take up the banner of social reform and color his writings to sway the people toward their approach to reform. As a result they turned on him. They attempted to destroy him through the spread of their own view of him. A view which has lingered through time.

Chekhov's image began to crystallize when some of the prominent Populist critics took notice of his work. The two most significant Populist critics were

55

Alexander Skabicheviskii [2] (1838-1910) whose perceptions are of lower quality than his fellow Populist Nikolai K. Mikhailovskii (1841-1904). While Chekhov liked Mikhailovskii, he disliked Skabichevskii, whom he considered a hack.

Skabichevskii considered Chekhov's work empty and reprehensible because he refused to take an obvious moral stand in his writing. His initial comment on Chekhov's more serious work was that he was a mindless literary clown who would eventually die drunk under a fence, forgotten by everyone. Skabishevskii lived long enough to witness Chekhov's views obscured by the Reductionist Criticism which represented him as the elegiac bard of a vanishing old order.[3]

The foremost of the Populist critics was N. K. Mikhailovskii who saw in the intelligentsia a "light in the night" and who stressed that "in addition to the need for knowledge there was a need for moral judgement." This, of course, put him at odds with Chekhov who rejected moralizing or subjectivity in his works. In an article, "About Fathers and Children and about Mr. Chekhov," which appeared in 1890, Mikhailovskii recognized Chekhov's talent, lack of political tendency, cold-bloodedness, and empirical approach. He felt Chekhov was the only really talented member of the literary generation of the 1880's but he found nothing more pathetic than "this talent which is being lost in vain." Chekhov's salvation, from the Populist point of view, would have been for him to put his talent at the disposal of the "cause" by writing beautiful but polemical tracts in support of the "movement."[4]

Michailovskii was scandalized by Chekhov's selection of topics and his literary methodology. He asserted that Chekhov ". . . himself does not live in his works, but seems to stroll past life picking out at random now this and now that." The weakness of Chekhov's method for Mikhailovskii is linked to this "stroll." This critic goes on to say "For all his talent Mr. Chekhov is not a writer who independently analyzes his material and selects from the point of view of some general idea, but from some kind of almost mechanical apparatus."[5] Mikhailovskii was criticizing Chekhov for his objectivity which appeared to Mikhailovskii to be a machine-like process of selection. Chekhov refused to follow his advice to be selective in his method in support of some subjective, pre-determined idea. It was only after Chekhov failed to follow any of this advice that Mikhailovskii's most virulent attacks began to appear in the press.[6] Mikhailovskii concludes, "Then let him at least be a poet of anguish for the general idea and of tormenting consciousness of its need. In this case he will not have lived in vain and will leave his mark in literature."[7] According to Professor Karlinsky, Mikhailovskii "staked his entire literary reputation on discrediting Chekhov in the eyes of enlightened readers; his failure to achieve this goal . . . probably opened the door for the eventual liberation of Russian literature from utilitarian dictatorship . . ."[8]

Despite his negative criticism, Mikhailovskii saw many of the unique qualities of Chekhov's work especially his impressionism as indicated by his seemingly random choice of material and details. Chekhov's impressionism has also been noted by Merezhokovskii, Tolstoi and others.[9] Soviet critics do not emphasize this aspect of Chekhov but it is recognized among Russian critics.

The Populists then saw little value in Chekhov as a writer. Because of his refusal to color his work politically, he was either a clown or a talent gone to waste. He did not see the truth and would not put the truth of moral judgment into his work. Because of his objectivity he was attacked and an erroneous image of him was created as a punishment for not conforming to their demands. Chekhov replied to this type of criticism in a letter on April 1, 1890. He began, "You upbraid me about objectivity, styling it indifference to good and evil, absence of ideals and ideas, etc." He scolds them, "You would have me say, in depicting horse thieves, that stealing horses is an evil." He continues, "But then, that has been known a long while, even without me. Let jurors judge them, for my business is only to show them as they are." He stresses that, ". . . if I add a pinch of subjectivity, the images will become diffused . . . . . . I rely fully on the reader, on the assumption that he himself will add the subjective elements . . ."[10]

Chekhov was objective; he did truthfully represent reality, but if there was to be moral judgment, and subjectivity, the reader was to make that himself. Chekhov only portrayed the truth as he observed it.

Mikahilovskii gave impetus to the development of the gloomy reductionist image with his dictum to Chekhov to become the "Poet of Anguish." This theme was continued and then transcended by Leon Shestov who forms a bridge from the populist to the reductionist view.

Leon Shestov, the Russian existentialist philosopher (1866-1938) took the melancholy image of Chekhov one step further by calling him destructive. In an essay written shortly after Chekhov's death, entitled "Creation from the Void,"[11] he declares Chekhov was "a singer of hopelessness," who "smashed human hopes." Shestov believed that all that Chekhov touched died: art, science, love, inspiration, and ideals. Persons for Chekhov were the despairing persons who were left alone with nothing and must create all themselves.

One is led from a Chekhov who is pictured as portraying "anguish" by Mikhailovskii to a Chekhov whom Shestov pictures as portraying the "despair" of the person in the void. Then the reader moves to a Chekhov whom the Reductionists picture as the bard of twilight Russia.

With the Reductionist image, Chekhov is reduced to the poet of the ultimate gloom, the end of a world. The image of Chekhov as the poet of twilight moods, the so-called *Voice of Twilight Russia*,[12] was created by Russian critics at the turn of the century which reached its most famous manifestation in the 1930's work of Princess Nina Andronikova Toumanova, a work characterized by platitudes and cliches. That image is still very much part of the modern view of Chekhov. Chekhov "hated it, thought it stupid, and made a point of leaving the room if anyone brought it up."[13]

Chekhov's own unfortunate medical condition, which appeared to place a twilight aura on his life, added to the unfortunate gloomy image which became all-pervasive. Even his wife Olga Knipper, who is quoted as saying in 1901, "My heart aches when I think of the quiet sadness that seems to be so deeply entrenched in your heart." To which Chekhov replied, "But, darling, that is utter nonsense! There is no sadness in me, there never was . . ." (Letter to Olga Knipper, August 14, 1901).[14]

The image of gloomy twilight went so far as to generate a mode of conversation – some began to talk "the Chekhovian way." Gorkii records an instance of a woman speaking this way to Chekhov. The woman began, "Life is so dull, Anton Pavlovich. Everything is so dingy, people, the sky, the sea, even flowers seem dingy to me. And there's nothing to wish for – my heart aches. It's like a kind of disease . . ." Chekhov rebutted, "That's just what it is. The Latin name for it is morbus shamitis." Fortunately for herself the lady did not understand Latin, or perhaps she pretended not to.[15]

The Reductionist image of Chekhov as gloomy, pessimistic and the poet of twilight Russia seems to connote the weakness, internal corruption, and sad beauty of the swan song of the empire as well as its poet. Toumanova identified Chekhov with the old order, which is absurd. He was not of the old order's dominant group and he was critical of its cruelty and corruption. By identifying him as the poet of the old order the image implies a bias toward it. This would of course cast doubt on Chekhov's value as a source of accurate information on conditions in turn of the century Russia. He has been reduced by members of the old order to be its balladeer when he was actually its creative critic.

Part of Chekhov's image as pessimistic or gloomy came from his refusal to record accepted "positive" myths.[16] His negative views did not necessarily imply weakness or disinterest. Charles du Bos, who has been called one of the few critics who really understood Chekhov said, "Chekhov's grandeur is that he could remain negative . . . and nevertheless could give forth . . . a gathering of strength . . . ." Du Bos depicted Chekhov "as a strong man whose strength is applied only to the depicting of the weak."[17]

The contradictions between the two dominant images, Chekhov the tragic clown with no social consciousness created by the Populists and the gloomy poet of twilight Russia created by the Reductionists were not accurate and needed a corrective balance. A creative compromise was achieved in 1914 when the twenty-one year old Vladimir Maiakovskii published an irreverent little essay, "The Two Chekhovs." Maiakovskii saw behind the gloomy, grumbling, discontented irrelevant Chekhov created by the philistines and discerned the "joyous" Chekhov, ". . . the powerful master of the art of literature."[18]

Like Maiakovskii, some post-revolutionary scholars have tried to sort through these images of Chekhov which were formed by groups for their own purposes. By the time the Soviet critics started to focus on Chekhov there were three Chekhovs: Mikhailovskii's, Toumanova's, and Maiakovskii's. In their attempt to deal with the three Chekhovs, the Soviet critics modified the three approaches and placed their own peculiar stamp on them to fulfill their own purposes and needs.

Orthodox Soviet critics tended to reject the image of the gloomy Chekhov and did not agree with the concept that he was the old order's twilight poet. Rejecting the Populists Skabichevskii and Mikhailovskii, they also go beyond Maiakovskii's "two Chekhovs," and coopt an element of the destructive function mentioned by the existentialist Shestov. Soviet criticism has stressed, instead, a positive Chekhov. Unfortunately, the critical reappraisal begun after the Revolution would eventually be overtaken by the advance of Stalin's dictatorship which culminated in the formulation of another terribly distorted image of Chekhov.

The reappraisal of Chekhov began to gain momentum in the mid-twenties when an early Soviet literary luminary, A. V. Lunacharskii, wrote "What Meaning Can Chekhov Have for Us?," which reflects the problem that Chekhov the "singer of the twilight" presented to the forward looking Revolution. Lunacharskii did not have anything new to say about Chekhov but his article helped to bring about a re-evaluation of Chekhov's image,[19] thus providing a bridge to the later work of Grossman, Eichenbaum, Chukovskii, and others.

The Soviet critic and scholar, Leonid Grossman, views Chekhov as a writer despairingly preoccupied with the tragedy of man's nature. "Not only a poet lived in this naturalist . . . ," he writes, ". . . but also a rare genius of creative gentleness . . ." Grossman views Chekhov as a "searching Darwinist" who had the love of "Francis of Assisi for every living creature," a writer who seemed ". . . to confirm with all his creative work the remarkable words of Beethoven – that the only heroism in the world is to see the world as it is, and still to love it."[20] This reflects the most significant trend in Soviet criticism, its stress on the positive Chekhov.

The adoption of Chekhov by the Revolution has had its negative effects. It led to an oversimplification and sentimentalization of his image. He is compelled to emerge as a didacticist with a message of how bad it was. The Soviets, seeing him confused by his faulty historical perspective, blame him for failing to perceive the true Bolshevik path to a "bright future." All his effort to show the complex, contradictory and confusing nature of life is shelved in the name of the revolution. This is particularly true in the post World War II period when only one side of his work, the positive, optimistic and teaching side, is stressed. B. I. Aleksandrov writes in "Chekhov in Russian Criticism" that the "main content" of Chekhov's art ". . . is not his passive reflection of reality, it is instead his 'active and destructive element (in respect to the Old World)'." He continues, ". . . Chekhov belongs to us, to the people of the revolution, and not to the old bourgeois society overthrown by its forces."[21]

The political mold of the Stalin era recast Chekhov and created the most perverted picture of him to suit Stalin's political needs. Such an image is partly seen in Vladimir Yermilov's Chekhov. Yet at the same time, Yermilov's scholarship corrects some of the misconceptions of previous distorted images. As an example of official Soviet opinion on Chekhov, a summary of the key points of Vladimir Yermilov's *Anton Pavlovich Chekhov* has been presented below.[22] The thing that is noteworthy is not the political verbiage of the work but the validity of some of the points made in spite of the politics imposed on its author. According to Yermilov, Chekhov considered himself a "pleb" and was poles apart from aristocratic literature, and as such Chekhov went beyond his pleb contemporaries' "bourgeois vulgarity" and revolutionized the entire genre of miniature stories.

Yermilov begins his rehabilitating of Chekhov by indicating that Chekhov was an enemy of the old order because he exposed its way of life that debased human beings. Effectively diminishing the twilight Russian image, Yermilov placed Chekhov in the great traditions of Russian literature, especially the satirical traditions of Gogol and Shchedrin by setting Chekhov up as the champion of the little man. This, of course, strikes at Mikhailovskii's image of the indifferent clown. Yermilov observed that the young Chekhov "Antosha Chekhonte," had three artistic aims of notable value as a writer. These aims were humor, satire, and the drive to paint an accurate picture of Russian reality. Yermilov stated that Chekhov's third aim supported the importance of the "little man" in his work and reaffirmed Chekhov's importance to the Soviet mind. This was possible because by supporting the little man Chekhov was in proper social focus.

By emphasizing Chekhov's accurate depiction of the little man, Yermilov challenged the approach to Chekhov taken by the Populists. After 1885, Yermilov saw Chekhov developing his tragic sense as a compliment to his humorous sense because there were two sides to one life. Yermilov seems to assert that, both in his work and his life, there were not two Chekhovs as Maiakovskii said, one in his work and the other in life. The two sides of life are reflected in both his work and life.

Although Yermilov elaborated on Chekhov's humor he had to bend his view to the prevailing political wind, nationalism. Thus, he saw Chekhov's humor as "profoundly national," reflecting ". . . the soul of the Russian."[23] Because Chekhov's humor was inspired by a "profound" and inexhaustible love for the little people, Chekhov is the best exponent of the "plebian democratic Russian intelligentsia." In effect, Yermilov makes the worthless comedian with no social consciousness, the Poet of twilight Russia, and the two Chekhovs into a scion of the plebian democratic Russian intelligentsia.

According to Yermilov, Chekhov's works reflected both the weaknesses and strengths of the new class of intellectuals because Chekhov described their truly democratic tendencies and their mistrust of upper-class bourgeois liberalism. Their remoteness from the path of revolution brought them under the influence of "abstract humane theories" and "liberal prejudices." Yet Chekhov was, in many ways, ahead of them in his ideas. Yermilov sees Chekhov as the leading edge of a new group of intellectuals who accepted liberal and humane theories. Chekhov expressed these tendencies not through revolution or upper-class liberalism, but instead by writing about his heroes, "the little people." The moral, social, and democratic spirit of Chekhov's work was often concealed under humor or beneath the carefully contrived Chekhov manner of "ostensibly impartial, strictly objective narratives." Beneath Chekhov's "reserve and objectivity," he exhibited clearly his love for the working man and his contempt for his enemies. In his assertion that Chekhov cared for the little man and revealed that care precisely in his writing, Yermilov rebutted both the Populist and Reductionist charges.

In trying to contribute a needed corrective to the Populist and Reductionist images of Chekhov, Yermilov tended to warp Chekhov because he went too far in eroding Chekhov's "objectivity and reserve." From the Soviet viewpoint Chekhov had one major tragic flaw, he was not a Marxist. Although Yermilov is concerned about Chekhov's lack of correct ideology, he appreciated his plebian instincts because Chekhov favored ordinary people as opposed to the exceptional few.

Yermilov further holds that Chekhov not only viewed ordinary people as individuals but also gave an accurate picture of the individuals' background, presenting, as it were, complete slices of life. Chekhov uses the little people as his heroes but they cannot be separated from their environment. Yermilov feels that Chekhov thinks the environment educates and influences; reality must be changed to eliminate the bad in life. The masses, the ordinary people, are "beautiful." Yermilov is building the traditional Marxist model of environment influencing persons and if you change the environment you change the person. One almost wants to say through the revolution we will achieve the new Soviet person.

The scholar in Yermilov points out that the belief that Chekhov had no social outlook comes from Chekhov's criticism of "tendencies" in literature. He asks, "What were the tendencies criticized by Chekhov?" They were either liberal, liberal-populist or reactionary "tendencies." Chekhov rejects everything that went to trim and misrepresent reality to make it fit this or that scheme or dogma.

Yermilov now points out that it was the insignificance of "popular" or liberal ideals that provoked Chekhov's rejection of "tendencies." Since he had nothing to put up against them, he could not avoid reflecting liberal and Populist tendencies. Unfortunately for Yermilov, Chekhov wasn't rejecting ideals. He was rejecting parties and the demands which groups place on literary figures to take up a cause in their work at any price, even a distortion of the truth!

Chekhov rejected "tendencies" and wanted "freedom" from all parties. Yermilov says Chekhov's stories were critical of Zemstvo liberals and that his stories explode Populist myths about "the Peasants." Yermilov felt that Chekhov had most strongly rejected the tendencies of the Populist critics such as Mikhailovskii and Skabichevskii. Yermilov believes that Chekhov should have been a Marxist. Why didn't he become one? First, because he had rejected political parties and therefore didn't investigate Marxism and the Marxists. Secondly, he longed for a scientifically-based outlook. Yermilov feels Chekhov's attempt at objectivity caused a narrow-mindedness in him which cut him off from Marxism. Thus he turned to despair. If he had met and described the positive, strong, struggling Marxist revolutionaries he could have avoided despair. Gorkii met these men and they were the heroes of his stories. Chekhov showed instead those who were not heroes.

Yermilov stretches and bends Chekhov so that he could write about Chekhov. If Yermilov hadn't been able to develop some Marxist "reason" for Chekhov's not being a Marxist, Chekhov would have been dumped into the Stalinist ash can. Chekhov did write about revolutionaries and, in general, the impression is negative because Chekhov disliked fanatics. One can answer Yermilov's question simply with a question. Would Anton Chekhov, the physician, consider "Scientific Socialism" scientific?

Yermilov, probably under political pressure, builds a case for Chekhov as a major critic of the Zemstvo. He believes that Chekhov mirrored Lenin's view that the Zemstvo did a *little* good. Yermilov believes Chekhov rejected them for not going beyond bourgeois democracy to socialist revolution. But A. P. Chekhov, Zemstvo physician, does not fit the Leninist mold created by Yermilov.

This distortion of Chekhov is continued when Yermilov says that since Chekhov was not a Marxist he did not understand the historical role of the working class and peasantry. As a result he felt Chekhov had difficulty creating an image of the socially active character of the true role of the working class. But Chekhov did understand the achievements of science and the progress of civilization. Yermilov says Chekhov was hostile to bourgeois conditions and rejected bourgeois theories of progress in a bourgeois society through science and technology.

It appears that Chekhov rejected middle-class society but not progress. Science and technology could continue to grow but only in a new environment, probably brought about by revolution. The facts of Chekhov's life and work make it clear that Chekhov did not follow this obviously Marxist image of himself. It must be said in justice to Yermilov that he uncovered Chekhov's belief in progress, science and technology under a layer of required political verbiage. Yermilov did this frequently in his study.

Yermilov closes his study by saying that in the final analysis Chekhov was an optimist, an "optimist of the hard kind, uncompromising and austere." When the time came "... the stormy wave lifted Chekhov aloft and carried him. He who had shunned politics, now threw himself into politics; he had become a believer."[24]

In conclusion it is fair to say that each of these images of Chekhov are distorted, but each contains some grains of truth which emerge in a dialectical interaction of these theories through time. What is clear is that the Soviet critics were moving in the right direction in their analysis of Chekhov but were constantly thwarted by the political line dominant at any point in time. This study draws on the grains of truth and provides a corrective for the distortions.

NOTES

1   The Reductionist critics reduce Chekhov to being the bard of the sad songs of the last days of the Empire; the apologists of its action, i.e. Toumanova.

2   A. M. Skabichevskii, *Sochineniia* (St. Petersburg, 1903), pp. 933-936.

3   Simon Karlinsky, ed., *Letters of Anton Chekhov*, with introduction by Simon Karlinsky. Translated by Michael Henry Heim in collaboration with Simon Karlinsky (New York: Harper and Rowe, 1973), p. 11. (Hereafter cited as Karlinsky, *Letters of Anton Chekhov*.)

4   N. K. Mikhailovskii, "Ob otsakh i detiakh i o g. Chekhove," in *Literatur-*

nokriticheskie stati'i (Moscow, 1957), pp. 594-607.

5 N. K. Mikahilovskii, "Ob otsakh i detiakh i o g. Chekhov, "in *Literaturnokriticheskie stat'i*, pp. 594-607.

6 Karlinsky, *Letters of Anton Chekhov*, p. 113.

7 Robert Louis Jackson, "Introduction: Perspective on Chekhov," in *Chekhov: A Collection of Critical Essays*, p. 3.

8 Karlinsky, *Letters of Anton Chekhov*, p. 11

9 D. S. Merezhkivskii, "Chekhov i Gor'kii," *Polnoe Sobranie Sochinenii* (St. Petersburg, 1911), XI, 39-92.

10 Avrahm Yarmolinsky, ed. *Letters of Anton Chekhov*, Trans. B. G. Guerney and Lynn Solotaroff (New York: Viking Press, 1973), p. 133, (hereafter cited as Yarmolinsky, *Letters of Anton Chekhov*).

11 Leon Shestov, *Chekhov and Other Essays*. New Introduction by Sidney Monas (Ann Arbor: University of Michigan Press, 1966), pp. 3-60.

12 Nina A. Toumanova, *Anton Chekhov, The Voice of Twilight Russia* (New York: Columbia University Ph.D. dissertation, 1937).

13 Karlinsky, *Letters of Anton Chekhov*, p. 2.

14 *Ibid.*, p. 2.

15 Anton Chekhov, *Selected Works*, Vol. I: *Stories* (Moscow, 1973), p. 14; also found in Maxim Gorky, *On Literature* (Moscow, 1956), p. 285.

16 Prince Mirsky shows how fun-loving Chekhov was when he writes of Chekhov's deceptions and jokes. D. S. Mirsky, "Chekhov and the English," in D. Davie, ed., *Russian Literature and Modern English Fiction* (Chicago: The University of Chicago Press, 1965), pp. 203-213. For a positive image of fun-loving Chekhov, Kornei Chukovskii, *Chekhov the Man*, translated by Pauline Rose (London: Hutchinson, 1945).

17 "The Chekhovian Sense of Life from the Journal of Charles du Bos," in *Chekhov: A Collection of Critical Essays*, pp. 184-185.

18 Vladimir Maiakovskii, "Dva Chekhova," *Polnoe Sobranie Sochinenii* (Moscow, 1955), I:294-300.

19 A. V. Lunacharskii, "Chem mozhet byt' A. P. Chekhov dlja nas?" *Pechat'i revoliutsiia* (1924), IV, 19-34.

20 Leonid Grossman, "The Naturalism of Chekhov," in *Chekhov: A Collection of Critical Essays*, pp. 32-48.

21 B. I. Aleksandrov, *Seminarii po Chekhovu* (Moscow, 1957), p. 76.

22 Vladimir Yermilov, *Anton Pavlovich Chekhov* (Moscow: Foreign Language Publishing House, ND), pp. 7-415.

23 Some important shift in emphasis has come with Soviet criticism despite its

"management." Eichenbaum's essay was supposed to be written to reveal Chekhov's national Russian characteristics and, only then, to discuss his literary technique. What actually developed was a positive contribution to Chekhovian criticism; this is to an extent true of Yermilov also. Boris Eichenbaum, "O Chekhove" in *Zvezda* (Leningrad, 1944), No. 5-6, 75-79.

[24]   For a short history of Chekhovian criticism in Russian up to 1957 omitting those who emigrated, see: B. I. Aleksandrov, *Seminarii po Chekhovu* (Moscow, 1957).

CHAPTER VI

EXPLODING THE MYTH

OF THE PEASANTS

This time was
on the outside the
"Pobebonostsevshchina"
on the inside the
"Chekhovshchina"

Semen Vengerov

Chekhov was in essence a story teller but the truth and power of his tales made him the ultimate iconoclast of late 19th century Russia. This study has thus far revealed and dispelled many of the confused perceptions held about Chekhov. This was done through a careful study of his personal communications and the reflections of contemporaries. Next then is a study of his views as presented publicly through his tales which were both truthful and effective in shattering stereotypes.

What were the things Chekhov cared about which led him to the topics he examined in his stories? He was concerned with: religion; political, artistic, and spiritual freedom; equality for all races and creeds; special devotion to equality for the peasantry, Jews and women; and personal action to achieve public good. He was particularly concerned about prejudice and ignorance, education, medical care, poverty, the quality of life of all classes and the establishment of a society, free from tyranny, under law. Because Chekhov was so deeply committed to these concerns he was impelled to write about them in his stories.

Careful analysis of the details and generalizations in Chekhov's stories present a remarkably complete and realistic picture of significant classes and institutions in Russian society. In the course of this study, in order to test the accuracy, objectivity, and validity of Chekhov's observations and judgments, his views will be carefully compared with scholarly research. Chekhov's views have been distilled from a careful analysis of all of his stories.

Because of his experience and training, Chekhov's style was very compressed. He was used to producing a story in 100 lines, a limit set by his publisher.[1] Commenting on the extremely compressed nature of Chekhov's writing, Korni Chukovskii observed that, "In general, every Chekhov story is so laconic, so consistently concentrated, and its forms are so many-layered, that if someone wanted to comment on any of them, the comment would be much longer than the text." Ironically he notes, "To any fleeting and little-noticed detail, taking up two lines in the text, one would have to devote five to six pages in order to find out . . . what idea it contains."[2]

This need for extensive commentary on the details in Chekhov's carefully polished words will be evident throughout this study. This is but another tribute to Chekhov's genius.

The details of Chekhov's stories would be familiar to a Russian of his time. As Boris Pasternak pointed out through *Dr. Zhivago*, Chekhov wrote of simple everyday details. Such details would be useful to the social historian. Professor Ernest Simmons notes that Chekhov will be remembered because his characters are so transcendent in nature.[3] But these characters are also useful, even to the social historian, because as is stressed by G. A. Bialyi, the Soviet critic, Chekhov sees his characters in terms of their jobs.[4] Like his description of Russian life, Chekhov's characters are also a source of general information and detail about policemen, prostitutes, and doctors as types.

As Professor Hingley points out, the usefulness of Chekhov's attention to realistic detail is enhanced by the fact that he was not an advocate of any political party's program.[5] Chekhov focused instead on presenting the reader with specific problems facing Russian society. The story "The Peasants" is a classic statement of one of those problems, "the peasant problem." To educated Russia, this story, as an "apparently innocent sketch, produced something of the effect of the child who pointed out that the Emperor had no clothes on."[6]

To understand how Chekhov's perceptions could be correct and yet cause a great furor, it is necessary to examine how the peasant was viewed by other nineteenth-century authors. This is not as simple as it sounds because the image of the peasant is clouded. In keeping with Professor Field's observations,[7] quoted earlier, Professor Fanger indicates the "almost complete" lack of works "depicting peasant life from the inside."[8] The Soviet Literary Encyclopedia of the 1930's, in an article on "Peasant Literature," rues the fact that the majority of peasant writers produced hackneyed stereotypical pictures of peasant life which were often reactionary in nature. This lack of a true picture triggered a surge of activity among Russian writers to try and capture the true peasant atmosphere.[9]

The Soviet scholar A. N. Pypin feels this led to ridiculous attempts to be "authentic," even to the use of a virtually incomprehensible muzhik-language which could not be read without a dictionary of rural slang. The commentator Annenkov felt that the depiction of true peasant life and the demands of art were irreconcilable, and I. Z. Serman held that the great age of the Russian novel shows not a single significant novel of peasant life.[10]

Uspenskii updated Tolstoi's theme of the gulf between classes holding that the land was the root of the difference. The peasants were subject to the power of the land. It is the earth and weather that govern the peasant's life. It is the land that gives the peasant his unique character and dignity. If he drifts from the land, he loses his character and dignity. The converse might be true for the intelligentsia.[15] The intelligentsia might accrue character and dignity by returning to the land.

Tolstoi and Dostoevskii developed the last step in the intellectuals' image of the peasant. Tolstoi goes beyond the power of the land and says that real Russian truth was to be found in the peasant. Peasants such as Platon in Tolstoi's *War and Peace* could teach the intellectual and aristocracy the secret of life. Tolstoi committed himself to show the beauty of the peasant soul, simple yet profound. Dostoevskii adds to this by trying to find the highest national and human truths in the peasant. The image of the peasant is created out of the intellectual's need for direction and higher truth. Each intellectual, having different views, had a different view of the peasant but clearly the dominant view was close to Tolstoi's. He felt the peasant was a noble Christian example who could teach Russia the truth.[16]

Professor Donald Fanger of Harvard University believes that it is only with Chekhov and later Bunin and Gorkii that the peasant is seen without tears, without expectations or lost illusions. It is only with the appearance of Chekhov's "The Peasants" in 1897 that the myth of the peasant is broken.[17] For Chekhov the peasants were not noble savages or Christian examples, they were just people living in grinding poverty. A contemporary critic noted, "As the author presents the matter, not only learning from the people, but even teaching them appears almost impossible." He went on ". . . all these characters are represented as somehow rudely possessed by a life that gives neither time for reflection nor freedom for demonstrating anything except purely instinctive urges with unusually faint glimmerings of human reason."[18]

Chekhov presented the peasants on their own merits. As Olga said in "The Peasants," "Yes, to live with them was terrible, yet all the same, they were people; they suffered and wept as people do; and in their lives, there was nothing for which excuse might not be found."[19]

Fanger says Tolstoi had painted the peasant existence for the sake of Christian examples. Chekhov wrote as an expression of what is and nothing else.[20] Chekhov killed the myth of the peasant with "The Peasants."

The response to Chekhov's exploding the century-long myth was immediate. In fact, it began before publication. On the strength of a report by a deputy censor, S. Sokolov, the entire censorship committee voted to cut the core of the ending out of "the Peasants." If Chekhov refused, the entire printing was to be confiscated. The full story appeared only later when it was published as part of a collection.[21]

When it was published, even in a censored form, Tolstoi was shocked and called the story "a sin against the common people." Chekhov "does not know his peasants."[22] "The Peasants" shook the intelligentsia because many had idealized the peasants as something special for the same reasons as had the writers of the nineteenth century.

Since, as these commentators point out, there were no good "inside" stud
the peasant, writers outside the peasantry developed a peasant from their
lights. Many times writers created peasants that conformed to the writer's
ideological needs. The cumulative result was the creation of the "Myth o
Peasant." In order to establish the view of the peasant in nineteenth-cei
Russia up through the end of the age of the great novels, a brief review of the ļ
authors' views of the peasants is in order.

The myth probably had its roots in Radishchev's *Journey from Petersbuɪ
Moscow*. In his "Journey" he tried to report conditions in the villages but iɪ
naivete he tended to idealize the peasant. This idealization interfered with
reporting. Karamzin was next on the scene and is an extreme example of the m
His "Poor Liza" in 1792 evoked great sympathy for the peasant but told nothinǫ
them.[11]

In the 1820's and 1830's, the raznochintsy writers Pogodin, Polevoi, and Pav
took a more realistic attitude. They stressed the contrast between the idealiː
picture of the peasant and the real circumstance of the villages. In addition, tl
stressed how every person deserved attention and placed no stress on peasantne
They ennobled every peasant without idealizing peasantness. This takes t
development to the 1840's, for Pushkin and Gogol spent no time on the peasan
who make only sporadic appearances in their works.[12]

In the 1840's, social thought began to be expressed in the form of literaɪ
criticism. Critics like Belinskii now found substance more important than form ɪ
literature. As a result of this influence, the young author Gregorovich emphasize
a social message in his "The Village" in 1846. Pypin noted that this was the firː
inside account of peasant life, but was marred by his fixation with dialect terms.[1]

Turgenev's *Sportsman's Sketches* was a positive and poetic statement about thɪ
Russian people and land. It outlined the well-known evils of serfdom but G. A
Bialyi believes its purpose was to provide a positive picture of the peasant as ɛ
contrast to Gogol's negative view of landowners in "Dead Souls."[14]

Each of the views of the peasant mentioned so far have been seriously flawed.
Radishchev and Karamzin tended to over-idealize the peasant, the raznochintsy
writers were on the right track but were swept aside by the socially conscious age
of Belinsky. The need to prove serfdom evil colored the 1840's and 1850's view of
the peasant. The abolition of serfdom in 1861 led to another view with Tolstoi,
Uspenskii, and Dostoevskii.

Having liberated the serfs, Russian society had to reach some accommodations
with them. The intellectuals sought to give the peasant meaning in terms of what
the intellectuals saw as the key problem of Russian society. They did not seek the
peasantry on its own terms but theirs.

Tolstoi postulated that the poor condition of the peasants and Russia in general,
could be corrected if the landlords would stay on the land and work. This would
close the gap between the upper-class, especially the intelligentsia and the lower
classes of Russian society. It was a new view of the aristocracy as the group which
could work and change things.

In spite of the outrage by government and dissenting intellectuals alike, Chekhov's perceptions about the peasants and the other classes and institutions of Russian society were correct. His work can be used as a source for social historians and is especially valid as a source on the peasants. This premise is supported by scholarly opinion and by the analysis presented in succeeding chapters.

"So accurate is Chekhov as an observer" wrote R. Hingley, editor of The Oxford Chekhov series, "that a social historian would in fact be unlikely to make any serious mistakes if he should draw on Chekhov as a source."[23]

Hingley's view gains some support from the work of W. H. Bruford.[24] Professor Treadgold, indicated that "The Peasants" is widely accepted as "depicting at least an important part of reality." Nicholas Vakar, a Soviet emigre, indicates that "The Peasants" is still a valid picture of the rural Soviet village today.[25]

Even Professor Field, while at Barnard College, admitted that he prefers Chekhov over other literary texts he uses in the teaching of Russian history. In particular, he prefers "The Peasants," "In the Ravine," and "The New Villa." He finds Chekhov's later stories most useful and sees Chekhov's line of descent flowing from Grigoreivich, through Turgenev, Yakushkin, Uspenskii, Leskov, and some of Tolstoi's tales. Social history is the least and worst-cultivated aspect of Russian history. He recognized that the tradition in which Chekhov wrote is of most importance for the light it casts on social history.[26] Professor Richard Stites, Russian social historian from Georgetown University, emphatically agrees with the idea that Chekhov was an objective observer who correctly portrayed the reality of lower-class Russia.[27]

Professor Stites quotes Chekhov frequently and uses several of Chekhov's stories to explain the facts of Russian life. Interestingly, he also uses one of Michael Chekhov's stories in a similar way. Professor Stites recognizes that Chekhov mirrored his age. He agrees with the perception of the critic Semen Vengerov in calling the end of the century in Russia in its inner form as the Chekhovshchina.[28]

Chekhov's vision is not fixed solely on the peasantry. George Fischer in his "The Intelligentsia and Russia" sees Chekhov as recording "vividly" the "non-civic" philosophy which stressed private affairs and political quietism later expressed by Berdyaev and others of the Vekhi group.

Klaus Mehnert in his "Changing Attitudes of Russian Youth," believed Chekhov "brilliantly" described the "officialdom" of Tsarist Russia from "the top men in ministries down to the thwarted little officials in the provinces . . . ." Among these and other men, Chekhov identifies an aimlessness in society according to John S. Reshetar in "Russian Ethnic Values." This perception of Chekhov is shared by Sir John Maynard.[29]

The breadth of Chekhov's observations is also recognized by Basil Dmytryshyn, who states that "his instant popularity and success stemmed from his ability to describe typical representatives of all professions and classes of Russian society . . ."[30] In sum, a significant segment of scholarly opinion assents that Chekhov truthfully records the broad spectrum of Russian society and can serve as a source for social historians.

Even the censor's report on "The Peasants" did not claim Chekhov's perceptions were false. The censor felt Chekhov deserved special attention and he was censored because the picture he painted was too gloomy. For this reason, the Moscow Censorship Committee decided on April 3, 1897, to eliminate the summation at the end of "The Peasants." Chekhov's summation was presented through the reflections of Olga, a peasant worker who was leaving the village.[31] Even the censors could not deny Chekhov's truth. They could only suppress it.

Chekhov gives two general descriptions of the peasantry. One is from the "inside" in "The Peasants" through the eyes of Olga, a tragically widowed peasant woman. The other is from the "outside" in "My Life," where a wealthy girl and her lover live a Tolstoian existence working the land on a country estate.[32]

Olga and her husband had lived in the city. When her husband became ill and lost his job, they returned to his village. Olga found that at times "these people seemed to live worse than beasts."[33] The peasant family working dawn to dark could not grow enough grain to feed them for the year. They were half-starved but the men would do anything for a drink. When they were drunk, they abused their wives. They were especially oppressed by taxes, the burden of them resting on the peasant families.

What are the reasons for the peasants condition? Ignorance. In addition, most of the peasants do not believe in God and are blind to religion. The peasants long for enlightenment and knowledge, but cannot find it themselves because they are mostly illiterate.[34]

Who keeps the pot-house and makes the peasant drunk? The peasant.

Who squanders his village, school and church funds on drink? The peasant.

Who steals from his neighbors, sets fire to their property and perjures himself in Court for a bottle of vodka? The Peasant.

Who is the first to run down the peasant at council and other meetings? The peasant.[35]

They were, however, men and women, and excuses could be found for everything in their lives: "back-breaking work"; "cruel winters, poor harvests"; "overcrowding"; "no help and nowhere to turn for it." "The richer and stronger" ones are no help and "the pettiest officials or clerks treat the peasant like tramps . . . as if by right." Reflecting her judgment on officials and clerks, Olga exclaims: "What help or good example can you expect from grasping, greedy, depraved, lazy persons who come to the village only to insult, rob and intimidate?"[36] According to Chekhov, the peasant looked helpless and got drunk. But fifteen or twenty years before every peasant looked as though he had a secret and there was talk of a charter with a gold seal, land and buried treasures. In Chekhov's time, the only talk was of poverty. The peasants believed they were worse off than in the days of serfdom. Then, at least, they ate; in Chekhov's time, all they got was robbed and flogged.[37]

The voice from the outside in "My Life" echoes and elaborates on the theme from the inside in "The Peasants." "What do you expect from these people?" asks a wealthy girl living a Tolstoian existence among the peasants. She had grown used to the peasants and found herself drawn to them. She considered them "mainly highly-strung, irritable people who had had a raw deal and whose imaginations had been crushed." They were men of limited, dull horizons and as a result were obsessed "with gray earth, gray days, black bread." They tried to cheat but were not very good at it because they could not count. They would not work for twenty rubles but would do the job for a half keg of vodka. Yet twenty rubles could buy four full kegs of vodka.[38]

Thus, we have the peasant from inside and out. The picture Chekhov painted was utterly human and true. It did not owe its form to the nineteenth-century folk myth that dominated literature until Chekhov shattered it. The overview of the peasants that emerges from the descriptions in Chekhov's stories is totally consistent with the facts of peasant life outlined in the scholarly literature covering the end of the nineteenth century and the beginning of the twentieth century in Russia.[39]

D. M. Wallace states, ". . . the peasantry of European Russia can no longer live by the traditional modes of agriculture." This is true even in the "most fertile districts." They need additional occupations such as those "practiced in less fertile provinces." Even then their conditions were "far from satisfactory."[40]

G. T. Robinson quoted an Imperial Commission investigating the peasants' economic condition which found that condition to be "extremely unsatisfactory" and it was found to be a widespread problem affecting the "whole central agricultural region."[41] Professor Karpovich believed the peasants were "not always able to earn subsistence for themselves" and at times "conditions became almost catastrophic" as in 1891-1893. At best, "the standard of living in the villages remained in most cases extremely low."[42] Vyshnegradsky, and later Witte, established policies which enriched the treasury, but, as William Blackwell pointed out, they impoverished the rural economy. Witte's critics said "twenty million peasants were starving after a half decade of Witte's policies." Blackwell believed that "it was obvious" by 1900 "that rural Russia was descending into an economic and political catastrophe."[43] Dr. Shingarev's report indicates that "the land has lost fertility, its productiveness has fallen, the natural wealth is exhausted, and the people are impoverished." He believed the peasants were being progressively ruined.[44]

Part of the reason the peasant was slipping into economic disaster was the taxes he had to pay. D. M. Wallace indicated that the money dues and "taxes are often more burdensome than the labor dues in the old times."[45] There were direct taxes, indirect taxes, assessments for state insurance and the arrears on payments on these taxes as well as redemption dues. Indirect taxes were important and brought in three and one-half times the amount of revenue to direct taxes. Indirect taxes were levied on all types of things: vodka, sugar, tobacco, kerosene, matches, and import duties on tea as well as many other items.[46] The state insurance was necessary but very expensive. Its cost amounts to one-half of the whole of all direct charges to the peasant.[47] The tax burden was heavy on the people. G. T. Robinson uses the arrears on the debts the peasants owed as an index of the peasant economic situation. The arrears were widespread and ever-increasing, indicating "the increasing distress in the village."[48] The peasants, after deducting what is needed to feed the family, must pay from 25% to 100% of his agricultural income into the Imperial treasury (depending on the district).[49] The tax burden was, as Chekhov had indicated, unbearable.

If illiteracy is an element in ignorance, then the peasant was ignorant. The overwhelming majority of peasant families were illiterate. In two villages studied by Dr. Chingarev, less than one-quarter of the males were literate and that was in an industrial area. When schools existed, they were poorly attended and in some instances, they had no books.[50] Ironically, when only a few can read and write, they use their knowledge to control or exploit the others.[51] Urban Russia was much more highly developed culturally than rural Russia. This was consistent with the government policy which deliberately kept the peasants ignorant.[52] The peasants were, as Chekhov had indicated, illiterate and ignorant.

The religion and morals of the peasant are an uncertain commodity. D. M. Wallace observes that the majority of parish priests were quite unfit to uplift the peasants. They rarely gained any moral influence over their parishioners. If Orthodox churches could make the peasants refrain from getting drunk as well as get them to abstain from animal food, it might then be able to teach them the barest moral principals as effectively as they get them to accept the sacraments.[53]

The peasant did like to drink. He would do more than sell his clothes for vodka. A person could bribe the village assembly by "treating the Mir," buying a barrel of vodka for them. The peasant attitude toward politics permitted this to happen. The intelligent, hard working peasant would not run for office because it would take up the time he would normally use to make money. The only time *this* type person would run for office was if he chose to use his office to gain power or wealth. "The Village Assemblies, too, have become worse than they were in the days of serfage."[54] There was peasant corruption and exploitation of peasants by peasants as Chekhov had indicated.

Sir John Maynard indicated that the Russian peasant "was not as depressed a class as the lower castes of India . . . but in some respects his case was worse than theirs." Arbitrary restrictions, lack of defined rights and duties, oppression by the Land Captains and other officials, these were complaints of the peasants. These complaints of the peasants were transmitted by Count Witte to the Tsar.[55] Officials did abuse peasants and treated them arbitrarily as Chekhov had indicated.

Listed in that same memo to the Tsar were peasant complaints "about arbitrary punishment (generally corporal)." Indeed you could be flogged.[56] But, as an old peasant said to D. M. Wallace, "There is no order now . . . it was better in the time of the masters."[57]

Chekhov is clearly an Iconoclast. He smashed the image of the noble peasant and Christian example for the rest of society with the truth. It is abundantly clear that Chekhov's views concerning the general condition of the peasantry are consistent with scholarly opinion. The next chapter deals with some of Chekhov's more specific analysis of peasant life and the historical validity of his perceptions.

NOTES

[1]   A. P. Chekhov, *Polnoe Sobranie Sochinenii i Pisem*, 13:41-42.

[2]   Kornei Chukovskii, *O Chekhove* (Moscow, 1967), pp. 129-130.

[3]   Ernest Simmons, *Introduction to Russian Realism*, p. 185.

[4]   G. A. Bialyi, "Iumoristicheski rasskazy A. P. Chekhova," *Isv. Akademiia Nauk USSR*, Otd.lit. i iaz. (1954) Vol. XIII, Vyp. 4, 307. For discussion of this see pp. 305-316.

[5]   Anton Chekhov, *The Oxford Chekhov*, trans. and ed. Ronald Hingley, 9 vols. (London: Oxford University Press, 1965-78), 9:10 (hereafter cited as *Oxford Chekhov*).

[6]   *Ibid.*, 8:4-5.

[7]   Daniel Field, *Rebels in the Name of the Tsar* (Boston: Houghton Mifflin Company, 1976), pp. 4, 213.

[8]   Donald Fanger, "The Peasant in Literature" in *The Peasant in Nineteenth-Century Russia*, ed. Wayne Vuchinich (Stanford, Stanford University Press, 1968), p. 231.

[9]   *Ibid.*

[10]   A. N. Pypin, *Istoriia russkoi etnografi*, II (St. Petersburg, 1891), pp. 357-358; Also I. Z. Serman's interesting article, "Problema Krest'ianskogo romana v russkoi kritike serediny xix veka," in B. J. Bursov and I. Z. Serman, eds. *Problemy realizma russkoi literatury xix veka* (Moscow-Leningrad, 1961), pp. 162-182. And P. V. Annenkov, "Romany i rasskazy iz prostonarodnogo byta v 1853 g.," in his *Vospominariia i kriticheskie ocherki*, II (St. Petersburg, 1877), 50.

[11]   Donald Fanger, "The Peasant in Literature" in *The Peasant in Nineteenth Century Russia*, pp. 233-39.

[12]   *Ibid.*, pp. 241-44.

[13]   *Ibid.*, pp. 244-45.

[14]   G. A. Bialyi, *Turgenev i russkii realizm* (Moscow-Leningrad, 1963).

[15]   Donald Fanger, "The Peasant in Literature" in *The Peasant in Nineteenth*

Century Russia, pp. 248-252.

16   *Ibid.*, p. 257.

17   *Ibid.*, p. 257.

18   I. N. Ignatov in *Russkie Vedomosti*, 1897, No. 106, 19 April, quoted in *Ibid.*, pp. 257-58.

19   "The Peasants," in *Oxford Chekhov*, 8:221.

20   *Ibid.*, p. 258.

21   *Ibid.*, 8:2.

22   *Ibid.*, 8:5.

23   *Ibid.*, 8:2.

24   W. H. Bruford, *Chekhov and His Russia*.

25   D. Treadgold, "The Peasant and Religion," in Vucinich, *The Peasant in Nineteenth Century Russia*, p. 103; Concerning Soviet Village see: Nicholas Vakar, *The Taproot of Soviet Society* (New York: Harper and Row, 1961), p. 174.

26   Daniel Field to Lee Williames, April 3, 1976.

27   Richard Stites, "Commentary" on "Chekhov as a Source for the Social Historian" by Lee Williames, a paper delivered at the Middle Atlantic Historical Association of Catholic Colleges and Universities Conference, Philadelphia, Pa. April 18, 1980.

28   Richard Stites, *The Women's Liberation Movement in Russia* (Princeton, Princeton University Press, 1978), p. 157.

29   George Fischer, "The Intelligentsia and Russia," pp. 263, 266, Klaus Mehnert, "Changing Attitudes of Russian Youth," p. 498, John S. Reshetar, "Russian Ethnic Values," p. 57, all in *The Transformation of Russian Society*, ed. Cyril Black (Cambridge, Harvard Univ. Press, 1960); and Sir John Maynard, *The Russian Peasant and Other Studies* (New York, Collier Books, 1962), p. 583.

30   Basil Dmytryshyn, *A History of Russia* (Englewood: Prentice Hall, 1977), pp. 451-452.

31   *Oxford Chekhov*, 8:300-01.

32   "The Peasants," and "My Life," *Oxford Chekhov*, Vol. 8 or see "Peasants," in *Polnoe Sobranie Sochinenii i Pisem*, 1944-51, ix.

33   "The Peasants" in *Oxford Chekhov*, 8:221.

34   *Oxford Chekhov*, 8:300-01. The censors' report provided a convenient summary of the points in "The Peasants" which were of contemporary interest. Portions of that report are paraphrased above; see also *Polnoe Sobranie Sochinenii i Pisem*, 1944-51, 9:579.

35 "The Peasants" in *Oxford Chekhov*, 8:221.

36 "The Peasants" in *Oxford Chekhov*, 8:221.

37 *Oxford Chekhov*, 8:300-01; also *Polnoe Sobranie Sochinenii i Pisem*, 1944-51, 9:579.

38 "My Life" in *Oxford Chekhov*, 8:70.

39 Sir John Maynard, *The Russian Peasant and Other Studies* (New York: Collier Books, 1962), pp. 57-70;

Anatoli Leroy-Beaulieu, *The Empire of the Tsars and the Russians*, 1893-1903, Trans. Zenaide Ragozin, 3 vols. (New York: G. P. Putnam's Sons, 1893), 1:504-21, 521-33, 546.

Sergei Pushkarev, *The Emergence of Modern Russia, 1801-1917*, Trans. Robert H. McNeal and Tova Yedlin (New York: Holt, Rinehart and Winston, 1963), pp. 206-219;

G. T. Robinson, *Rural Russia Under the Old Regime* (Berkley: Univ. of California Press, 1969), pp 94-116, especially 116;

Dr. Shingarev, "The Dying Village," quoted in Sir John Maynard's *The Russian Peasant and Other Studies* (New York: Collier Books, 1962), pp. 62-69. Dr. Shingarev, an employee of the provincial Zemstvo in Voronezh did a study of two villages in the province and published his results in June, 1907. It covers the specifics of peasant life and the specifics are consistent with the view Chekhov presents in his stories;

Michael Karpovich, *Imperial Russia, 1801-1917*, (New York: Holt, Rinehart and Winston, 1931), pp. 58-62;

Sir Donald Mackenzie Wallace, *Russia* (New York: Henry Holt & Co., 1905), pp. 446-490;

William Blackwell, *The Industrialization of Russia* (New York: Thomas Crowell Co., 1970) pp. 30-33.

40 Sir Donald MacKenzie Wallace, *Russia*, p. 471; Michael Karpovich, *Imperial Russia, 1801-1917*, p. 59; Lazar Volin, "The Russian Peasant," in *The Peasant in Nineteenth Century Russia*, p. 297.

41 G. T. Robinson, *Rural Russia Under the Old Regime*, p. 115.

42 Michael Karpovich, *Imperial Russia, 1801-1917*, p. 59; G. T. Robinson, *Rural Russia Under the Old Regime*, p. 116.

43 William Blackwell, *The Industrialization of Russia*, pp. 31-33.

44 Dr. Shingarev quoted in Sir John Maynard, *The Russian Peasant and Other Studies* (New York: Collier Books, 1962), p. 69; Also: G. Pavlovsky, *Agricultural Russia on the Eve of the Revolution* (London, 1930), pp. 96, 86; D. W. Treadgold, *The Great Siberian Migration* (Princeton: Princeton University Press, 1957), Chapter 2, "The Peasants in the Homeland."

45 D. M. Wallace, *Russia*, p. 466.

46 G. T. Robinson, *Rural Russia Under the Old Regime*, p. 96.

47 Sir John Maynard, *The Russian Peasant and Other Studies*, p. 64.

48 G. T. Robinson, *Rural Russia Under the Old Regime*, p. 111; D. M. Wallace, *Russia*, p. 481; A. Leroy-Beaulieu, *The Empire of the Tsars and the Russians*, passim.

49 D. M. Wallace, *Russia*, p. 481.

50 Sir John Maynard, *The Russian Peasant and Other Studies*, pp. 68, 62.

51 D. M. Wallace, *Russia*, p. 474.

52 Lazar Volin, "The Russian Peasant," in *The Peasant in Nineteenth Century Russia*, p. 297.

53 D. M. Wallace, *Russia*, p. 473.

54 *Ibid.*, p. 475.

55 Sir John Maynard, *The Russian Peasant and Other Studies*, p. 70.

56 John Maynard, *The Russian Peasant and Other Studies*, p. 70.

57 D. M. Wallace, *Russia*, p. 473.

CHAPTER VII

The Facts of Peasant Life

*"His life is a long-drawn question
between a crop and a crop"*

Kipling

Having outlined the myth of the peasant and how Chekhov attacked the myth as a general concept, the focus of the study now shifts to the details of Chekhov's view of peasant life. Chekhov's concept of peasant life exploded like a bomb among intellectuals. Were his concepts and details correct? Was Chekhov as objective and truthful as he and others maintained? This and succeeding chapters will examine the facts of peasant life. Chekhov's views will be compared with generally accepted scholarly opinion to try to determine the validity of his perceptions. These chapters will look at Chekhov's idea of lower-class rural life. His treatment of it is so comprehensive that our study of it in this chapter can also serve as a social history of rural Russia on the eve of the 1905 Revolution. It will include such areas as: family life, the hut, food, education, bureaucracy, relations between gentry and intelligentsia, health care and disease, Zemstvo, arrears and corruption. Some of these images are among Chekhov's most devastating and powerful.

The Family

The picture of the family presented in "The Peasants" is that of an extended family breaking up into smaller units under economic pressure. In the story the family is composed of the grandmother and grandfather; the daughters-in-law, Marya, who had six children, and Fyokla, who had two children; joining this group was Nicholas, his wife Olga, and their daughter. Marya's husband, Kiryak, worked elsewhere, and Fyokla's husband, Denis, was in the army. Nicholas, Olga and their child returned to the village after Nicholas lost his job in the city.[1]

This pattern of an extended family with fragmentation into nuclear families, because of the decline of agriculture and rise of urban employment, is consistent with scholarship on the family. Robert Redfield indicates that the majority of European peasant families had patrilocal residences and followed the male line of descent. Nicholas Vakar states that the peasants' basic social unit was not the individual but the family, "developed to save the individual by suppressing him." Both Tokarev and Tolstoi discovered the domination of the extended family form. Mary Matossian confirms the picture that Chekhov presents. Although it seems clear that the extended family concept was the prevailing familial structure, this structure was under severe strain during the time Chekhov was recording it. D. M. Wallace points out that under the pressures of the decline of the agricultural village the extended family was gradually being fragmented into a series of nuclear families.[2] Chekhov points out how these changes can be seen in the movement of the peasant family members back and forth from the city to the village. Be this as it may, the change was slowly taking place and during Chekhov's time the extended family structure was still dominant.

Fyokla and her children were dependent on the extended family for survival. Fyokla had to work at the manor house to support herself because her husband, Denis, was in the army. There would have been little difference in her condition if he were dead. Her plight is totally consistent with the facts generally accepted by scholars. John Curtiss states that "When a man was taken for the army, his family bewailed him as though he were already dead . . ." The married soldier's wife was usually "doomed to a life of bitter poverty."[3]

To provide money for the extended family, Nicholas sought a job in the city. Unfortunately, he became ill and was forced to return to the village. Peasants who moved to the city rarely cut fully the bonds that tied them to the village. Government policy encouraged such ties and Chekhov's analysis is wholly consistent with the government's policy. Maintaining workers' ties with the village was part of the government's peasant-worker alternative to the proletariat of the West. D. M. Wallace recognized this attempt to achieve industrialization on the Western model without uprooting a significant segment of rural population. The village, as G. T. Robinson points out, saw an ever-increasing army of peasant laborers who took "going-away work" and became involved for a period of time in manufacturing and mining.[4]

Through his stories, Chekhov accurately portrayed the roles individuals played in the functioning of Russian family life. Within the family, Chekhov showed the old woman "Gran" as the dominant force. She tried to do everything herself. She drove the old man, the daughters-in-law, and the grandchildren, fearing they would not work. She guarded her kitchen plot, worried about the food supply, and was the engine of the family in general.[5] This is consistent with the Matushka image of the mother as the binding and driving force of the Russian family.[6]

Chekhov used the character of "Gran" to document the vital role women played in Russian peasant family life. He emphasized that role when he showed that the Father, who was nominally the head of the house, often partially surrendered his authority to the Mother or some other competent female. For example, in "In the Hollow" the father surrenders power to a daughter-in-law who protects it at all cost. In "The Peasants," the children learned to perform their roles as helpers.[7] When the children did not properly protect the kitchen garden, the family's food supply, they were beaten. In both stories, one can see the tensions between the mother and the daughters-in-law, which is a result of latent power and sexual struggle. The roles of father, mother, daughter-in-law, and children as represented by Chekhov are consistent and true to life.

Mary Matossian, in her study of peasant life, indicates that a senior female in actual practice could have control of the family and that she could be the binding force of the family. She also shows how the children had to learn to accept tasks reliably and that their performance of routine tasks could make the difference between survival or catastrophe. She also confirms the tension, described above, between the mother and the daughter-in-law. Matossian's work specifically supports Chekhov's observations with regard to the peasant family and the various roles within it.[8]

The Village

Chekhov observed and described "real poverty." In the peasant village, there was "poverty – sheer, grinding poverty that you could not escape from."[9] The worry caused by poverty made the villagers sleep fitfully; even the children did not sleep because of hunger.[10] The quality of life ground Olga down until "there was something blank and torpid about her glance, as if she was deaf," perhaps as deaf as the village cat which had been deafened by a beating. Both had been beaten and abused by the life in the village. Yet Olga "was sorry to leave the village and the villagers."[11] She had ties there and people there cared, unlike the city.

The villages described by Chekhov in "The Peasants" and "Thieves" follow the traditional patterns for small villages (derevni) of the period. They are predominantly linear in their layout and are located by water or along a hollow. Both the villages and the huts described by Chekhov are consistent with the patterns of the period recognized by scholars.

The Hut

Taken as an example, the hut (izba) in "The Peasants" is consistent with the pattern. The only exception was the size of the stove relative to the size of the hut. The hut is small and the stove takes up half the area of the hut as opposed to the normal one-quarter to one-fifth of the area occupied by stoves. Chekhov himself noted this as an exception. Chekhov's description of the location of stoves, the icon corner, the sleeping bench and even family sleeping patterns are typical of Russian customs and mores.[12]

John Maynard, quoting Dr. Shingarev's report on the villages in Voronezh Province, paints a picture at least as gloomy as Chekhov's. The wooden huts of the villages had no privies. In most houses, the excrements were left in the outer passages of the house and were "eaten by swine, dogs and fowls." Generally, the houses were packed close together, with little air to breathe, "smoky and yet not sufficiently warm, poorly lighted, entirely without ventilation, and in many cases, old." People slept on the stove, benches, shelves and the floor. The cattle spent the winter inside.

Huts were insect infested. Ninety percent had cockroaches but only fifteen and a half percent had bugs. Apparently bugs only go to the best locations. Black beetles spread themselves around but did not stay where there was no food. The peasants said you could tell extreme poverty when there were no black beetles in evidence.

The general characteristics of the villages and the izba are consistent with this author's observations at the Russian Museum of Ethnography in Leningrad and the Museum of Wooden Architecture in Novgorod. As is indicated above in other sources, Chekhov's view of the village was a valid representation of conditions as they actually existed.[13]

The quality of life of a society can be seen through the food it consumes. In stories like "The Peasants," "Murder," and "In the Hollow" Chekhov graphically described the type of and quality of peasant food. Chekhov used food as a symbol. In general, overeating was viewed negatively and starvation was sometimes seen as a relative indication of virtue.[14] For Chekhov, the ultimate sign of his disgust at the conspicuous consumption that overeating represented was the eating of oysters. Chekhov hated oysters.[15]

In stark contrast to the luxury of "oysters," Chekhov presented the poor peasant eating fish head soup from a common bowl. This documented the importance of fish as opposed to meat in the peasant diet. For the poor, even fish was reserved for holidays. Even then the fish broth would be served as one meal and the fish as another.[16]

Frequently, "the peasants" ate only bread soaked in water. They had little variety and only rarely ate meat. As one moved to better economic straits, the food improved as in the Tsybukin's home in the story "In the Hollow," or at the small inn in "Thieves." Such improvement in the quality of food was a sign of the emerging differentiation of poor and rich peasants. Tea ceased to be a special commodity. The rich peasants could drink real tea, not just herb tea, many times a day. They had individual bowls in which cabbage soup was served. Frequently meat, sausage, or fish would be served at the three or four daily meals. They had a drink of homemade spirits. In the final analysis, however, only a wealthy peasant could eat meat all the time.[17]

Even the lowest rank of rural professionals had much more than the poor peasant. In the home of a down-and-out teacher's family cabbage soup and porridge, or potatoes fried in mutton drippings that smelled of tallow was served along with vodka.[18]

In Chekhov's stories the variety of food and use of meat increased as one continued up the social ladder. It is only with the new rich and worst of aristocratic society that Chekhov will bring on the oysters, the ultimate symbol of his disgust.[19]

Excluding the "oysters," Chekhov's description of foods is consistent with the studies of scholars on the subject.

Dr. Shingarev's report indicates that he was not surprised to find little meat in the peasant diet. Contrary to those who assumed that the peasant made up for the lack of meat protein by drinking readily available milk, Shingarev reported that in many of the households he visited there was no milk at all.

Shingarev found them suffering from fat hunger. He was completely surprised when he found that in most of the homes, there were no cabbages or cucumbers. The peasants depended on a diet of rye to maintain them. The consumption of sugar per person per year was two and one-half ounces, and tea was one half ounce. There was no drink shop in the village, and they consumed two fifths of a gallon of vodka per person per year. Tea, sugar, and vodka were evidently considered luxuries and used only on holidays.[20] There can be little doubt that at the turn of the century the peasants functioned at subsistence level and occasionally existed below subsistence level.

The School

One can see through Chekhov's eyes the rural school building in "My Life," and the operation of a rural school in "In the Cart." Though many areas did not have a school for miles as in "The Savage,"[21] Chekhov drew on his own experience of building three schools and on his brother's experience as a teacher to write about education.

In "My Life," one sees a rich girl following her Tolstoian lights trying to build a school for the peasants. It is apparent that the peasants do not really want a new school. They resent having to work on the school in addition to their normal labors. The school was her idea, not theirs. As the story evolves, it is apparent she is not building the school for the peasants but for civilization and her own ego. The peasant attitude was to get whatever they could as extra income during the building of her school. The new school brought no new benefit, but added income would. They were not grateful for the school they did not need and they surely were not working to build her school for free.[22]

"In the Cart" examines the life of a rural teacher and in the process reveals the horror of the operation of the schools. The teacher, a well-educated, gentle soul, was crushed by the conditions of her job. She had to collect money from the children to pay for firewood which she paid to the school manager. She practically had to beg him to deliver the wood, and when he did, he stole some of the money. The school caretaker was cruel to the children and threatened the teacher when she protested his cruelty.

The local school examiner, a kind and incompetent member of the gentry, was no help to her. His principal contribution was giving the school globes they did not need.

The teacher lived in one cold, damp room which was attached to the school. She made very little money and had little hope. She was victimized by petty officials and left unaided by the gentry. The peasants, on the other hand, felt she was paid too much and that she cheated the children out of the firewood money.[23]

At the same time, Chekhov made it clear that some peasants saw the value of education. They wanted education, but could not get it because of cost or lack of schools, as in "The Savage." The problem was not so much with the idea of the school, but with the peasants having to pay to run the school, do extra work building it and then be cheated by the local corrupt administration.[24]

The peasants needed education the most and could least afford it. In a satirical fragment "From a Retired Teacher's Notebook," Chekhov stressed the need to educate the lower-class. The focus should not just be on teaching them to read newspapers but to develop their minds with ideas through books.[25] Such a policy was contrary to that of the Ministry of Education decree of 1887.

It should be noted that, as Donald Treadgold states, Populism was initially not a peasant idea. The peasants did not ask the Populists and other intellectuals to come to the country and educate them. The peasants could easily reject a wealthy intellectual's good intentions to help them. It should also be mentioned that most villages did not have any school at all as pointed out by S. Tolstoi and M. Matossian.

The attitude of the peasant toward the school was determined by the general environment. This attitude is understandable when one realizes, as Leroy Beaulieu points out, that at times the peasant's obligation for taxes and arrears amounted to one hundred percent of his agricultural production. Any cost in money or in labor could push them below subsistence level. The peasant bore the majority of the tax burden and could afford it least. Wallace indicates that some people viewed the zemstvo as an enemy and a failure, saying that it did little and raised taxes to do it.[26]

As can be seen in *Istorii Rossii v XIX vike*, in 1880 there were 22,700 rural primary schools in European Russia, with some 1,140,000 pupils. Their expenditures amounted to 6.2 million rubles annually, of which forty-four percent was paid for by the zemstvos, thirty-four percent by rural communes, twelve percent by the central government and ten percent by miscellaneous sources, largely private. The peasants viewed the school, any school, in light of the burden they would bear. They usually bore most burdens.

Using P. Miliukov's statistics, one can compute that there were in 1899 a total of 8,250,100 students in 175,600 primary schools in Russia. Of these, about half were located in rural areas. The number of schools had increased but so had the burden on the peasant at a time when his economic fortunes were not rising. Even if outsiders paid for building materials, the peasant viewed any unpaid labor as a cost to himself. He could have been doing something else during that time that would help him survive. In addition, once the school was built, the commune would have to pay the teacher's salary. The peasants would accept education but could not accept the added costs. This was borne out when, as Pushkarev notes, the peasant supported the drive for universal free primary education which occurred in the Duma beginning in 1907.[27] Peasant resistance to added financial or labor burdens does not alone explain the lack of proper educational facilities in rural Russia. It is important to remember that the Tsar's government tended to discourage the lower classes from seeking an education beyond their station. This excerpt from the notorious instruction was published by the Ministry of Education in 1887:

> Gymnasiums and progymnasiums are freed from receiving the children of the coachmen, servants, cooks, laundresses, small tradesmen, and the likes, whose children, with exceptions, perhaps of those gifted with extraordinary capacities, ought by no means to be transferred from the sphere to which they belong and thus brought, as many years experience has shown, to slight their parents, to feel dissatisfied with their lot, and to conceive an aversion to the existing inequity of fortune which is in the nature of things unavoidable.[28]

Pushkarev notes at the same time the government "raised tuition to forty rubles per year, which was more cash than many peasants saw in a year."[29]

The government attitude was summed up by the famous sociologist, a friend of Chekhov's, N. N. Kovalevsky:

> The principal objective of the government was not to spread popular education as widely and as rapidly as possible, but to ward off some kind of a danger to the nation because the people will acquire too much knowledge unnecessarily through schools and books, and will broaden their intellectual horizon. There are still not a few persons who are convinced that popular ignorance is the best guarantee of social order.[30]

A. A. Manuilov, the eminent Russian economist and educator, wrote that the authorities deliberately tried to keep peasants from having access to books, lectures, and even talks on specialized topics.[31] Chekhov's perceptions of education appear to have been correct when viewed in light of the opinions of scholars on the subject. In addition, his "From a Retired Teacher's Notebook" was aimed at the government's policy of retarding lower-class education.

Relations Between Gentry Intellectuals and Peasants

The relations between the gentry and peasants were not particularly good. Chekhov knew and recorded this fact. Some persons mistakenly believed that the peasants welcomed the leadership of the gentry. Chekhov arrived at a different conclusion in stories like "My Life." The peasants had not accepted the "to the people" movement nor were they accepting Tolstoi's surge back to the land. In "My Life," a Tolstoian intellectual and an engineer's daughter try to live a useful existence on the land. The peasants treat the well-meaning pair as outsiders and view their activities as self-serving. In the end, when the romance breaks up, so does the effort on the land. The peasants had known what the outcome would be.

Chekhov also makes an excellent point about how difficult it really was to maintain an intellectual existence while farming the land as the peasants did. Chekhov had faced this problem himself at Milikhovo. Chekhov sold this estate because it was evidently too much for him.[32]

At the root of the problem between gentry and peasant was the lack of communication. Chekhov reveals the separation of their two different worlds in stories like "Gusev." Gusev and Paul Ivonovich are both dying while returning home from Siberian duty. Gusev, a discharged peasant soldier, and Paul, a former bureaucrat from the clerical class, try to talk. They cannot communicate. Their words are the same but have different meanings. Their analogies are different. Huge fish and beast-like winds are all part of Gusev's world while Paul is furious with Gusev's illogical world of myth and ignorance. All they can do is die together.[33]

The differences between the intelligentsia and the peasant can be seen in the contrasts between their worlds. In "On Official Business," the contrast between the two is seen in the division of waiting rooms in the local council hut. The peasants's side had a pile of hay in the corner with the rustle of cockroaches. The gentry side was a well-furnished parlor and had a samovar. Two separate worlds in one building.

For the intelligentsia, Russia was not the land which the peasants inhabited. Russia was Moscow and Petersburg, the twin capitals of Russia. The intelligentsia were urban in orientation, educated and privileged because of that education, and often educated because of class privilege. The peasant was illiterate, rural and powerless.[34]

The split between the peasants and the intelligentsia was recognized and recorded by Chekhov and his perceptions are consistent with scholarly opinion. Donald Treadgold writes that a social gulf existed between "the Moscovite tsars and their serving men, later the emperors and their bureaucracy on the one hand and the peasantry on the other . . ." This gulf emerged in the eighteenth century between the peasantry and westernized gentry, from which most of the intelligentsia came. The gulf was both social and cultural in nature. Treadgold says "thus the Russian peasant for centuries was separated from the best intellectual and moral forces of his civilization." Low culture peasant dissidents were alienated and suppressed while the higher culture intelligentsia became alienated from the peasant's general outlook. Daniel Field accepted this gulf and believed it was deep-seated, large, and filled with suspicion. The aristocracy tended to view the peasants as objects of their compassion but not their respect.[35]

Health Care and Disease in Rural Russia

In general, in his stories, Chekhov paints a positive picture of the attempts of the Zemstvo and others to provide medical care in rural Russia. He generally represents physicians in a positive frame and recognizes the contribution that they made against tremendous odds. He even portrays the promise of the Feldsher concept in rural health care.

Chekhov also indicates the problems which hampered health care. Problems like the shortage of money, poor educational facilities, lack of government cooperation, corrupt officials, peasant ignorance and the inability of the doctor to cure one of the primary causes of disease, poverty.

As a physician, Chekhov was acutely aware of the medical problems of Russians and the inadequacy of the Russian health care system, and he was expert in his commentary. Chekhov as a practicing physician, in fact, provides a sound primary source on the subject of health care in turn-of-the-century Russia.

Sometimes the commentary of experts in a field is criticized as too abstract or disinterested. Chekhov's tubercular condition added an additional dimension to his commentary. On March 22, 1897, Chekhov met Suvorin for dinner at the Hermitage Restaurant, one of Moscow's most elegant. During dinner, Chekhov had a massive hemorrhage with a convulsive emission of blood. He collapsed and was diagnosed as having tuberculosis in advanced stages in both lungs.[36]

Chekhov had suppressed his own suspicions about his tubercular condition since the early 1890's. But his disease gave him a perspective and sensitivity not present in some other commentators on the topic of disease.

This perspective is seen in Chekhov's story "A Dreary Story." The central figure, a professor, wonders whether he really should consult a colleague about his health. Then he pictures another physician sounding his chest, who tries to conceal the truth from him. His colleague would say something like, there is nothing to worry about at the moment, but you should give up working. Chekhov's professor then questions "what man lives without hope?" Since the professor was treating himself, he hoped that he might be deceived by his own ignorance, but he could not ignore the telltale signs.[37]

Finally, fear turns to rage and the professor wants to cry out. The world is silent at the cruelty of this famous man being condemned to death. They should be running about in horror and despair at his fate. Perhaps Chekhov is expressing his own need for self-delusion, and then his rage and sense of imminent death.[38]

Chekhov had the practical and expert knowledge of a practicing physician as well as the perspective of a terminally ill person, a victim of one of the plagues of his society. Tuberculosis will be mentioned in many of his stories, reflecting his interest and the fact that it was one of the great killers in Russia at the turn of the century.

Health care for the poor was portrayed in stories like "The Peasants." Chekhov records that peasants were not so afraid of death as they were of illness. Disease was a frequent topic of conversation, and there was constant fear of catching cold. Gran, in "The Peasants" loved to go to the hospital and get medicine for herself and some of the children. Good medical care was available.[39]

Gran made a hobby out of illness and cures. She had taken her son Nicholas to the doctor and received some drops which he said helped his illness. Gran knew all the doctors, medical assistants, and quacks in the area and was always looking for a cure. When she heard of a new healer in the area, she just had to have him see Nicholas. He came, this old man, a converted Jew and former army medical orderly, who was supposed to be good at cures. He examined Nicholas and said he had to be bled, a conclusion which satisfied all folk wisdom. The children watching said they could see the sickness drain out of him as twenty-four bleeding cups drew it out of him. The healer left and Nicholas felt euphoric, weak, then very cold, and turned blue. He lay down on his sheepskin and was dead by morning.[40] One can almost see the frustration roll from Chekhov's eyes. Ignorance!

Thus Chekhov introduced us to rural health care, the domain of the sorcerer and witch, who were only now being challenged by the Zemstvo doctor. Fear, superstition, ignorance and poverty all resisted the improvement of health care and favored the retention of witchcraft.

Chekhov showed the problem of health care as multilayered. Even when care was available, the peasants' own habits worked against it. In addition to Nicholas in "The Peasants," there was the old woman in "Rothschilds Fiddle." An old man, Jacob, took his wife to the doctor because she was ill. The doctor, drunk, was unavailable so they saw the doctor's assistant (feldsher) who pronounced that the old woman had a flue or typhus, a fever of some sort, and besides she was old, it was her time to die. The old man observed that even a bug has a will to live, could he help her. The doctor's assistant then gave Jacob some powders for her and told him to put cold compresses on her head. This leads one to question the quality of the physician and his assistant.

But Jacob objected out of his peasant folk wisdom and said that powders were for the guts. He felt the old woman was having chills and everyone knows you should bleed her for that. They each got angry and old Jacob was ordered off with his dying wife. As he left, he mumbled that if they were rich, the old woman would have been bled, the bastards![41]

The episode in the story helps reveal some of the problems of public medical care. In the story, there was a doctor permanently stationed at the local public hospital. But in this case he was drunk and not available. Chekhov often observed that poor pay and bad working conditions led to drunkenness at isolated rural hospitals. Usually, only the worst or the most dedicated worked in public hospitals. Most physicians were drawn off into private practice and many tried to go to Petersburg or Moscow.

In the absence of a physician, the prime source of "qualified" health care were the "feldshers" or doctor's assistants. They were meant to perform the role of our contemporary doctor's assistant or nurse practitioner. Unfortunately, in many cases, the promise of the system was not realized. The doctor's assistants as portrayed by Chekhov were many times as poorly trained, as lazy and as problem-ridden as the worst of the doctors. In several stories, Chekhov represented these doctor's assistants as ignorant pompous fools who caused as much harm as good. In "Rothschilds Fiddle," the doctor's assistant was correct in not bleeding the old woman, but giving the old woman bicarbonate of soda and telling her she was old and it was time she was dead was hardly a positive alternative to the healer who bled Nicholas to death. The old man and woman went home and died.[42]

The peasant, on the other hand, with his rich store of misinformation from witches, peasant holy men, and quacks, thought he knew how to treat illness. The ignorance of the peasants contributed substantially to the problem. The peasants felt safe treating themselves with ancient charms, spells or group rituals whose roots go back to pre-Christian times. Even the Church's sacrament of Extreme Unction was used at times as folk magic, as with Gran in "The Peasants." The ignorance of the peasants and the doctor's assistants both had the same taproot, poverty.[43]

A key problem was lack of money to pay and train good doctors and/or doctor's assistants. When the system worked, it worked well, but frequently it failed with fatal consequences. Staff and facilities were desperately needed. Chekhov was not demanding new, big hospitals mentioned in "In the Hollow."[44] What he seemed to prefer was the idea of many dispensaries which, for instance, might have helped the scalded baby in "In the Hollow." A clinic like the one Lydia wanted in "An Artist's Story" could have saved her servant from dying in childbirth.[45] A local clinic with a competent doctor or doctor's assistant might have saved some of the six children who died out of Marya's thirteen children in "The Peasants."[46]

Chekhov presented some of the views of a rural doctor in his "Ward Six." He described the condition of a rural town hospital and gave an in-depth look at the problems of the health care system. He also gave some sense of the difficulty of reforming it, but he also makes it clear that it could and had to be reformed.

As one approached the hospital in "Ward Six," the stench was so bad one could hardly breathe. The ambulance men, the nurses and their children slept in the wards with the patients. Everyone complained about the roaches, bed bugs and mice. Infection was endemic in the surgical department and there were only two scalpels and no thermometers in the hospital. The hospital manager, the head nurse and the doctor's assistant, all stole from the patients. The doctor who was being replaced had sold the medical alcohol and had a harem among the nurses and patients. This was accepted matter-of-factly in the village.

Some people in "Ward Six" defended the conditions by pointing out that the only people who used the hospital were low-class town dwellers or peasants. They should not complain because conditions were worse in their own homes. Some said the town could not support the hospital they had and needed support from the Zemstvo. The Zemstvo refused to build a hospital or help because the town already had one in operation. They felt the people should be grateful for having any hospital at all.[47]

The new physician, Dr. Ragin, realized that conditions were bad but believed he did not have the will power to change it. He adopted an attitude of apparent indifference to the irregularities. He worked hard seeing patients, but, over time, the mortality rate did not decline. Struck by the futility of his efforts, he became bored. He saw forty people a day but could not give them in-depth care. He began to feel he cheated forty people a day, twelve hundred per year.[48]

Dr. Ragin began to question all this, became depressed, and started to let things slide. He stopped attending the hospital everyday. He attributed conditions at the hospital to some greater evil; it was not his fault, it was the fault of the age.[49] In his absence, the doctor's assistant took over. He was a religious fanatic and tended to attribute diseases to not praying properly. Even when the doctor attended, he saw only a few patients and then let his assistant take over.[50] The general result here was the same as before. No reliable medical care because of ignorance, poor training, and poor pay for doctors led to poor medical care.

If the hospital was bad, the mental ward, "Ward Six," was terrible. The attendant was stupid and beat the patients to maintain order. The entrance to the ward was the hospital junkyard. Inside, there was an acrid stench and bugs. It was a "zoo." The maniacs lay about in faded blue smocks, some racked by tuberculosis. They were seen by the doctor only a few times a year because it depressed him.[51]

The doctor knew "Ward Six" was an abomination which could exist only in a rural backwater one hundred twenty miles from the railway, one dominated by officials who were illiterate fools. There was great progress in the city, but it had no effect in the rural world.[52]

The real undoing of the doctor occurred when he realized that one of the madmen who was being treated as an animal was really a person. He discovered the madman was probably one of the sanest men in the town. Once he recognized this madman as a person, he began to improve conditions much to the mystification of his subordinates. He talked to the madman and visited the ward everyday. The doctor's actions could hardly be considered sane within the context of the society previously described at the hospital. The doctor was eventually committed for his actions by a committee composed of town officials, a young doctor who wanted to take over and a foolish ex-officer. The doctor was judged by the incompetent people he had previously tolerated and he was committed to the hospital he had refused to reform.[53] This may be Chekhov's allegory for all of Russia but specifically it reveals the desperate condition of medical care in Russia.

The system was dominated by incompetent doctors and ignorant doctor's assistants under the control of corrupt or stupid officials. Many hospitals were primitive; if new big hospitals were built, they served only the immediate vicinity. Even when care was available to peasants, some were too ignorant and suspicious to take advantage of it. They would sooner be bled to death than go to the doctor.

This whole situation was compounded by the tremendous effect disease had in this rural, poor society. Chekhov frequently notes diseases endemic to areas: malaria, anthrax, and always in the background, tuberculosis.

Chekhov's general picture of the problems in the health care system in Russia are consistent with scholarly comment on the same topics. This is especially true when dealing with physicians, physicians's assistants and the problems of the hospitals and clinics in Russia.

Dr. Shingarev in his report, "The Dying Village," on the Voronezh district, outlined an environment of poverty, malnutrition and disease-bearing filth. Animals eating human waste, the dam for cattle ponds made of dung, rotting animal flesh all provide a breeding ground for disease. Malaria was endemic to the villages he studied. The people lived in cramped, insect-infested huts.[54]

Leroy Beaulieu's view of conditions is remarkably consistent with Chekhov's and presents, if anything, a bleaker picture than Chekhov's. He saw as the first major problem the peasants' prejudices and the generally anti-hygienic village traditions. The power of the witch was still strong. According to Matossian, the peasants depended on good and bad witches as well as magic rituals to rid themselves of disease.[55]

Secondly, Leroy Beaulieu saw the difficulty of getting adequate medical staff as a critical problem. Physicians were paid ridiculously low wages. The Zemstvos were forced to rely on medical students, midwives and doctor's assistants assisted by licensed male hospital nurses and vaccinators. Even with these persons, the salaries were so low as to warrant the attention of only the most desperate. "Money is the universal stumbling block in Russia . . ." The notable exception to this was the excellent quality of women doctors and doctor's assistants who unfortunately, like the village teacher, were limited by prejudice against them.[56]

D. M. Wallace, through personal experience and in conversation with a doctor's assistant (feldsher), learned just how poorly trained they were. He was told by a peasant to go to the witch instead of the doctor's assistant. The doctor's assistant was viewed as a useless and dangerous member of society. The peasant believed that the witch (znakharka), through herbs and charms, could cure disease and even raise the dead. For Wallace, the doctor's assistant and the witch represented two ages of medicine, the magical and the scientific. Under the pressure of disease, when science seemed to fail, the peasant would return to magic. Chekhov's perceptions in this area were consistent with these and other scholarly views on the topic.[57]

The Zemstvo

On balance, Chekhov was very positive about the Zemstvo in his stories. He was critical in areas where criticism is generally accepted as true. He lauded their efforts to provide health care and education but also recognized the weaknesses of the system. Chekhov was especially concerned about the corruption of government officials and the chronic lack of operating funds. Corrupt officials frustrated the Zemstvo's attempts to improve conditions. The lack of operating funds not only hampered the functioning of the Zemstvos but also alienated the peasants because the Zemstvos could get money only by taxing them.

Chekhov recognized that the Zemstvos were also burdened because the gentry, whose interests were radically different than those of the peasants, dominated the institution. Those who fare best in Chekhov's view are the Zemstvo employees, the doctors, teachers, and other specialists, who try to do the work of the Zemstvo while fighting the officials, the Zemstvo, the peasants, ignorance, and disease.

For this monumental task, they are underpaid, abused, and ridiculed. Chekhov was, for a time, a Zemstvo doctor and had a clear sense of the problems. As in the previous sections on education and medicine, Chekhov, although critical, was in favor of the Zemstvo and his hope for Russia lay in positive individual action by reasonable persons through the Zemstvo structure.

Gentry domination of the Zemstvo was, in Chekhov's view, one of its major failings. For him, such members were nothing more than dilettantes. He presented in "The Name-Day Party," a scathing picture of a young nobleman, fresh out of the university with little experience, who become a member of the Zemstvo. Thinking himself a forward-looking progressive, this stereotypical, rich mama's boy, so newly-arrived, had the temerity to preface his remarks in the Zemstvo with phrases like "we active members of the Zemstvo."

Within a year, the new member was bored and looking for an excuse to return to the excitement of St. Petersburg. His excuse for leaving was that the Zemstvo was useless and not worth his time and efforts. His wife, who initially thought her husband was so wonderful and generous in being an "active member of the Zemstvo," also conveniently concluded that the institution was wasteful of her husband's progressive talent.

This young nobleman was indeed progressive. A scientific farmer, he possessed the newest breeding stock, beehives, utilized the newest methods for raising crops, and built a new cheese factory. He even followed the latest financial management techniques. Unfortunately, as Chekhov indicated, all the nobleman's progressive measures were used to support old and corrupt patterns of behavior. Every summer he sold timber and mortgaged part of this land so he could go to the Crimea with his mistress in the autumn.

For Chekhov, a key problem for the Zemstvo and for the rural economy was the high proportion of gentry representation on the Zemstvo. The gentry's lack of interest and commitment, represented by the young progressive nobleman, hurt the Zemstvo, and their pleasures squandered the resources of the rural economy. Thus, the gentry would not, indeed could not, lead the economic revival of the area through the use of progressive farming. They would eventually go bankrupt instead. What will be remembered would not be the gentry's profligacy but their comments about the uselessness of the Zemstvo which would echo for years. Ultimately, the gentry would also conclude that the Zemstvo itself was responsible for the institution's failure, not their selfish aspirations and desires.[58]

On the other hand, the peasants tended to blame the Zemstvo for any local difficulty, even when the Zemstvo could not have had anything to do with the problem.[59] It was a convenient way of dealing with frustration. Chekhov suggested in one story that the source of the habit of blaming the Zemstvo, even when they were blameless, came from the factory owners and the businessmen.[60]

Although the Zemstvos often received unfair blame for peasant problems, there were occasions when the Zemstvo deserved criticism, especially when individuals got control of the Zemstvo for their own benefit. In one of his stories, Chekhov had the chairman of the Zemstvo appoint relatives to all local jobs.[61]

On other occasions, it was just Zemstvo's inability to deliver proper support for their employees. The teachers, doctors, and their assistants performed under difficult circumstances at low pay, yet they constantly had to worry. They worried about where their next meal was coming from, about illness, about lack of fuel and about bad roads. They even missed the satisfaction of thinking they were working for an ideal or for the people. The work was hard, the life dull and only drudges put up with it for long.[62] Chekhov's sympathy was clearly with the professional employees of the Zemstvo.

In his stories, Chekhov proposed the values of individual action and it was with this that he proposed to solve the Zemstvo problem. Through Lydia in "The Artist's Story," Chekhov proposed that the motivated individuals get together and fight the corruption and neglect, that these individuals should join the Zemstvo and make it work.[63]

The control of the Zemstvo was, as Chekhov had noted, clearly in the hands of the gentry. D. Shakhovskoi, in his articles on the Zemstvo, indicated that in the Zemstvo, the aristocratic and non-aristocratic estates met with the full force of their differences. These two groups had completely different political and civil rights as well as economic and social differences. In addition, persons of completely different political and social views were brought together. To a large extent, the representation reflected the feudal estates system of the past. Boris Veselovsky indicated that the 1864 statute guaranteed the landed gentry a relative majority in the Zemstvo assemblies. The 1890 document gave them an absolute majority, only in a very few did the peasants retain a majority of votes.

Veselovsky believed a series of acts kept the Zemstvo from centralizing and maintained gentry and ultimately, government control over it. On November 21, 1866, the government imposed drastic limitations on the right of Zemstvo assemblies to tax commercial and industrial enterprises. In 1867, an act prohibited the Zemstvo from different provinces from linking together. On June 13, 1867, the government granted more power to the chairman of the Zemstvo who was usually a person favored by the Provincial Governors. Finally, the government put the Zemstvo in its place, as it were. In September, 1869, it was ruled that "neither by their composition nor by their basic principles are Zemstovs government agencies, and therefore, they have no other legal rights than private persons and societies . . ." This list of restrictions presented by Alexander Vucinich goes on to include limiting Zemstvo control over the schools. Finally, in 1879, the government was given the right to hire and fire as well as transfer Zemstvo employees.

This list of acts reflects a trend toward officials controlling the Zemstvo. The lowest ranking official in effect had control of the Zemstvo. N. N. Avinov believed that the government officials' attitudes toward the Zemstvo were generally negative, viewing it as an incidental, nonessential appendage of local government. However, in the final analysis, Vucinich felt that the Zemstvo achieved a remarkable amount in education, sanitation, construction of roads, veterinary service, mutual insurance, and public charity, in spite of its weaknesses. The key weaknesses Vucinich identified were: domination of the Zemstvos by the gentry; their inability to reach down and become part of the community; their lack of real power; their dependence on local officials to carry out their decisions; and from their perception by the government as a potential rallying point for opposition and as a force for change. To this list should be added Leroy Beaulieu's view that because they lacked money they had to tax the peasants. They also lacked competent professional staff because of the pay and conditions. Chekhov's perceptions are consistent with scholarly opinion on the Zemstvo and its problems.[64]

Local Officials and Government

Chekhov developed a picture of local officials as inept and often corrupt, but he also realized that the corruption flowed from the top down. The state bureaucracy at the center was probably more corrupt than at the local level. It was all part of the system of state bureaucracy represented by the hierarchy of rank within the government service.

The system of chin, or rank, emerged with the centralized state of Peter the Great. The system placed every member of official society in a specific rank on the table of ranks and they could ascertain their relative position on that table.[65] Rank (chin) became the critical fact of official life in the nineteenth century. Chekhov pointed up this fact in a story fragment wherein an aging civil servant living in the country was seeking happiness. But, when asked if he would like his youth restored to achieve happiness, he refused because, as a young man, he would not hold his present high rank.[66]

This sense of rank dominated the entire society. It affected everyone from the Tsar to the lowly elder of the commune. The pattern of behavior, the ethics, and the method of advancement became a highly stylized world apart from the rules which had to be followed.

Chekhov sketched the character of those involved in the system. In "An Anonymous Story," he examined a senior civil servant, Kukushkin, and a lawyer influence peddler, Pekarsky. The senior civil servant was described as short, stout, and generally ugly with the manners of a lizard who slithered about. He did nothing and was paid well for it. He was a careerist to the core of his being and would do anything to be seen with someone influential. He groveled in cowardice and ambition, and his general conversation was vulgar and disgusting. This "creature," Kukushkin, played up to men like the influence peddler, Pekarsky.

Pekarsky was a lawyer whose power was enormous in the nether world of influence, bribery, corruption and groveling. He could deliver high-level jobs through his patronage and cut red tape with his card. Pekarsky was very intelligent in a calculating way but could not understand human emotions. He did not even have a sense of humor. Drinking and whoring were all right as long as they did not interfere with business. He did not believe in God, but he felt religion must be preserved to keep the lower orders under control.[67] Pekarsky was a machine.

This bleak picture of officials was continued as Chekhov moved through the inferno. In "My Wife," Chekhov outlined a mid-range civil servant who was educated and well-bred. He was honest, fair, high-principled, but as a result, radiated stuffiness which offended and humiliated others. He disliked the world, because he was a man of integrity; religious believers, because they are immature;

nonbelievers, because they lack faith; the old, for their backwardness; and the young, for being free thinkers. He valued Russia and the peasant yet feared the peasants as potential robbers and thieves. He related only to his own kind, civil servants.[68] Even when they were honest civil servants, they were officious.

In a very humorous story, Chekhov gave an example of the "practical" application of chin. He demonstrated this through the comic device of a dog in "Chameleon." A tradesman claimed he was bitten by a dog and chased it, finally cornering the animal. The question of what to do came to the attention of a local police official and a crowd formed.

Initially, the official believed he could curry favor with the crowd and the tradesman by threatening to punish the dog's owner, whoever that might have been. Then someone yelled that it was the general's dog. Immediately, the dog belonging to the general outranked the tradesman. The discussion shifted to what the tradesman must have done to incite the poor little dog to defend itself by biting the tradesman. Then someone said, no, it's not the general's dog, and the police official again flipped over to the theme of the poor man bitten by the vicious dog. No, it is the general's brother's dog! The police official warned the poor tradesman not to abuse poor animals again and he took the dog to return it to his excellency.[69]

In this story, Chekhov captured the whole system of rank (chin) and how absurdly broad its application was in Russia. The general's dog outranked the tradesman and the police official would use the dog to gain advantage with the general.[70] Another civil servant would use his wife's beauty to get ahead in the system.

In "The Order of St. Anne," a civil servant married an attractive girl with social graces, such as speaking Russian with a French accent, which she had cultivated. She was brought into a society where the highest achievement was to come to the attention of his Excellency, the minister. In this environment, the civil servant deliberately tried to have his wife catch the minister's eye. Initially, the girl was shy and performed socially only because she feared her husband. However, she learned the operation of the system and her power in it. Eventually, she gained his Excellency's attention. Her husband was promoted and decorated with the Order of St. Anne.[71] The story ended happily by the standards of the bureaucracy; he was maneuvering for a new medal and his wife was the queen of that strange, unreal world of the bureaucracy.[72]

Chekhov revealed the perverse life and values of the bureaucracy and in stories like "My Life," he revealed the scope of the corruption in bribes. All civil service jobs were the same, observed one young man who had held nine and whose father had been a civil servant. He revealed the operation of the system. He explained his father had taken bribes because he felt people offered him money out of respect for his moral caliber, so it was not corruption. The over-all system touched everyone and few succeeded without it. If students wanted to be promoted, they paid their teachers. At recruiting time, the military commander's wife took bribes. The doctor took bribes at the hospital. The health inspector was bribed by the butchers and restaurants. Applying for anything at any institution required a bribe. Even in the church, bribes were necessary.

Those who did not take bribes were viewed as arrogant, callous, narrow-minded, and were accused of exercising a corrupting influence on society. In addition, if you did not pay bribes, you could not survive in the system. An example can be seen in "My Life." The town council decided that the top bribe they would pay to the railroad construction engineer was forty thousand rubles, when he wanted fifty thousand rubles.[73] As a result, the station was built three miles outside of town instead of on its outskirts. The town had to pay even more for a road to link to the railroad. Pay and survive![74]

The engineer in the story lived a good life in the system. He had fine foods, imported wines and the best cigars, all as kickbacks. He and his daughter had all the best things in life for free. They had adapted to their environment. Bribes were part of the income they expected from the job.[75] This attitude and environment trickled down to the lowest level.

Chekhov developed the theme of local officials in many of his stories but he focused on them in "On Official Business." In this story, a local government insurance agent had committed suicide and a doctor and the coroner came to the village to hold an inquest. The person responsible for guarding the body and making sure order was maintained was the village constable. The constable was a semi-literate of peasant stock while the doctor, the coroner, and the dead man were all educated. The doctor and the coroner were county-wide officials, the constable was of this community. The peasants were ignorant and in their ignorance were upset at the presence of a suicide's body being left in the village overnight.

Chekhov expressed what was strong and weak in the makeup of local government through the constable and the same for county government through the doctor. The constable was semi-literate, local, honest, hardworking, and concerned about all classes in the community. He was given his position in 1866 and served with honor and a sense of duty.[76] He had a purpose and he filled it, as seen when he trekked all night in a blizzard to get the doctor to return to conduct his inquest because the peasants were restless. He was worried about the peasants and was going to make sure that the county officials did what they should and thus quiet the peasants.

The doctor, on the other hand, left the village so that he might sleep in comfort with his own kind in a gentry home. He could not accept that the peasants would get excited about a dead body in the village overnight. He ignored their ignorance, superstition and fear. He did not understand and could not, or would not, help.

The constable's strength lay in his sense of duty and purpose but he could not help with the ignorance of the peasants because he was ignorant and a peasant himself. The doctor had the education but was not local and could not identify with the peasants so he ignored them and, therefore, could not destroy their ignorance either. Local officials were in contact with the problem but too ignorant to solve it. County officials had the knowledge but were too remote and lacked the consciousness to understand the problem. Neither solved anything.

A third side to the problem appears with the man who committed suicide. He had been educated. He worked locally and saw the problem. He lacked the sense of mission the constable had so he was overwhelmed by the problems and committed suicide. The constable, for all his sense of duty, received abuse from all but the peasants.

This was the problem of local government. How do you get a corps of dedicated, educated, honest, locally-rooted individuals who will work for low pay in the village? The role of the local officials, and perhaps the lower class in general, was expressed by Chekhov in a dream of the doctor's, who saw the constable marching through the blizzard while the likes of himself sat in light and comfort. The constable and his like bore all the burdens; their own and the upper classes.[77]

They took upon themselves all the hardest and most bitter elements in life. They left for the privileged the easy, enjoyable things, so the privileged might sit at their dinner tables rationally discussing why the constable and his like suffer and perish, and why they were less healthy and happy than the privileged.[78]

Chekhov pointed out a key element of the problem of working in the village in his story "Terror." The problem in the story and in local government is the need for a sustained effort everyday, not just a surge to meet a crisis. The "terror" in the story was the terror of everyday life that dragged people down, the routine from which no one could escape. The grinding routine coupled with no sense of purpose led to fear of those who have a purpose.[79] This again was the merit of the constable in "On Official Business." He could take the grind; he had his duty. This sense of duty could not be based on the myth of the peasant because when the myth collapsed, so would the sense of duty and the "terror" of everyday life would destroy the person, perhaps leading to suicide. Chekhov wanted clear-eyed professionals with a genuine purpose, not one based on a myth. These persons could not appear for a moment of crisis but must be there for the protracted day-to-day struggle that was needed in the village.

Chekhov also supplied another view of the problem of service in the village. In the event there was an involved, educated, and honest person willing to work in the community, he would run into a problem. If he planned to live in the midst of misery, how could he plan a happy life for himself and his family?[80]

It is significant that the coroner and the constable discuss the changing pattern of suicide in the village. In the old days, the gentry might shoot themselves because they had been discovered embezzling money. Now they killed themselves because they were fed up with life, depressed and frustrated. In the end, the peasants had not committed suicide, and the constable reminded the coroner that he had to do his work and solve the peasant problem.[81]

Chekhov appeared to want to combine the best of both the doctor and the constable. But if a choice must be made, he appeared to favor the constable's dedication and identification with the peasants to the remote, educated indifference of the coroner and the doctor. Chekhov was supporting local government.

The constable represented the better part of local officialdom. The alternative was the corrupt and inefficient government which Chekhov also observed and recorded. The ineptitude of local officials can be seen in "The Peasants" when the village elder tried to lead the fight against the traditional village enemy, fire. His response to the crisis was to break every window in the burning hut, with no purpose. Having completed that task, he began to chop down the porch while he sent the women to get the fire engine. Order was restored only when the men from the manor house arrived led by a young student, a member of the gentry. This contrast set off in bold relief the incompetence of the village elder.[82]

In addition to incompetence, laziness was a problem among village officials. Constable Zhukov in the "Murder" only got out of his chair when his superiors came for inspection.[83] If it was not ignorance, incompetence, or laziness, then it was corruption among local officials.

Clear-cut examples of criminality among local officials can be seen in Chekhov's story "In the Hollow." The son of the storekeeper, Anisim Tsybukin, was a police agent. He decided to supplement his income by counterfeiting rubles. For this, he ultimately lost his rights and property, as well as being sentenced to six years hard labor in Siberia. This, however, was not the typical type of crime.[84]

A more typical problem was bribery. In the same story, a local police inspector and the health officer took ten rubles a month from the tannery owner whom they permitted to operate a tannery which had been ordered closed. The tannery was polluting the village's meadows and the village cattle were getting anthrax. This and malaria were a major threat to the village. This was all permitted for ten rubles a month.[85] Chekhov identified the problems of the local government as difficulty in getting qualified people, ignorance, laziness and corruption. Scholarly opinion supports Chekhov's view of officials.

According to Leroy Beaulieu, official corruption appeared to be a way of life in Russia. The causes of that corruption have been categorized in two groups. First, those that might be unique to Russia; and second, those which might be common to all bureaucracy. The tradition growth from which the Russian bureaucracy emerged may have contributed to the growth of corruption. The bureaucracy at all levels from the time of Ivan IV emerged out of a rabble among whom embezzlement and fraud had been a matter of tradition. The tradition of Oriental despotism and its corruption (perhaps reflecting the Byzantine and Mongol legacy) were strong in Russia. Finally, there was the corrupting effect of serfdom which touched all groups.

There were also more traditional areas common to most bureaucracies which were problems in Russia. First, the inadequacy of salaries led to a standardized structure of bribes which were expected if one wanted services from the state. Bureaucrats viewed it as similar to fees for religious services. Even the state recognized the existence of the system. Second was the more modern practice of paying for big government contracts. Third, a market had arisen for bribes to escape the measures enacted against revolutionaries. Fourth, at the highest level, corruption took the form of buying offices, titles, companions, and almost anything else one might want or need. This encouraged corruption on all levels throughout the empire.

Leroy Beaulieu believed that this pattern, in conjunction with absolutism, delivered the empire into the hands of an arbitrary and corrupted bureaucracy, which preferred its own interests to those of both Sovereign and nation. As a result, the peasant and the poor townsman did not trust officials of any type.[86]

The pattern of corruption reached down into the local community because the central government bureaucracy controlled the local government and recreated it in their own image and likeness. Corruption flowed down the hill.

This pattern of control and corruption is documented in an investigation conducted by S. N. Prokopovich at the beginning of this century. It indicated that the commune usually fell under the leadership of the wealthiest or most aggressive elements who tended to lord it over the average peasant. The Mir, in turn, was dominated by the Volost (several villages) which was dominated by government officials. These government officials were elected in name only. Peasant officials were unable to defend their own interests. S. N. Prokopovich wrote that, "As a result, the better element of the village, as a rule, shuns service and the positions are occupied by the scum of the peasant population."[87]

The elected authorities of the village community and the township were obliged by law to carry out all tasks assigned to them by numerous government officials, including the ubiquitous police and court investigators. Alexander Vucinich pointed out that the very word 'bureaucracy' took on a negative meaning. He quoted the *Entsiklopedicheskii slovar'* definition of bureaucracy as a method of administration unique to political communities in which "the central government authorities have concentrated all power in their hands," and in this, there exists a "privileged segment" of officials who behave with "caste exclusiveness" and they are "poor members of communities" because of their alignment, not with the society, but with the authorities they are employed by.[88]

Chekhov again was correct in his perceptions and his opinions concur with scholarship in the field.[89]

Taxes and Arrears

The biggest problem that ordinary people had with officials was the collection of obligations. These obligations to the government were paid by the peasant through the commune. They included fire insurance payments which were substantial but from which some benefit accrued to the peasant. In "The Peasants," the hut that burned down was insured.[90]

Among the obligations, the largest and most resented item was the redemption payment which raised the annual obligations substantially. All the obligations the peasant owed, but could not pay, could be lumped together as arrears. As in "The Peasants," the debt was put on the commune and shared by its members, even those who moved to town. Town workers were paid well, but they sometimes did not send their share back to the village.[91] The last thing a peasant would pay was his portion of the commune's redemption payment.

The village elder in "The Peasants" was responsible for collecting each share of the debt from the peasants. He was, in turn, responsible to the government official who came to collect the money.[92] For all intents and purposes, the commune and government officials had taken the place of the serf owner in the peasant's life. The elder was placed in the position of being afraid of the authorities because of the arrears of his fellow commune members.[93]

The elder utilized various methods to pressure peasants to pay their obligations. In "The Peasants," it was the elder who took the samovars from the peasants' huts to make them pay their arrears. At tax time, he would have a whole collection of them in his hut. Other huts had had livestock seized to force payment. The animals were taken to local government offices but were sickened because they had been roughly handled or not fed. The elder, under pressure from above, was driven to express his own power by abusing the peasants.[94]

"Whose fault was it?" they asked in "The Peasants." The answer was always the Zemstvo. The habit of blaming the Zemstvo had grown up years before. Some wealthy peasants who had been on the Zemstvo were forced to leave held a grudge. That led to the habit of blaming the Zemstvo.[95]

Scholarly opinion on this problem of arrears and the difficulty of payment by the commune attest to the accuracy of Chekhov's observation.

There were three kinds of direct taxation: Imperial to the central government; local to the Zemstvo, and commune to the Mir and Volost; and besides these, the peasant had to pay a yearly sum for the redemption of the land allotment which he received at the time of the Emancipation. Taken all together, these were a heavy burden for the peasant. For the first decade, the peasants bore their burden without getting too deeply in arrears. By 1872, some problems began to emerge. It took the government over a decade to react with measures which were really effective.[96]

During the next twenty years (1881-1901), the arrears of the whole of European Russia rose from approximately 27 million to 144 million rubles. The increase was greatest in the dark earth agricultural regions. William Blackwell maintained that it was apparent that the peasant, his land, and his ability to pay taxes were all exhausted. The rural population exploded, grain prices and wages fell, tax arrears and rent obligations built up. The peasant sold his livestock, watched his topsoil erode, and began to grow hungry and desperate. It was in the midst of this decline that Vyshnegradsky and then Witte tried to collect the arrears that had accumulated over the years.[97]

Alexander Gerschenkron lays a good portion of the blame for the depression of the economy around 1900 on the "exhaustion of the tax-paying powers of the rural population. The patience of the peasantry was at its end."[98] Wallace indicates that the peasant population of the agricultural areas were paying from 25% to 100% of their agricultural income beyond subsistence to the Imperial Treasury.[99] Maynard says there was very little private indebtedness other than rent of land and obligations from redemption. The obligations were the straws that broke the camel's back.[100]

From the central government down, the pressure was on to collect the arrears. Lazar Volin maintains that it was arrears which forced the commune to intervene in the affairs of individual households. To guarantee payment, a member of the defaulting family could be hired out or the head of the household could be replaced and a different member appointed in his place.[101]

William Blackwell believes that, "such hopeless conditions produced violence, riots, burnings, and pillage . . . particularly during the last years of Witte's administration." Chekhov was correct in his portrayal of the impact of the taxes and arrears on the peasants and is in agreement with scholarship in this area.[102]

In this chapter some of the specific areas of the peasants' environment have been discussed and Chekhov's observations have proven to be true.

NOTES

[1] "The Peasants," in *Oxford Chekhov*, 8:196.

[2] Robert Redfield, *The Little Community Peasant Society and Culture* (Chicago: University of Chicago Press, 1960), p. 60; Nicholas Vakar, *The Taproot of Soviet Society* (New York, Harper and Row, 1961), p. 41; S. A. Tokarev, *Etnografiia narodov SSR: I storicheskie osnovy byta i kul'tury* (Moscow, 1958), p. 51, 28; S. P. Tolstoi, et al, eds. for the Akademiia nauk SSSR, Institut etnografii, *Narody Mira: Narody evropeiskoi Chasti SSSR*, I (Moscow, 1964), pp. 462-64, quoted in Mary Matossian "The Peasant Way of Life" in Vucinish, *The Peasant in Nineteenth Century Russia*. p. 17; Sir Donald Mackenzie Wallace, *Russia* (New York: Henry Holt & Co., 1905), p. 467, see break up of large family; Anatoli Leroy-Beaulieu, *The Empire of the Tsars and the Russians*, trans. by Zenaide Ragozin, 3 vols. (New York: G. P. Putnam's Sons, 1893-1903), 1:486-504.

[3] John Curtiss, "The Peasant and the Army" in *The Peasant in Nineteenth Century Russia*, p. 110; Additional comment on this is in the section on the military; see also Matossian, "The Peasant Way of Life," in *The Peasant in Nineteenth Century Russia*, p. 31.

[4] Reginald Zelnik, "The Peasant and the Factory," in *The Peasant in Nineteenth Century Russia*, pp. 158-159; Additional comment on this in the section on workers; D. M. Wallace, *Russia*, p. 472; G. T. Robinson, *Rural Russia*, p. 107.

[5] "The Peasants," in *Oxford Chekhov*, 8:202.

[6] Vera S. Dunham, "The Strong-Woman Motif," in the Transformation of Russian Society, ed. Cyril Black (Cambridge, Mass., Harvard University Press, 1960), pp. 459-83.

[7] "The Peasants," in *Oxford Chekhov*, 8:206.

[8] Matossian, "The Peasant Way of Life" in *The Peasant in Nineteenth Century Russia*, pp. 17-20; Quoting Eric Wolf, *Peasants* (Englewood Cliffs, N.J., Prentice-Hall, 1966), pp. 65-70, Tolstoi, *Narody evropeiski Chasti SSSR*,

p. 468, Lev A. Tekhomirov, *Russia, Political and Social*, (London, 1888), 1:187, and A. F. L. M. Baron Von Haxthausen, *The Russian Empire*, trans. Robert Faire, 2 vols. (London: Chapman and Hall, 1856), 1:123.

9   "The Peasants," in *Oxford Chekhov*, pp. 195, 200.

10   "The Peasants," *Ibid.*, 8:212.

11   "The Peasants," *Ibid.*, 8:220-21.

12   "The Peasants," in *Oxford Chekhov*, 8:195, 198; "Thieves" in *Oxford Chekhov*, 5:89.

13   Sir John Maynard, *The Russian Peasant and Other Studies* (New York: Collier Books, 1962), pp. 62, 67-68; Chekhov's general descriptions are also consistent with typical villages and huts of the Russian Museum of Enthnography in Leningrad and the Museum of Wooden Architecture in Novgorod. These are recorded in the notes and photographs of this author; See also: Wright Miller, *The Russians as People* (New York, 1961), p. 64, Haxthausen, *The Russian Empire*, p. 21, Tokarev, *Etnografiia narodov SSR: I storicheskie osnovy byta i kul'tury*, p. 51, Tolstoi, *Narody Mira: Narody evropeiskoi Chasti SSSR*, pp. 283-90, quoted in Matossian, "The Peasant Way of Life," *The Peasant in Nineteenth Century Russia*, pp. 1, 2, 5-8.

14   *Oxford Chekhov*, 6:10-11.

15   Ironically, when Chekhov died, his body was shipped back to Moscow in a refrigerated car marked "Oysters."

16   "Murder," in *Oxford Chekhov*, 8:45-46; "The Peasants," in *Oxford Chekhov*, 8:202; "In the Hollow," in *Oxford Chekhov*, 9:154.

17   "Theives," in *Oxford Chekhov*, 5:91; "In the Hollow," in *Oxford Chekhov*, 9:154, 156.

18   "The Order of St. Anne," in *Ibid.*, 8:34-35.

19   "His Wife," in *Ibid.*, 8:18; "Ariadne" in *Ibid.*, 8:79.

20   There can be little doubt that at the turn of the century the peasants functioned at subsistence level and occasionally existed below subsistence level. *The School.*

21   "The Savage," in *Oxford Chekhov*, 8:225.

22   "My Life," in *Oxford Chekhov*, 8:167-168.

23   "In the Cart," in *Ibid.*, 8:251-256; "The Artist's Story," in *Ibid.*, 8:98.

24   "The Savage," in *Ibid.*, pp. 226-231.

25   "From a Retired Teacher's Notebook" in *Oxford Chekhov*, 6:260.

26   Donald Treadgold, "The Peasant and Religion," in *The Peasant in Nineteenth Century Russia*, ed. W. Vucinich (Standford: Standford Univ. Press, 1968), p. 78; Matossian, "The Peasant Way of Life," in *The Mira: Narody*

evropeiskoi Chasti SSSR, pp. 408-09, 468-69; Leroy Beaulieu, *The Empire of the Tsars and the Russians*, 2:177-79; Wallace, *Russia*, p. 500.

27 *Istoriia Rossi v XIX veke*, 9 vols. (St. Petersburg C., 1910), 7:165; Cited in: Sergei Pushkarev, *The Emergence of Modern Russia 1801-1917*, Trans. Robert H. McNeal and Tova Yedlin (New York: Holt, Rinehart and Winston, 1963), p. 288; Paul Miliukov, *Ocherki poistorii russkei kul'tury* (3rd ed.; St. Petersburg, 1902), 2:382; Cited in: Pushkarev, *The Emergence of Modern Russia*, 1801-1917, p. 289.

28 Alf Edeen, "The Civil Service," in *The Transformation of Russian Society*, edited by Cyril Black (Cambridge: Harvard Univ. Press, 1960), p. 281.

29 Sergei Pushkarev, *The Emergence of Modern Russia, 1801-1917*, pp. 163-164, 188-189.

30 N. N. Kovalevsky quoted in Volin, "The Russian Peasant," in *The Transformation of Russian Society*, p. 297.

31 A. A. Manuilov, Pozemel'nyi vopros v Rossii (Moscow, 1905), p. 47, quoted in Volin, "The Russian Peasant" in *The Transformation of Russian Society*, p. 297; see William H. E. Johnson, Russia's Educational Heritage (New Brunswick, N.J. 1950), pp. 281-90, 154-56.

32 "My Life," in *Oxford Chekhov*, 8:159-74.

33 "Gusev," in *Oxford Chekhov*, 5:103, 108-09

34 "On Official Business," in *Ibid.*, 9:112, 117, 120, 121, 123; "The Duel," in *Ibid.*, 5:138.

35 Treadgold, "The Peasant and Religion" in *The Peasant in Nineteenth Century Russia*, pp. 78-105; Daniel Field, *Rebels in the Name of the Tsar*, pp. 212-213.

36 Karlinsky, *Letters of Anton Chekhov*, p. 292.

37 "A Dreary Story," in *Oxford Chekhov*, 5:65-86.

38 "A Dreary Story," in *Ibid.*, 5:43.

39 "The Peasants," in *Ibid.*, 8:219.

40 "The Peasants," in *Ibid.*, 8:219-20.

41 "Rothschilds Fiddle," in *Ibid.*, 7:95-96.

42 "Rothschilds Fiddle," in *Ibid.*, 7:95-101.

43 "The Peasants," in *Ibid.*, 8:219.

44 "In the Hollow," in *Ibid.*, 9:179.

45 "The Artist's Story," in *Ibid.*, 8:105.

46 "The Peasants," in *Ibid.*, 8:203.

47 "Ward Six," in *Ibid.*, 6:130.

48 "Ward Six," in *Ibid.*, 6:130-32.

49   "Ward Six," in *Ibid.*, 6:138-39, 132.

50   "Ward Six," in *Ibid.*, 6:132-33.

51   "Ward Six," in *Ibid.*, 6:121-22.

52   "Ward Six," in *Ibid.*, 6:137-38.

53   "Ward Six," in *Ibid.*, 6:143, 134, 129, 137, 139-47, 152, 163-64, 167.

54   Dr. Shingarev, "The Dying Village," quoted in Sir John Maynard, *The Russian Peasant and Other Studies* (New York: Collier Books, 1962), p. 67.

55   Anatole Leroy-Beaulieu, *The Empire of the Tsars and the Russians*, 2:186-89; Matossian, "The Peasant Way of Life" in *The Peasant in Nineteenth Century Russia*, pp. 310-11.

56   Leroy-Beaulieu, *The Empire of the Tsars and the Russians*, 2:186-189.

57   D. M. Wallace, *Russia*, pp. 65-78 ("Feldsher," pp. 65-68, "Witch" pp. 72-74, "Plagues," pp. 74-76, "Feldsher and Zemstvo," pp. 76-77, "Lunatic Asylum," pp. 77-78).

58   Anton Chekhov, "The Name-Day Party" in *The Portable Chekhov*, ed. Avrahm Yarmolinsky (New York: The Viking Press, 1968), p. 204, (Hereafter cited as *Portable Chekhov*).

59   "In the Cart," in *Oxford Chekhov*, 8:251.

60   "The Peasants," in *Ibid.*, 8:304.

61   "The Artist's Story," in *Ibid.*, 8:99.

62   "In the Cart," in *Ibid.*, pp. 254-55.

63   "The Artist's Story," in *Ibid.*, p. 99.

64   D. Shakhovskoi, "Politischeskie techeniia v russkom zemstve," p. 444, B. B. Veselovsky, "Detsentralizatsiia upravleniia i zadachi zemstva," pp. 35-36, 43; N. N. Avinov, "Glavnyia cherty v istorii zakonodatel'stva o zemskikh uchrezhdeniiakh," pp. 3, 28, 17, in B. B. Veselovsky and Z. G. Frenkel, eds. *1864-1914, I ubileinyi zemskii sobornik* (St. Petersburg, 1914), all quoted in Alexander Vucinich, "The State and the Local Community," in *The Transformation of Russian Society*, edited by Cyril Black (Cambridge: Harvard University Press, 1960), pp. 201-206; Anatoli Leroy-Beaulieu, *The Empire of the tsars and the Russians*, 2:186-189; See also: for a detailed description of Zemstvo achievements, Prince G. E. Lvov Wallace, *Russia*, pp. 491-509; Richard Stites, *The Women's Liberation Movement in Russia: Feminism, Nihilism and Bolshevism, 1860-1930*, (Princeton: Princeton University Press, 1978), p. 87, "Women doctors and the Zemstvo."

65   "My Wife," in *Oxford Chekhov*, 6:47.

66   "Fragment," in *Ibid.*, 6:255.

67   "Anonymous Story," in *Ibid.*, 6:190-192.

68   "My Wife," in *Ibid.*, 6:47.

69   "The Chameleon," in *The Portable Chekhov*, ed. A. Yarmolinsky, pp. 85-89, (Hereafter referred to as Portable Chekhov).

70   "The Chamelon," in *Ibid.*, p. 89.

71   "The Order of St. Anne," in *Oxford Chekhov*, 8:35, 37-41.

72   "The Order of St. Anne," in *Ibid.*, 8:42

73   "My Life," in *Ibid.*, 8:125-126.

74   "My Life," in *Ibid.*, 8:127.

75   "On Official Business," in *Ibid.*, 9:54.

76   "On Official Business," in *Ibid.*, 9:124.

77   "On Official Business," in *Ibid.*, 9:122.

78   "On Official Business," in *Ibid.*, 9:122-123.

79   "Terror," in *Ibid.*, 9:122-23.

80   "On Official Business," in *Ibid.*, 9:122-23.

81   "On Official Business," in *Ibid.*, 9:112.

82   "The Peasants," in *Ibid.*, 8:207-09.

83   "Murder," in *Ibid.*, 8:52.

84   "In The Hollow," in *Ibid.*, 9:157, 173-75.

85   "On Official Business," in *Ibid.*, 9:153.

86   Leroy-Beaulieu, *The Empire of the Tsars and The Russians*, 2:98-116, see also for added information 2:172-175, 179, 185, 192-193, 87-97.

87   S. M. Prokopovich, *Mestnye liudi o nuzhdakh derevni* (St. Petersburg, 1904), p. 99, quoted in Lazar Volin "The Russian Peasant," in *The Transformation of Russian Society*, p. 297.

88   Alexander Vucinich, "The State and the Local Community," in *The Transformation of Russian Society*, p. 197; for additional information see pp. 197-199, 202-203, 204, 206; A. Ia., "Biurokratiia" in F. A. Brokgauz and I. A. Efron, eds. *Entsiklopedicheskii slovar'* (St. Petersburg, 1895), 5:293, quoted in Vucinich, "The State and the Local Community," in *The Transformation of Russian Society*, p. 204.

89   For further substantiation of Chekhov's view, see also Alf Edeen, "The Civil Service" in *The Transformation of Russian Society*, pp. 278-279; Wallace, *Russia*, pp. 325-345; Walters "The Peasants and Village Commune," in *The Peasant in Nineteenth Century Russia* p. 157; Terence Emmons, "The Peasant and Emancipation," in *The Peasant in Nineteenth Century Russia*, pp. 46-47, 70-71; Michael Karpovich, *Imperial Russia, 1801-1917* (New York: Holt, Rinehart & Winston, 1960), p. 52; G. T. Robinson, *Rural Russia Under the*

Old Regime (Berkley: University of California Press, 1969), p. 147; Push-karev, *The Emergence of Modern Russia, 1801-1917*, pp. 202-206; Maynard, *The Russian Peasant and Other Studies*, p. 64.

90 "The Peasants," in *Oxford Chekhov*, 8:209. As a point of information, Leroy-Beaulieu in *The Empire of the Tsars and the Russians* (pp. 191-92) states that 80 million rubles a year were lost to fire in Russia, one-fifth to one-third of the fires were arson, a total of one hundred thousand homes per year were destroyed in the empire.

91 "The Peasants," in *Ibid.*, 8:215.

92 "The Peasants," in *Ibid.*, 8:213.

93 "The Peasants," in *Ibid.*, 8:213-15.

94 "The Peasants," in *Ibid.*, 8:215-16.

95 "The Peasants," in *Ibid.*, 8:216.

96 Wallace, *Russia*, pp. 480, 470-71.

97 William Blackwell, *The Industrialization of Russia: an Historical Perspective*, pp. 33, 31.

98 Alexander Gerschenkron, "Problems and Patterns of Economic Development," in *The Transformation of Russian Society*, pp. 52-53.

99 Wallace, *Russia*, p. 481.

100 Maynard, *The Russian Peasant and Other Studies*, p. 64.

101 Lazar Volin, "The Russian Peasant," in *The Transformation of Russian Society*, p. 296.

102 Blackwell, *The Industrialization of Russia*, p. 31.

CHAPTER VIII

FORCES IMPACTING ON THE PEASANT

"We Were Better Off As Serfs"
Chekhov "The Peasants"

At this point the focus of this study shifts to forces which impact on the peasants from outside themselves as they try to live their lives. These forces, as described by Anton Chekov, are compared here with the perceptions of scholarly opinion to determine the validity of Chekhov's thought and observations. As the specifics which Chekhov described are proved to be accurate it will add credibility to his general posture as an iconoclast.

This portion of the study presents a series of separate views formulated by Chekhov on specific problems or institutions which affected the peasant. The chapter will include an investigation of: the differentiation of the peasantry into wealthy and poor peasants; the pressures on the peasant of industrial society and the village; the army and the peasant; religion and the peasant: Jews and the peasant; the peasant and the gentry; the question of being "better off as serfs"; peasant reaction to poverty; and Chekov's view of 'what was to be done' about the peasants.

Differentiation of the Peasantry

The differentiation of the peasantry, the emergence of different levels of wealth among the peasants, is a phenomenon clearly evident in several of Chekov's stories. Chekhov utilizes these stories to document various ways in which peasants acquired wealth at the end of the century.

In "Murder," Chekhov presents a classic case of plowback by an old believer family. The old believer family had run a successful inn for generations. However, the building of a railroad changed travel patterns and the inn declined. Despite the change, the family did not suffer because it had accrued a sizable sum by working hard at the business and not dividing the inheritance. Actually one of the heirs cheated the other and retained the wealth of the previous generation and built on it. The owner was strongly religious but cheated people to make and maintain his fortune.[1]

Chekhov's story "In The Hollow," shows how a peasant family works its way from poverty to wealth by taking every opportunity, both legal and illegal, to accumulate money. Both means were pursued with vigor. The head of the family, Gregory, and his daughter-in-law pursued the business ruthlessly, using dishonest means to achieve their success.[2] Chekhov noted this pattern of peasants cheating other peasants in several stories including "The Peasants."[3]

Chekhov develops this theme especially well in "In The Hollow." The owner of the store was Gregory Tsybukin who hated peasants, even though he was in the process of raising himself from their midst. He was willing to utilize any means to gain wealth. On holidays he sold the peasants putrid salt beef with a stench so vile it was difficult to approach the barrel. He accepted goods such as scythes, caps, and women's scarves from drunks in payment for vodka. Gregory cheated everyone, both peasants and mill workers. When he ordered clothes for a family wedding he paid the dressmakers in useless goods. He also sold vodka illegally at a great profit. In fact, the whole grocery store was just a front for illegal dealing in vodka, cattle skins, grain, pigs and whatever else would make a ruble.[4]

His daughter-in-law was as committed to the business as Gregory. From their relationship one can see that their accumulation of wealth had to be protected from division or ineffective use.

"In the Hollow" and "Murder" reveal how murder was sometimes employed to preserve accumulated wealth. Perhaps Chekhov was also trying to emphasize, in both stories, the drive and sacrifice required by the capitalist ethic. At any rate, in the story "In the Hollow," the family rose, in one generation, from the poverty of the type expressed in "The Peasants" through effective use of cheating and murder.

In the daughter-in-law's plans one can see what happened with capital once acquired. She diversified the family interests in a store and a brick factory. Both businesses were built by means of careful aggression and ruthless management. Once wealth and property were achieved, the family thought of itself as better than the peasant and artisan class from which they came.[5]

The story "At the Mill," also reveals how the drive for profit and wealth led to the use of base methods to gain success. A miller had a monopoly and used it to charge higher prices for his services. He tried to increase his wealth by building a monopoly over the fishing rights in the river. The miller respected nothing more than profit. A cheater and a miser, he became a beater of monks and even refused to help members of his own family in their hour of need. Nothing meant more to him than money.[6]

The drive by individuals and families in rural Russia to accumulate and expand their wealth by legal and illegal means led to the emergence of a new class of wealthy peasants. By committing their energies to developing a business through hard work and careful management, such peasants rose above the masses in the villages. The relations between these people and the peasants of the village were poor in many instances. Chekhov accurately and correctly recorded this process of differentiation in the peasant community. His record is confirmed by scholarship.

The growth of this new class of peasants received encouragement from government policy. Tentatively by 1897 and definitely after 1905, government policy tried to accelerate the growth of a class of wealthy peasants. This can be seen in Alexander Gerschenkron's "Patterns of Economic Development."[7]

Leroy-Beaulieu believed that if Russia was to prosper and evolve politically and economically she had to develop a rural agricultural middle class. Such a class he thought was taking root because hard-working peasants were buying land under individual titles. He felt that this trend was a positive alternative to the purchase of the land by speculators who had no interest in the long-term condition of the land.[8]

Writing about the new class D. M. Wallace states that the communal equality of Russia had been artificially maintained, but as individual freedom was expanded, "the struggle for life has become intensified . . . the strong men go up in the work while the weak ones go to the wolf." He saw the birth of a new aristocracy appearing throughout the country which would be more properly titled a plutocracy, in contrast was the ever increasing pattern of pauperism. "Some peasants possess capital, with which they buy land outside the Commune or embark in trade . . . ." Others "have to sell their livestock and sometimes have to cede to neighbors their share of the communal property."[9]

A. N. Engel'gardt in his *Letters from the Village* saw the process of differentiation in operation before 1870.[10] A. A. Kornilov records a conversation in which a peasant who is supposed to be a socialist because of his communal ties is asked what he would do if he had five hundred rubles. His non-socialist reply was "he would open a bar."[11] It was this mentality that led to the rise of the middle-class peasant.

Sergei Pushkarev notes that while many peasants became poorer other peasants became wealthier. They might buy land privately or engage in trade or usury. They would hire poorer members of the commune to work their land and perhaps lease, at low rates, the land of less fortunate members of the commune.[12] Competition for land became intense says G. T. Robinson. Townsmen began to speculate in land but over the long run, from 1877 to 1905, peasants bought land at a faster rate than townsmen. Some peasants acquired enough land so that their interests were closer to the gentry's than those of poorer peasants.[13]

This differentiation, although initially opposed by the government in an attempt to preserve the commune, continued unabated. By the turn of the century, the government came to recognize the economic potential of this differentiation among the peasants. After the revolution of 1905 the government committed itself to accelerating the process. Pushkarev quotes Stolypin as saying that the government decided to place "its wager not on the wretched and the drunkards, but on the strong . . . ."[14] Scholars confirm Chekhov's perceptions of the growing differentiation of the peasants.

The Effect of Industrialization on the Village

Modernization came slowly to the villages. As Chekhov indicates the first contacts probably were the railroad, the telegraph, and later, in a few villages, electricity and the telephone. The interaction between the peasant and these wonders was evidenced in one of Chekhov's stories, "The Culprit." A peasant was arrested for unscrewing nuts from the rails of the railroad track. The peasant admitted he had stolen nuts but could not understand why the authorities would be upset by his action. When the judge explained that the peasant's action could have caused a train wreck, the peasant was quick to tell the judge that he had only taken some of the nuts and that the peasants had been removing nuts from the tracks for years.

The peasants were using the nuts for fishing sinkers. They saw absolutely nothing wrong in the practice, especially since they only took a few at a time. The judge finally found out why a train was derailed the previous year. It is obvious to the reader that neither side comprehends the actions of the other. The peasant does not understand why he was arrested for such a trifle as stealing nuts; the judge does not understand the rationale of the peasant's action. The peasant finally says he does not understand railroads and the judge should not be angry because he was the peasant's protector and should explain these things. The peasant felt that he would have been judged more fairly by his former master.[15]

Thus Chekhov shows the problem of linking the industrial world to the still primitive agricultural village. He also, once again, underscored the fact that the bureaucrats replaced the old serf-owner relationship as the chief influence on peasant life but with less success.

The introduction of the telegraph and electricity into a town did not have the same impact on peasant village life that the introduction of a paved highway had. The telegraph crossed the countryside but more often than not it carried messages across the rural world, not it. The introduction of electricity for the rich did not immediately change anything for the peasants. In the story "In The Hollow," the factories in town brought in the telephone for themselves and connected it to the parish office. As a symbol of the whole problem of modernization in the rural area, the village phone malfunctioned because the villagers have allowed bugs and roaches to take up residence.[16]

There had been some industry in villages since Peter the Great. But in post-reform Russia all types of manufacturing were important elements in the countryside and Chekhov wrote effectively about the pervasive presence of industry in rural areas.

The deteriorating economic condition of the agricultural peasant discussed earlier forced the peasant to supplement his income in any way that he could. Some peasants turned to cottage industry.

The winding of silk, as described by Chekhov in "The Peasant," was one such industry. To supplement their agriculture and cash income the entire family participated in this type of activity.[17] The fact that the peasants turned toward cottage industry after emancipation is well documented throughout scholarly studies. Chekhov's description is accepted in its details by scholars.[18]

Manufacturing outside the home was also an important part of rural life and Chekhov gives strong indications of this in his stories. The daughter-in-law in "The Peasant" worked outside the home to supplement the family income. This was an important part of the family's survival and it was consistent with government policy. The government encouraged rural factories and itself had used serf labor in them. After emancipation the government still encouraged rural factories, using peasant labor in order to avoid the formation of an urban proletariat. The capitalistic daughter-in-law in "In The Hollow" started a brick factory using local peasant labor. In "Gooseberries," a man bought an estate with a brickyard on one side and a bone ash works on the other.[19]

In many of Chekhov's stories one sees the effects of industry more than the industry itself. In many works, Chekhov talks of fouled streams, polluted pastures, disease and death as a result of pollution. Even madness, as with the hatter in "Ward Six," can be attributed to this pollution.[20]

The demands made on the peasant because of the decline in agricultural prices, coupled with the population increase, drove peasants to seek new sources of revenue. Chekhov indicated this in "The Peasants." Workers still tied to the rural areas migrated on a regular basis to the towns. Peasants wanted family members to go to the city to earn cash wages at the higher urban rate and then send money back to the village to help with the arrears. For this reason, all the lads of Zhukova village were sent to Moscow to work as waiters and servants. Unfortunately, Nicholas in "The Peasants," became sick and had to return to the village and became a burden to the family. The move to the city reversed the trend of the extended village family and effectively eroded it.

This dual existence was brought on by the need which Chekhov described and by the government policy to create a peasant-worker for political reasons. Chekhov's development of the idea of the link between the peasant and cottage industries, rural factories, and urban employment was accurate according to many scholars' views.

Mary Matossian points out that cottage industry had always been an important part of peasant life as a source of income beyond subsistence level. The 'putting out' system became significant as a source of income to maintain at least subsistence level when agricultural wages declined.[21] Peasants also worked in factories in the towns and in rural areas as far back as the reign of Peter I. At that time forced industrialization was achieved by means of forced serf labor.[22] However, in the nineteenth century, under the influence of liberal political economists, the government came to believe that Russian economic growth could only be achieved by means of free labor. This contributed to the liberation of the serfs. At that point, according to Terence Emmons in his "The Peasant and Emancipation," the government feared the consequences of a landless proletariate with revolutionary potential as happened in the West in 1848. Accordingly, the state committed itself to preserving the commune drawing its labor from the rural areas. Workers were to be rooted in the country and only temporarily linked to industry.[23] According to Zelnik in his "The Peasant and the Factory," the consequences of this policy would have a negative effect for both the peasant and for industrialization in Russia.[24]

Dr. Shingarev in his "The Dying Village" noted that large numbers of peasants worked in gentry-owned, large scale agriculture, but even more worked as laborers in other manufacturing.[25] This view is confirmed by G. T. Robinson who adds that as agricultural wages dropped even more, people took on non-agricultural work in mining and manufacturing.[26]

D. M. Wallace indicates that because many workers could not find work locally they left their wives and children to farm the allotment and went away to work. At times, the length of the journey would use up much of the money earned.[27] Robinson maintains it is impossible to know how many went away for wage work but according to the passport application it was a large number.[28] Wallace says over two million villagers were absorbed by industry.[29] As a possible indicator, Robinson quotes the 1897 census in which five million city dwellers were classed as villagers in the cities of European Russia.[30] Both L. Haimson and T. Von Laue agree that a large portion of the factory workers were peasant-workers with strong ties to the village. This was particularly true from 1892-1903.[31] Chekhov's record of the peasants' need to perform other type of work because the decline in agriculture is consistent with scholarly opinion.

The Army and the Peasant

The peasant soldier was as important as he was abused. Some scholars feel that the main reason for the abolition of serfdom was to enable the peasant to serve more effectively as a soldier. The emancipation did little to enhance the peasant image of military service.

Chekhov records the effects of military service on the peasant and his family. Being drafted into the army was looked upon as a disaster. In "Peasant Woman," the drafted individual was shaken to the core. In the story "The Peasants," when a young woman's husband was drafted there was great weeping and the young man called into the army took a last look around his home as if he was never going to return.

Wives and children of peasant soldiers were left alone to take care of themselves. If they were lucky they had families to live with as in "The Peasants." Mostly, they had to make do as best they could. The soldiers did not appear to be able to send money home. Apparently, even the officers needed money from home. When the soldiers left for duty, they were sometimes forgotten by their families.[32]

The soldiers were not treated well. In "The Savage" one learns that the enlisted men were beaten; that the soldiers themselves became brutal and often brutalized others. Chekhov pointed out that the army tried to move away from brutality. But he also adds that human nature had not changed. A soldier who became sick was not well-treated and was discharged as soon as possible. An example of this can be seen in "Gusev" and the "Peasant Woman."[33]

According to Chekhov, the troops were kept ignorant. They did not even know if their officers stole from them. Soldiers were beaten and cheated. Some were even used as servants. Chekhov found this particularly disgusting. Put through the hell of going into the army, some troops became servants for officers – performing menial duties like wakening them, and making their breakfast. All this, while the soldier's family wasted away at home.[34] Scholarly research bears out Chekhov's picture of conditions in the army. According to Matossian, when a man was drafted, the whole village mourned him. He was expected to go on a "drunken debauch" until the date he was to report for duty. The village would hold a sorrowful repast for him, "at which professional wailers bewailed his loss in the name of his mother, wife, sisters, and dear ones." He was blessed by his parents and then a crowd would walk him to the outskirts of the village.[35]

John Curtiss, in his "The Peasant and the Army," states that when a man was taken, there was good cause to wail as if he were dead, "for few of them returned to their homes." If a soldier were married, he had little chance of seeing his wife again, and she was "usually doomed to a life of bitter poverty." "The peasants hated military service and considered it almost as bad as penal labor for life." For some the army was punishment for some offense committed in civilian life.[36]

The soldiers' apprehension was justified. They were brutalized by both officers and non-commissioned officers. Prior to 1863 the punishments were truly horrible. But in 1863 things like the gauntlet were eliminated. After 1874 abuse was cut even further but soldiers were still beaten. Probably the most vicious were the sergeants who had been beaten themselves as youths.[37]

The soldiers were viewed as inferiors and were addressed as children. The living conditions were terrible, and the NCO's would abuse and extort money from them.[38] There was a high incidence of lung disease as a result of the poor conditions in the barracks. Chekhov's Gusev died of lung disease.

John Curtiss reveals that the poorly-paid officers would steal from their troops in order to support a higher life style for themselves. Commanding officers, as a matter of course, would cut rations and pocket the money. The reforms of the 1870's lessened such abuses, but the peasant soldiers continued to suffer hunger and cold while their families continued to waste away at home.[39]

Conditions were getting better in the army in Chekhov's time, as he noted, but they still had a long way to go, as can be seen in the demands of 1905. Chekhov was accurate in his portrayal of the effect of the army on the people. This was borne out in scholarly opinion on the subject.

Religion

Chekhov deals with religion frequently in his stories and even has clerics as central figures in some. Chekhov's basic point might be summed up thus: the

Russian people did not believe in a theology but practiced a ritual. In "The Peasants" the old man did not believe and when asked about belief he said that was woman's business. Gran believed, but in what, she was not sure; it was all rather vague. The daughters-in-law, Marya and Fyokla crossed themselves and took communion but it meant nothing to them. They did nothing to teach their children about God or prayer. The only thing they did was keep the fasts and other rituals. "It was much the same with other families – few believed, few understood."[40]

Olga in "The Peasants" and Barbara of "In The Hollow" both loved Scripture but did not understand it. Olga would read them to the others and none of them understood.[41] Some who believe do not understand and others who should believe do not. In fact, in "In The Hollow" it is apparent that it touches even the church; "The parish chairmen don't believe in God either . . . nor does the clerk, nor does the sexton."[42]

If disbelief was widespread then, why did they practice the ritual and keep fasts? Chekhov answered that, ". . . they only do it so folks won't speak badly of them, and to be on the safe side. . ." in case there is a Judgment Day.[43] In "Poor Compensation" and "In The Hollow" men went to a religious service because it was the thing to do.[44]

Going to church was generally looked upon as a social occasion. Young girls, for example, would dress up in their finest and would go to church in a group. Religious feast days were primarily viewed as key social events and always drew large crowds. As Chekhov shows in "The Peasants," peasants were also attracted to feast days because they could get drunk at the festivities.[45]

The peasants usually prayed when they wanted something. One woman banged her head on the floor and prayed for her children's education.[46] The poor prayed to get well when they were sick. Chekhov seems to indicate that the rich were less prone to prayer. It seemed that "the richer they grew, the less they believed . . ."[47]

The rich seemed to fear death more than the peasants. Accordingly, they often tried to buy their salvation. "The rich . . . grabbed everything, even the church" which was the "only refuge of the poor."[48] In "The New Villa," Chekhov emphasized this idea by saying that "the rich are well off . . . even in the next world," because they paid for their "church candles" and paid to have "special services" for them. The rich also gave to the poor as additional insurance for their salvation in the afterlife. The poor of course could not pay such things. Chekhov notes that the peasants did not have the time to make the sign of the cross and were as poor as church mice. "There's no happiness for us in this world or the next . . ." he says, "the rich have took it all."[49]

The church was also viewed as being closely tied to the state. In "The Duel" Chekhov criticized the hierarchy for thinking of themselves as pillars of the state. They defended the state position on nationality and science but spent little time worrying about church affairs.[50] In fact some believed as Orlov in "An Anonymous Story," that belief in God was not important but religion must be preserved, since the common people needed some restraining principles or else they wouldn't work.[51] The church was viewed as tied to the state.

The clergy received mixed reviews at the time Chekhov wrote. There were good clerics and bad but they were all human. Chekhov described them within the context of the society. For example, the bishop, in the story of the same name, was an intelligent urbane man who found Russians rough and ill-educated in comparison to the western world.

The prelate was so beset with administrative duties that he was not able to write or even conduct services.[52] Other lower level priests showed an equal mix of human qualities. Some were holy and inefficient, others were efficient, yet unholy. The well-to-do hierarchy had difficulty understanding and working with the poor peasant parish priest. Many of the priests drank and were poor examples of religious life.[53]

In their contacts with the peasants, Chekhov recorded that the clergy were more interested in money than piety. The parish priests were most concerned with collecting fines from those who violated ecclesiastical rules or collecting a stipend for services. The local church officials were even worse. Chekhov presented an example of clerical callousness and indifference to suffering when he described the funeral of a baby in the story "In the Hollow." At the funeral it is quite obvious that the priest is not concerned in the least with the pain and suffering of the child's parents and is mumbling meaningless phrases. Weddings and wakes were all the same; food and a fee were expected.[54] Religion had some positive effects such as the development of a conscience and moral values, as in "The Letter" and "In The Hollow."

The clergy constituted a class. Some families had been in the service of the church for many generations. Being a member of this clerical class guaranteed a decent living if a cleric obtained a good position and, above all, received an education. Throughout Chekhov's stories, as in Russian society, one meets persons holding positions as bureaucrats who are from the clerical class. They won the jobs because they were educated in Church schools.[55]

Ironically, education caused some problems for the church. Chekhov records the crisis of the educated young exposed to the concepts of modern science yet inoculated with ideas in their youth which they may not have understood. This is seen in "The Letter" in the confrontation between the archpriest and his son, when the boy tells the father all is relative. The father's world is objective and fixed; the son's is relative and changing. The problem is the same with the nonbelieving doctor in "Ward Six."[56]

As a counterpoint to the decline of belief among many orthodox Christians is the almost fanatical belief of the Old Believers. In "Murder," Chekhov presents varied facets of their lives. Because of earlier persecution they tended to remain fixed in their beliefs. As a result of their isolation, both physical and spiritual, they became self-sufficient. Their lifestyle was frugal and, being hardworking as well as virtuous, they made money when they engaged in commerce.

Some took to extreme expressions of religious belief as in "Murder" when one young man becomes a peasant holy man in a pattern very similar to Rasputin's. In general, the old believers restricted themselves to much more conservative expressions of their belief, keeping to themselves and viewing the orthodox community as sinful. But they, too, had their problems as Chekhov indicates when an old believer kills to protect the wealth that the family has acquired over the generations.[57]

Donald Treadgold has written that, in Russian, 'Christian' and 'peasant' were synonymous. That does not mean necessarily that the peasants were deeply committed to Christianity.[58] As D. M. Wallace indicates, the peasants' Christianity was superficial in nature. They go to church on "Sunday and holy days, cross themselves repeatedly when they pass a church or Icon, take the Holy Communion, abstain from animal food . . ." on Wednesday, Fridays, Lent and the other long fasts. They "fulfill punctiliously the ceremonial observances which they suppose necessary for salvation. But here their religiousness ends." The peasants are ignorant of religious doctrine and Scripture. "For him the ceremonial part of religion suffices, and he has the most unbounded, childlike confidence in the saving efficacy of the rites which he practices." If he observes the ritual through life without regard to other actions he feels confident of his salvation.[59] Belinsky believed the Russians did not fear God and believed that the Icons were as good for covering pots as praying.[60]

Treadgold quotes S. M. Kravchinsky, the author of *The Russian Peasantry: Their Agrarian Condition, Social Life and Religion*, who believed that the Russian Orthodox peasant was not religious. If you chose to call an ethical system without a theology religion only then could you call them religious. There are, of course, those who would disagree with these scholars,[61] but for our point Chekhov's perceptions are confirmed by scholars. The peasant observed the rituals of religion and perhaps had an ethical system linked to Christianity but was not religious in the sense of belief in a theology.

The Orthodox church may have been on the decline due to its separation from its intellectual roots, the loss of its most faithful to the Old Believers and its subjugation to the state in 1721.[62] This subjugation to the state occurred when the church was put under the Holy Synod and then deliberately neglected. It eventually lost the capacity for leadership. The state came to use the church for its own purposes as when it released the Emancipation Proclamation through the church. The state feared violence and chose to use the church and the fear of God to control the peasants.[63] The peasants still rioted, however.

After 1861 the church continued to lose believers to various sects. It also saw an accelerating loss of intellectuals from the Orthodox fold, while the schismatics and sectarians grew.[64] Part of this may have been due to the quality of local priests. The local priest was the immediate contact between the church and the peasant. Kravchinsky gives us an appraisal of the peasant attitude toward the clergy. Quite simply, the peasants did not respect the clergy. "The orthodox clergy, as a body, have no moral influence over the masses, and enjoy no confidence among them."[65]

A. H. Williams gives a balanced view of the clergy when he indicates that there were some ignorant and stupid priests who held positions because of their relatives. Sometimes they got drunk. However, "the average priest was neither conspicuously devout nor conspicuously negligent." They were men burdened by their offices and families yet they were "shrewd, observant, with common sense and humor." The local priest was sincere but no theologian. There were many good simple priests. "The wonder, considering all the conditions of service, is not that there are so few good priests, but that there are so many of them."[66]

One of the great problems of the local clergy was their poverty. By mid-nineteenth century the parish clergy were a poverty-stricken hereditary caste whose sons were leaving for other professions. They were notorious for drinking or loose living and were the objects of scorn by all classes. That is the way Treadgold sums up the condition of the clergy. A report to the Grand Duke Constantine Nikolaevich confirms this picture and Chekhov's general view.[67]

The priests gained their revenue from the small plots of land they farmed, a small lsum of money from the state and from the fees they received for performance of services. The priests were in competition with each other and the poor for every coin. The economic crisis that swept the community also affected the parish priest.[68]

Kravchinsky saw the Old Believers as an interesting contrast to the Orthodox peasant. The Old Believers were very religious.[69] They had been ignorant peasants but because of their belief in the Scriptures they learned to read. Some turned from farming to trade and became successful. Their education, their movement to commerce and to the trades placed them in a favorable economic position in the nineteenth century.[70]

Scholarly opinion supports Chekhov's perceptions of the dominant religion in Russia.[71]

Jews and the Peasant

Chekhov gives us an insight into some of the anti-Semitic feelings of the peasants but does not dwell on them. At the same time he does give a perception of Jews in Russia. Anti-Semitism is evident in stories like the "Peasant Woman." In this story a Jewish woman was required to pay a kopek to water her horse. Within earshot, the well owner called her Jewish scum who was always trying to get free water. In "The Duel," the fact that Von Koren's friends were called German Jews was considered an offense grave enough to provoke a fight. The pressure of anti-Semitic behavior impelled some Jews to hide their heritage as the Jewish woman did in "The Duel" when she tried to pass herself off as a Georgian.[72] However, most Jews faced up to this discrimination.

Chekhov reveals the irrational base of bigotry and the uneasy relations between Jew and gentile in "Rothschild's Fiddle." The fiddler 'Bronze' came to hate Jews for no reason other than that he did not like the musical style of one Jew who played in a band with him. He became obsessed by hatred and contempt toward all Jews and the band musician, Rothschild, in particular. Bronze's hatred grew so strong that he tried to physically beat Rothschild.

The Jews responded to Bronze's hatred by not using him to play in their band. Yet every so often they needed him to replace a band member. He would play with the Jewish band not because he liked them but because he needed the work. They lived in the same area but associated with each other only when it was necessary. This reflected the uneasy relations between lower-class Jews and Gentiles in nineteenth century Russia.[73]

Chekhov also saw anti-Semitism in the upper levels of society. He portrayed it in "Mire," where a wealthy and educated Jewish girl showed her rejection of anti-Semitism by triumphing over two Russian nobleman, using sex as her primary weapon. She showed her conquest of them by making them want her – a Jew.[74]

Another type of reaction can be seen in "The Steppe" when Solomon, in the Jewish inn scenes, tried to destroy the image of the money-mad Jew. He tried to show society how wrong it was by burning his part of the family fortune. As a counterpoint his brother tried to fit in with the Gentile community and diminishes himself in the process. In this author's opinion the strongest image is to be found in "Rothschild's Fiddle" where Rothschild triumphed on the basis of his talent without having to compromise.[75]

Chekhov cast Jews as he cast others. But he also gave indications that stereotypes were false, as in the stories mentioned above and also in "A Dreary Story." In this story a Jewish storekeeper advanced credit to a young Gentile student. He clearly indicates the quest among Jews for an education. In "Dr. Startsev" the librarian comments that the library would close if it were not for the girls and the young Jews. He notes in "My Life" that no one went inside the town library or club reading room other than a few Jewish youths. Even the rich Jewish Protestant convert in "The Russian Master" paid for tutors for his children.

Jews portrayed by Chekhov did not fit the stereotype. They were human and were angered by repression, some rejecting it in different ways. The general image is positive. In his youth Chekhov had fought anti-Semites and later was engaged to a Russian woman of the Jewish faith, Dunya Efros,[76] who raged at her repression by anti-Semites. Chekhov was not anti-Semitic; he gave a sensitive and accurate picture of Jews in society as a counterpoint to the stereotype supported by anti-Semites. Unfortunately most Russian peasants were as irrationally bigoted as Bronze.

Scholarly opinion tends to bear out Chekhov's perception. Leroy-Beaulieu indicates that the pattern of repression of Jews helped to compound the problem of the image of Jews in Russian society. As Jews emerged in Poland and later in Russia they were restricted in what occupations they could go into. Many times they were limited to what Gentiles could not or would not do. Jews succeeded at commerce and trading. Others restricted from farming might end up lending money. The restrictions imposed by the government forced them out of the arts, sciences, and farming into the stereotypical roles of isolated, clannish merchants and money lenders.[77]

Pushkarev indicates that during the reign of Alexander III legal restrictions were leveled against Jews. They had been limited to the "pale" and even there they were further restricted in buying or renting land in rural areas. In 1887 a quota was introduced for Jewish children in government secondary schools.

In 1891 a decree expelled thousands of Jewish mechanics, masters, and artisans from Moscow where they had been permitted to settle twenty-six years before. The municipal regulation of 1892 deprived the Jews of the right to participate in municipal self-government.[78] Thus, Jews were forced in on themselves and into various postures in opposition to this repression. Anti-Semitism was a matter of private and public choice.

The classic example of anti-Semitism is described by G. T. Robinson when he writes of the mobs of the Union of the Russian People. The Union was founded in 1905 and supported Orthodoxy, Nationality, and Autocracy, but its most famous precept was anti-Semitism. It drew members from all classes including the clergy.

This group maintained that all ills in Russian society could be traced to the Jews. Liberals and Radicals were just accomplices of Jews. In a Union pamphlet, "The Plot Against Russia," they blamed Jewish Social Democrats for not attacking Jewish capitalists but instead going after Christian landlords. It was a Jewish plot to corner all the wealth and take over with a Jewish Tsar. It called for all Christians to arise and crush "the Jewish army of anarchists, socialists, and other revolutionists and deceitful liberals, directed and supported . . . by the Jews and . . . Russian and foreign Masons."[79]

Riots broke out in scores of Russian cities directed against Russian intellectuals but more often than not against Jews of all classes. The resentment against Jews and fear of change all came together and thousands of Jews were killed.[80] Anti-Semitism was present in Russia and it was tolerated by the government. Government regulations forced the Jews to be what the anti-Semites wanted them to be. Chekhov correctly perceived the scope and nature of anti-Semitism as well as the true condition of Jews in Russia.

Women in the Village

Perhaps the symbol of women in the village for Chekhov was the white cat in "The Peasants." The cat was unable to hear the gentle call of those who wanted to show affection because it had become deaf through beatings. The relationship that Chekhov stresses is one of brutality and subjugation of the women in the hut. Closely linked to the brutality was drink. In "The Peasants" both the old man and Kiryak drank too much. The men would curse and swear in front of their wives and children. The old men seemed to be the worst of all. Gran talks of the old man as being useless, all spend and no earn. To her the men were rotten, including the old man and her wife-beating son, Kiryak. When Kiryak was drunk he brutalized his family. Kiryak's wife was so afraid of him she refused to live with him.[8] When drunk he would come to the house late at night. The implication was that he wished to have intercourse. Failing that, he would beat her. Marya, his wife, lived in constant fear of him.

The daughters-in-law, Marya and Fyokla, both disliked their husbands. Both had husbands who were worthless to them, the one in the army and the other living far away. The wives were both backward and understood little. Marya had never been as far as the local town and could neither read nor write. She did not even know the Our Father.[82]

Wives were judged on their durability first and then their good looks. The Tsybukin's, who were rich by the standards of the village in "In The Hollow," could thus pick a bride for their son. They looked for a good worker through the marriage broker. They picked a poor but pretty bride and hoped she would work as well as the other poor girl they had picked for another son. The son, Anisim, was only marrying because of pressure from his parents. It was the village custom to take a wife to help in the house.[83]

Some women became resigned to brutality. Gran told Marya that she must put up with it because it was in the Bible. But there were other alternatives. Barbara in "Peasant Woman" indicates that she was dirt poor as a child and married to escape poverty. Instead she became a slave in her father-in-law's home. So she found escape in recreating with the priest's sons. Her friend Sophia knew Barbara sinned, but would have liked to have done the same when she was young and pretty.[84]

Accepting the conditions as they were or turning to infidelity were not the only alternatives described by Chekhov. Both Barbara and Sophia wanted to kill their husbands. It was not the fear of God that stopped them, but the possibility of being caught.[85]

In "In The Hollow" Aksinya, the daughter-in-law who had worked so hard to build the brick yard and the rest of the business, found that the old man was going to leave it to his infant grandson. Aksinya went into a rage at this obvious deference to males, especially to an infant who had done none of the work she had done to build the business. Screaming that the infant had stolen her land she scalded it to death with boiling water.[86]

Aksinya was not punished and, in time, reasserted her dominance in the group. Ultimately she was able to get even with the old man. As he aged, she did not feed him and forced him to spend most of his time in the cold.[87] Stolypin would clearly have wagered on Aksinya. Yet it must be remembered that Aksinya was probably deaf to the baby's cries just as the cat had been deaf and for the same reason, namely, brutality.

Professor Richard Stites in his *The Women's Liberation Movement in Russia* confirms Chekhov's view of conditions in the village. Women were considered inferior because of the doctrine of impurity of women implicit in Christianity in the Byzantine Empire which was absorbed by Slavic Orthodox Christianity. This evolved into adages like "love your wife but give her no power" eventually to "a bad man is always better than a good woman." As a result, women were considered inferior. The peasant was content in demonstrating this inferiority "by clubbing his wife with a bottle from time to time or breaking her teeth with his fists."[88]

Stites believes that the Orthodox Christian tradition of womens' inferiority was the wellspring for the general principle that "girls and women should do less, be less, and get less (as inheritance, for example) than men or boys." From the principle came the practice of treating the wife or equivalent "as a brood mare upon whom the sexual act could be performed at any hour." Eventually men conditioned the women "to behave in a manner as dissolute as the men."[89]

A. S. Rappoport comments that despite their hard work women were viewed as inferior. It was the custom in some areas to beat a man whose first child was a girl. Female children were treated less kindly and had less to eat than the male. Throughout her life she had to do her work above all else. She was subject to the male head of the house in everything; even in the choice of a husband. Love had little to do with marriage; it was generally arranged. "It is no exaggeration when we say that one of the worst things in Russian peasant life is the low estimation in which the women are held."[90]

Chekhov's perceptions of the conditions of women in the village were confirmed by contemporary observation and scholars.

Peasant and Gentry

Class was not an element in Russian society, it was *the* element. Chekhov shows the depth of class consciousness in "My Life." In this story, a member of the Gentry decides, for Tolstoyian philosophical reasons, to live the life of a laborer. He becomes a housepainter but is resented by gentry and workmen alike. The Gentry did not mind if he went to another province and took up the workman's life where he was unknown, but to remain at home and do so was impossible because it threatened the existing concept of social order. The Governor ordered him to behave according to his rank or he would take extreme measures against him.

On the other side of the coin, when the housepainter's sister becomes pregnant out of wedlock and tries to stay with her housepainter brother, she runs afoul of class again. The peasant landlord would not tolerate such indecency. Such behavior, he believed, was all right for the Gentry but not for God-fearing Common-folk.[91]

Chekhov recorded the fact that class distinctions were real and expressed themselves even to the point of having two waiting rooms in rural council buildings. Attitudes were also quite different between the classes especially after the serfs were emancipated. Before the emancipation the superiority of the Gentry was a matter of law – they owned the serfs. However, according to the old constable in "On Official Business," the Gentry became quite touchy after emancipation. They no longer tipped him and were abusive toward him. The peasants, on the other hand, would offer him some bread, cabbage soup, or a glass of something.[92] Chekhov indicates the deterioration of the relations between the peasants and Gentry as time moves close to 1905.

The price for violating class lines was painful alienation. This theme, seen in the story of "My Life," is also developed in the short story "Daydreams." In the narrative, an unknown man was accepted as something more than a peasant, because he spoke and acted differently than a peasant. Because he was educated and had manners, he had to be socially superior to the peasants, perhaps the son of a priest or a clerk. Since he was neither Gentry nor peasant he was in a social limbo.[93]

In actual fact the man's mother was a house serf, who, serving as a nanny, raised her son along with her Gentry charges. In the story, the Mother and her son are sentenced to hard labor because she killed the manor owner for jilting her. The reason for the murder gives the son dreams that perhaps he was the illegitimate son of the manor owner. He would have noble blood even though, by class, he was a peasant. Through "Daydreams" Chekhov once again brings out the problem of class in Russian society. The Gentry have as a birthright the rare opportunity of acquiring manners and an education. Chekhov showed the ridiculousness of the class distinctions which remained and perhaps intensified after emancipation.[94] There is no doubt that the peasants resented the Gentry. Chekhov recorded this resentment in stories like "At Home" and "The Peasant." In "The Peasant" Fyokla's resentment stemmed from the fact that one night while at the manor she was stripped and forced to return home naked.[95]

The resentment intensified when Fyokla's father-in-law begged vodka money from the young noblemen who, in turn, ignored the old man. Yet the young Gentry would reach into their pockets on impulse and give the children some change. This incidental sum was equal to the entire family's income in cottage industry for a week. While in the presence of the peasants, in order to speak privately, the Gentry would speak French, which the peasants did not understand. This was a further sign of the separation of these classes. Marya, the other daughter-in-law in the story, viewed the Gentry as monsters who could crush her. Feared by Marya, begged from by Old Osip, and damned by Fyokla; that was how the Gentry were viewed.[96]

Often, when someone from the upper classes of society decided to communicate with the peasants, the peasants rebuffed them as payment in kind for the way they were treated. This was the theme Chekhov developed in the "New Villa." An engineer and his wife bought a villa in a rural area where he was building a bridge. The peasants disliked them for several reasons. They were resented because he was building a bridge which would introduce change into their lives. The peasants also feared they would have to pay for the bridge, which they did not feel they needed. Also, the engineer and his wife were resented as outsiders and because of their wealth. The engineer purchased the villa with no intention of farming it. He wanted it just to enjoy the fresh country air. Such a purpose infuriated the local peasants and produced deep resentment because they were land-hungry.[97]

The engineer's wife, remembering her poverty as a governess in Moscow, took pity on the peasants and tried to help them by giving them money. The peasants took the money but did not love her for it. The peasants saw the engineer and his wife as outsiders and took what they could to survive. They picked his mushrooms, stripped the bark from his trees, cut his wood, then drove off his livestock and charged him for supposed damages. He was enraged and confused.

Why could they not or would they not understand? He treated them kindly and they stole from him. The simple fact for them was the land. It was there to be used for their survival.

When his wife proposed to build a school the peasants refused it. The peasant feared that the school would cost them money or extra work. They did not trust her even though she was well meaning. She wanted to help them to give a purpose to her life. An old man tried to encourage her but he said it would take years before the people would trust her. It would take time to dig out the old attitudes. Both the engineer and his wife were frustrated and he realized that they would start looking down on the peasants because they would not communicate.[98] They were "dark people."

Chekhov might conclude this discussion of class with a brief statement from his story "Thieves," where a Doctor's assistant laments being entrapped by class and society. He eventually thought of stealing to gain freedom from this structured society. Why were there doctors, assistants, merchants, clerks and peasants? Why were there not just free men?[99]

The relations between the Gentry land-owner and the peasant had been poor before Chekhov's time. They feared that if the peasants were not freed they would free themselves as Pugachev had less than a century before. The great emancipation was actually a conservative document to (1) avoid peasant revolt, (2) foster the growth of the army and (3) aid industrialization. In addition, relations between serf and master had deteriorated in the 1850's.[100] The peasants thought they would receive "real freedom" with the land. Instead they remained obligated to the landlord for almost a decade and had to pay for the land they did get. They received less than they had for their use before emancipation. They were bound by law to the commune and subject to obligations for the state instead of their masters. The peasants felt they had been cheated.

They had no capital and could not in many instances improve economically. Their education was restricted and they were encouraged not to change. The relation between Gentry and peasant remained problematical. The peasants had difficulty making ends meet so many worked as wage workers on the Gentry's land.[101] An official commission of the government reported in 1897 that "nowhere are relations between employer and employed so strained as in agriculture.[102] Poor labor relations and poor wages helped cause friction between Gentry and peasants.

As had been mentioned, as a result of emancipation the actual land farmed by the peasant was "cut" by almost one fifth so they had a more difficult time.[103] As Russia evolved from 1861 to the late 1880's, things changed for the peasant. The peasant struggled with a cash nexus and his liberty with social and legal limitations on it.[104] After 1890 grain prices dropped, agricultural wages dropped, peasant population increased and land rents increased.[105] Wallace notes that Russian agriculture had been extensive not intensive, so that there arose a land-hunger among the peasants of Russia.[106] As G. Pavlovsky writes, there was no land shortage, it was low productivity due to poor use of the land.[107] D. Treadgold says that technological backwardness was the key to the low productivity not lack of land.[108] But the fact remains, the peasant wanted land because he thought he needed it and he did, given the factors mentioned above.

Lazor Volin asserts that land-hunger was very real for the peasant. The peasant attitude has been drawn from the commune concept of land use. Those who need it and use it get to use it. At emancipation the peasant knew that they farmed the land of Russia and they believed that the Tsar would redistribute the land to them. They should have the land not the Gentry who did not farm it. When they did not receive it they always believed that some day they would get the land that they had a right to.[109] Land was one of the causes of friction between the Gentry and peasants.

Social status was also a problem. The peasant was discriminated against *de facto* and *de jure*. In fact the peasants were considered to be the "dark folk." In law, the Gentry were defined as the leading class in Russian society,[110] and the peasant was deprived of his rights by government policy.[111] Four decades after emancipation the peasantry was still "a peasant nation consistently segregated from the general life of the community," asserts I. M. Strakhovsky. V. A. Maklokov believed the peasant after emancipation was a "kind of caste." Volin would add "oppressed caste."[112]

Chekhov was correct in his representation of stress between Gentry land-holders and the peasantry. These views are consistent with scholarship on the topic.

"We Were Better Off As Serfs"

The physical conditions of the peasant environment described by Chekhov have been established as consistent with the views of recognized scholars. But what about the pervasive atmosphere of poverty which runs through his picture of peasant life? Is this consistent with the facts?

Throughout "The Peasant" one is struck by the poverty but it goes even beyond this. All readers, including the tsarist censor, find passages which leave one in shock. "We were better off as serfs" appears to be ridiculous until it is elaborated on. The old man who says he was better off as a serf explains how he ate better with more variety – even the forests had more game.[113]

Then one remembers other impressions of figures in "The Peasant" indicating that the hut had been in better shape in years past and food had been more plentiful. Types of food were cooked and eaten by the peasants then which were no longer available to them.[114] The old man and woman ate bread and water at this time, fearing that they could only produce enough food for six months for the family.[115] This reflection is not permitted to become too distorted because in the end they say "No, better be free than serf."[116]

It would appear that Chekhov was in fact correct in portraying peasant views in this way. Scholars examining the period of emancipation concur with the peasant view. Peasants actually remained bound to the land for a period of time.[117]

The peasants were worse off. For those paying the obrok, the redemption payment remained the same as their obrok payment had been but their land allotment was reduced in size and/or quality. Through the decades to the 1890's the allotments were insufficient to maintain a subsistence level with existing agricultural practices and the obligations of redemption payments and general taxes. This problem was further compounded by the fact that most of them were tied to the peasant commune with its outmoded practices. By 1890 population was increasing at one million peasants per year. These factors caused a land-hunger.

As a result, land prices shot up while, at the same time, grain prices continued a fifty-year spiral of decline. It was at this point that the government, pursuing rapid industrialization, tried to finance it by taxing the peasant population. Obligations increased while allotments were decreased. Even when taxes were reduced to give relief, grain prices dropped further, cancelling out the relief.[118]

The peasants had dreamed of complete freedom, "real freedom" with the land. This is not what they received and they knew it.[119] They were worse off than before economically. Yes, they were free but they did not have "real freedom" as they had hoped. Their quality of life had deteriorated. Chekhov was correct in his observations here as well. As the censors report indicated, it was not that Chekhov was wrong, it was that his writing was too gloomy. It was contrary to the myth of happy peasants. One is reminded of the Potemkin Village myth. The view that the peasant was worse off is supported by the weight of scholarship.[120] Chekhov also proves to be a valuable source of peasant attitudes.

NOTES

1   "Murder," in *Oxford Chekhov*, 8:48, 52-54, 59-61.

2   "In the Hollow," in *Ibid.*, 9:163.

3   "The Peasants" in *Ibid.*, 8:221. Chekhov as a boy worked in a store and makes it clear in his notebooks that peasants cheat; See Getovich, *Leyopis Zhizni i tvorchestva A. P. Chekhova*, p. 455.

4   "In the Hollow," in *Ibid.*, 9:153-65.

5   "In the Hollow," in *Ibid.*, 9:163-70.

6   "At The Mill," in *Portable Chekhov*, pp. 79-85.

7   Alexander Gerschenkron, "Patterns of Economic Development," in *The Transformation of Russian Society*, ed. Cyril Block (Cambridge: Harvard University Press, 1960), pp. 54-57

8   Leroy-Beaulieu, *The Empire of the Tsars and the Russians*, 1:556-57, 560-61.

9   D. M. Wallace, *Russia*, p. 468.

10 A. N. Engel'gardt, Iz derevni. 12 pisem 1872-1877 (Moscow, 1937), Cited in: Lazar Volin "The Russian Peasant" in *The Transformation of Russian*

Society, edited by Cyril Black (Cambridge: Harvard University Press, 1960), p. 213.

11   A. A. Kornilov, *Krest'isanskaia reforma* (Moscow, 1905), p. 175 quoted in Lazar Volin "The Russian Peasant" in *The Transformation of Russian Society*, p. 300.

12   Sergei Pushkarev, *The Emergence of Modern Russia*, p. 213.

13   G. T. Robinson, *Rural Russia Under the Old Regime*, p. 133.

14   Sergei Pushkarev, *The Emergence of Modern Russia*, p. 266, quoting the stenograficheski Ochety of the Third State Duma, December 5, 1908, pp. 2280-2284.

15   "The Culprit," in *Portable Chekhov*, p. 103.

16   "The Peasants," in *Oxford Chekhov*, 8:222; "The Bishop," in *Oxford Chekhov*, 9:192; "In the Hollow," in *Oxford Chekhov*, 9:156.

17   "The Peasants," in *Oxford Chekhov*, 8:210.

18   Mary Matossian, "The Peasant Way of Life," in *The Peasant in Nineteenth Century Russia*, pp. 11-12.

19   "Gooseberries," in *Oxford Chekhov*, 9:33.

20   "The Peasants," in *Ibid.*, 8:195-222; "In the Hollow," in *Ibid.*, 9:153-57; "A Frisky Affair," in *Ibid.*, 6:621.

21   Mary Matossian, "The Peasant Way of Life" in *The Peasant in Nineteenth Century Russia*, pp. 11-12.

22   Zelnik, "The Peasant and the Factory," in *Ibid.*, p. 160.

23   Terence Emmons, "The Peasant and Emancipation," in *Ibid.*, pp. 43-44.

24   Zelnik, "The Peasant and the Factory," in *Ibid.*, p. 188.

25   Dr. Shingarev, "The Dying Village," quoted in John Maynard, *The Russian Peasant and Other Studies*, p. 188.

26   G. T. Robinson, *Rural Russia Under the Old Regime*, pp. 105-106.

27   D. M. Wallace, *Russia*, p. 482.

28   G. T. Robinson, *Rural Russia Under the Old Regime*, p. 107.

29   D. M. Wallace, *Russia*, p. 487.

30   G. T. Robinson, *Rural Russia Under the Old Regime*, p. 108.

31   Zelnik, "The Peasant and the Factory," in *The Peasant in Nineteenth Century Russia*, pp. 158-159.

32   "Gusev," in *Oxford Chekhov*, 5:113; "Peasant Women," in *Oxford Chekhov*, 5 :119; "Home," in *Oxford Chekhov*, 8:245.

33   "The Savage," in *Ibid.*, 8:229-31; "Gusev," in *Ibid.*, 5:103; "Peasant Wo-

man," in *Ibid.*, 5:120.

34 "Gusev," in *Ibid.*, 5:106, 110; "The Kiss," in *Portable Chekhov*, pp. 168, 176.

35 Matossian, "The Peasant Way of Life," in *The Peasant in Nineteenth Century Russia*, p. 31.

36 John S. Curtiss, "The Peasant and the Army," in *The Peasant In Nineteenth Century Russia*, p. 110.

37 *Ibid.*, pp. 110, 111, 115-116.

38 *Ibid.*, pp. 127, 125-126, 118, 123-124.

39 *Ibid.*, pp. 121-124.

40 "The Peasant," in *Oxford Chekhov*, 8:217.

41 "The Peasant," in *Oxford Chekhov*, 8:217; "In the Hollow," in *Oxford Chekhov*, 9:165.

42 "In the Hollow," in *Ibid.*, 9:165-66.

43 "In the Hollow," in *Ibid.*, 9:166.

44 "Poor Compensation," in *Ibid.*, 9:250; "In the Hollow" in *Ibid.*, 9:161.

45 "The Peasants," in *Ibid.*, 8:217-18.

46 "The Savage," in *Ibid.*, 8:231.

47 "The Peasants," in *Ibid.*, 8:218.

48 *Oxford Chekhov*, 8:305, from his notebook on "The Peasants."

49 "New Villa," in *Ibid.*, 9:100-01.

50 "The Duel," in *Ibid.*, 5:183.

51 "An Anonymous Story," in *Ibid.*, 6:191.

52 "The Bishop," in *Ibid.*, 9:198, 202.

53 "The Bishop," in *Ibid.*, 9:193; "The Letter," in *Portable Chekhov*, pp. 142-44.

54 "The Peasants," in *Oxford Chekhov*, 8:217; "In the Hollow," in *Oxford Chekhov*, 9:163, 183.

55 "The Bishop," in *Ibid.*, 9:202; "The Letter," in *Portable Chekhov*, pp. 145-48.

56 "Ward Six," in *Oxford Chekhov*, 6:136-37; "The Letter," in *Portable Chekhov*, p.148.

57 "Murder," in *Oxford Chekhov*, 8:50-60, 62, 65, 67, 69.

58 Donald Treadgold, "The Peasant and Religion," in *The Peasant In Nineteenth Century Russia*, p. 73.

59 D. M. Wallace, *Russia*, pp. 58-59.

60 Donald Treadgold, "The Peasant and Religion," in *The Peasant in Nineteenth*

Century Russia, p. 75.

61   *Ibid.*, p. 80-81.

62   *Ibid.*, p. 99.

63   *Ibid.*, pp. 54-55, 99.

64   *Ibid.*, p. 99.

65   *Ibid.*, p. 79.

66   R. H. Williams, *Russia of the Russians* (London: Charles Scribner's Sons, 1917), pp. 47-148.

67   Donald Treadgold, "The Peasant and Religion," in *The Peasant in Nineteenth Century Russia*, p. 77.

68   *Ibid.*, pp. 100-102.

69   *Ibid.*, p. 80.

70   *Ibid.*, pp. 69-70, 75-76, 79, 81-83, 86, 93, 96.

71   See also Leroy-Beaulieu, *The Empire of the Tsars and the Russians*, 3:24-40, Nature of Religion in Russia, 3:40-50 Dualism of Belief, 3:51-325, On Orthodox Christianity, 3:326-507, Schismatics and Sects, 508-548, Western Sects, 3:549-586, Jews, Muslims, and Buddhists. Wallace, *Russia*, 3:227-273, the Heretics, 3:238-255, The Dissenters, 3:256-266, Church and State, 3:46-64, The Parish Priest.

72   "Peasant Woman," in *Oxford Chekhov*, 5:128; "The Duel" in *Oxford Chekhov*, 5:139, 197.

73   "Rothschild's Fiddle," in *Ibid.*, 7:93, 99, 100-01.

74   Anton Chekhov, "Mire" in *Select Tales of Tchekhov*, trans. Constance Garnett (London: Chatto and Windus, 1967), pp. 439-58.

75   Anton Chekhov, "The Steppe" in *Select Tales of Tchekhov II*, trans. Constance Garnett (London: Chatto and Windus, 1968), pp. 208, 302.

76   Note: Yevdokia "Dunya" Efros was murdered by anti-Semites in one of the "camps" during World War II.

77   Anatole Leroy-Beaulieu, *The Empire of the Tsars and the Russians*, 3:551, 556-557.

78   Sergei Pushkarev, *The Emergence of Modern Russia*, p. 190.

79   G. T. Robinson, *Rural Russian Under The Old Regime*, pp. 183-184.

80   *Ibid.*, p. 184.

81   "The Peasants," in *Oxford Chekhov*, 8:195, 197, 202.

82   "The Peasants," in *Ibid.*, 8:198.

83   "In the Hollow," in *Ibid.*, 9:162, 157-59.

84 "The Peasants," in *Ibid.*, 8:198; "Peasant Woman," in *Ibid.*, 5:126-27.

85 "Peasant Woman," in *Ibid.*, 5:127.

86 "In the Hollow," in *Ibid.*, 9:177, 179.

87 "In the Hollow," in *Ibid.*, 9:186-87.

88 Richard Stites, *The Woman's Liberation Movement in Russia: Feminism, Nihilism, and Bolshevism*, 1860-1930 (Princeton: Princeton University Press, 1978), pp. 12-13.

89 *Ibid.*, p. 13.

90 A. S. Rappoport, *Home Life in Russia* (New York: The MacMillan Co., 1913), pp. 32-36.

91 "My Wife," in *Oxford Chekhov*, 8:149-51, 183.

92 "On Official Business," in *Ibid.*, 9:111, 114-15.

93 "Daydreams," in *Portable Chekhov*, pp. 109-14.

94 "Daydreams," in *Ibid.*, pp. 109, 114.

95 "The Peasants," in *Oxford Chekhov*, 8:200, 209.

96 "The Peasants," in *Ibid.*, 8:213-14.

97 "New Villa," in *Ibid.*, 9:96-97.

98 "New Villa," in *Ibid.*, 9:97-107.

99 "Thieves," in *Ibid.*, 5:95, 99-100.

100 Terence Emmons, "The Peasant and the Emancipation," in *The Peasant in Nineteenth Century Russia*, p. 44. He draws his points from Alexander II's speech to the Gentry in 1856.

101 Terence Emmons, "The Peasant and the Emancipation," in *The Peasant in Nineteenth Century Russia*, pp. 43-47, see entire article pp. 49-71.

102 John Maynard, *The Russian Peasant and Other Studies*, p. 69.

103 *Ibid.*, p. 58; see also L. Volin, "The Russian Peasant," in *The Transformation of Russian Society*, p. 295.

104 John Maynard, *The Russian Peasant and Other Studies*, pp. 59-60.

105 William Blackwell, *The Industrialization of Russia*, pp. 31-33.

106 Wallace, *Russia*, p. 488.

107 G. Pavlovsky, *Agricultural Russia on the Eve of the Revolution* (London: George Routledge and Co., 1930), p. 86.

108 D. W. Treadgold, *The Great Siberian Migration* (Princeton: Princeton University Press, 1957). See Chapter 2: "The Peasant in the Homeland."

109 Lazar Volin, "The Russian Peasant," in *The Transformation of Russian*

Society, pp. 300-01.

110   Sergei Pushkarev, *The Emergence of Modern Russia*, p. 189, quotes Catherine's Charter of the Nobility.

111   Alf Edeen, "The Civil Service," in *The Transformation of Russian Society*, p. 189, quotes ministry of education guidelines, 1887.

112   I. M. Strakhovsky, in Krest'ianskii stori (St. Petersburg, 1905), I: 388, V. A. Maklakov, "The Agrarian Problem in Russia Before the Revolution," *Russian Review*, IX (January, 1950), 3-15, quoted in Volin, "The Russian Peasant," in *The Transformation of Russian Society*, p. 297.

113   "The Peasants," in *Oxford Chekhov*, 8:210.

114   "The Peasants," in *Ibid.*, 8:195, 210-12.

115   "The Peasants," in *Ibid.*, 8:196, 197, 199, 202, 206.

116   "The Peasants," in *Ibid.*, 8:213.

117   For an explanation of the process of emancipation see Alexander Gerschenkron, "Agrarian Policies and Industrialization, Russia 1861-1917," in *Cambridge Economic History of Europe*, Vol. VI, part 2 (Cambridge, 1967), pp. 712-13; P. Lyashchenko, *History of the National Economy of Russia to the 1917 Revolution* (New York: The Macmillan Co., 1949), pp. 376-402; D. M. Wallace, *Russia*, pp. 429-451; G. T. Robinson, *Rural Russia Under the Old Regime*, Chapter 5; *Velikaia reforma: Russkoe obshchestvo i brest; ianskii vopros v proshlom i nastoiashchem*, ed. by A. K. Kzhivelegov and others (6 volumes; Moscow, 1911) first four volumes describe and analyze various aspects of serfdom; For general overview of the agricultural economy prior to the Revolution see: Lyaschenko; Gerschenkron and G. Pavlovsky, *Agricultural Russia on the Eve of Revolution* (London: George Routledge and Co., 1930).

118   Terence Emmons, "The Peasant and Emancipation" in *The Peasant in Nineteenth Century Russia*, pp. 69-70; Watters, "The Peasant and the Village Commune" in *The Peasants in Nineteenth Century Russia*, pp. 139-141, 146, 149-151, 153-156.

119   *Ibid.*, p. 56.

120   Pushkarev, *The Emergence of Modern Russia, 1801-1917*, pp. 206-219; G. T. Robinson, *Rural Russia Under the Old Regime*, pp. 94-116; D. W. Treadgold, *The Great Siberian Migration*, Chapter 2: "The Peasant in the Homeland;" G. Pavlosky, *Agricultural Russia on the Eve of the Revolution*, pp. 86-96; Sir Donald Mackenzie Wallace, *Russia*, pp. 464-490; Wallace saw the process of differentiation in all villages but felt in general the black soil regions were worse off than the non-agricultural regions; Sir John Maynard, *The Russian Peasant and Other Studies*, pp. 57-70.

CHAPTER IX

WAGE WORKERS, MIDDLE CLASS,

GENTRY

*"Moscow is the lowest point in Russia
and everything rolls downhill"*

Russian Proverb

Three other major groups in Russian society will now be examined. They too were viewed at least in part through the smoked glass of myth and Chekhov's keen perceptions of their reality, once again have been supported as valid.

The first group consisted of those who worked for a wage: in rural areas this included those who worked in the mines but not those who worked on the farm; in the towns this included small craftmen and traders; in the city this included workers, servants, small craftmen and small traders as well as prostitutes.

The second group consisted of the new middle-class made up of affluent merchants, manufacturers and professionals.

The third group consisted of the gentry.

In all these instances Chekhov's views will be compared with general scholarly opinion.

Wage Workers

The movement from the village to the town and city was accelerated by the decline in agricultural wages and the boom in industry. Peasants who needed work took to the road.

Some of those in need of work found it in the mines. In "The Savage" Chekhov described how a landowner hired transient workers to work in his mine. He hired desperate men, some without passports. He wanted to make as much money as he could and begrudged the men their pay. He conspired with the foremen to cheat the workers. The owner told him not to pay the men. The workers would beat up the foreman but the owner paid the foreman ten rubles on Saturday if he did as he was told. The foreman did not pay the men, they beat him up, and he got paid the money. On Monday, a whole new group of migrant laborers signed on and every Saturday it was the same, the foreman got beaten for ten rubles. Both the foreman and the owner made an added profit. The men beat the foreman because they were starving. The fact that the men starved was not important; the fact that the foreman and the owner made added money was the whole reason for the system.[1]

Some persons tried to earn a wage in the provincial towns as Chekhov described in "My Life." Chekhov questioned, through his characters, the nature of these townspeople. He concluded that they were "respectable" people who were as stupid, as cruel, as lazy, and as dishonest as the drunken, superstitious, local peasants.

These people were like animals who lived by the instincts which governed their monotonous lives.[2]

Among the townspeople were such small craftsmen as house painters. One of the painters, Andrew Ivanov, called himself a decorating contractor to upgrade his clients and perhaps make a little more money. He and his crew of workers did painting, glazing, wall-papering, and even took on roofing work. He was a respected workman who could have made ten rubles a day. He could have been well-off, but he wanted to be boss at all costs and call himself a contractor. He paid the workers from 70 kopeks to 1 ruble a day. He spent too much time setting up jobs so he made little profit but he was happy and so was his crew.[3]

Andrew Ivanov was called Radish. Radish was an impractical man, lacking business sense. He would take on more work than he could handle and had to get added workers and end up not making money. On one occasion, he was unable to pay his men. The hungry painters were going to beat him up. They called him a Judas and a bloodsucker. The difference between Radish and the mine owner was that Radish borrowed money to pay the men. He would never be rich.[4]

The workmen were cheated by shops that palmed off rotten meat, stale flour, and used tea leaves on the workers. They were pushed around by police and junior clerks. In the hospitals, the nurses and junior medical staff sponged off the workmen. If the workmen could not afford to bribe the nurses, they were mistreated. The tradesmen, the bosses, other workmen, and clients were all dishonest. Yet, the workmen had to stand, hat in hand, at back doors waiting for wages.[5]

Not only was the workman abused, but he was expected to cooperate in this system of theft. The painter, in "My Life," papered a room. He was paid seven kopeks but was told to sign a receipt for twelve kopeks. When he refused, a distinguished looking gentleman threatened to smash his face unless he did sign. Everyone was expected to participate in the system of corruption.[6]

The workmen, for their part, played up to clients, flattering them to their faces in order to get tips. However, the workers would make fun of them after they left the job. When they were tipped, they would thank the person profusely. They all wanted to make a little more. If they did not receive a tip, they would take home some linseed oil. Even an upright person like Radish did that because he did not see that as wrong.[7]

The town in "My Life" supported many small businesses like the slaughterhouse, which was just three gloomy sheds with a gray fence around them. When the wind was right, the stench of dung and carcasses was choking. The yard was a mess of mud and blood.[8]

The meat was taken by sled to the butcher's stall at the market as dawn was breaking. Cooks and old women with baskets came to look. Prokofy, the butcher, in his white, bloodstained apron would claim he sold them meat at cost, but he gave them short change and short weight. They raised no objection. They just called him a shark.[9]

This systematic theft had negative effects on the small businesses. An example of this would be the case of the refreshment room at a mainline station in "Murder." The manager, Sergey, had worn a tailcoat and a gold watch, but he fell on hard times. He spent all his money on new equipment and was robbed by his own staff. His career began to decline; he was moved to a less-busy station, and then another less-busy one. His wife ran off with the silver. Finally, he ended up as a waiter.[10] As a waiter, he was harassed and humiliated by the station master. Theft and poor judgment ruined him.[11] If he continued the way he was going, he would lose his waiter's job too.

Chekhov gave his attention to the pattern of movement from the village to the city and town. He showed this through a sequel to "The Peasants," a story fragment called "Peasants." The principal figure that provides the transition from country to city was Olga. Olga had fled the poverty of the village and went to the city making contact with some other people from Zhukovo, her deceased husband's village. Through them, she found a job as a maid and found lodging for her daughter among people from Zhukovo.[12]

Sasha, Olga's daughter, slept on the floor of her aunt's room. Her aunt was a middle-aged prostitute named Claudia. Their landlady rented a six-room apartment and lived by subletting it. Five separate families inhabited the five bedrooms. Claudia and Sasha were in one small room; a layout man from the print works, Ivan Matveichev the old waiter, and the landlady were each in their own rooms; finally, a woman and three children lived in the last room. They were probably supported by a monk who visited periodically. Olga slept where she worked and could get free from work only occasionally. When she did visit, she slept on chairs in the hallway.[13]

Olga worked at a hotel as a maid. She worked very long hours and could not even find time to go to church. She received no wages and lived solely on tips she received from the guests. She saved money out of her tips to send back to the family in her village. When she was in the village, she longed for Moscow, but now she longed for the green of the country and the sense of belonging with her husband in the village.[14]

Claudia, the forty-two year old prostitute, was kind and loving. She only received a few "guests," now mostly older men and an occasional college boy.

She was fading fast and knew it, yet she had a purpose. She was good at treating her clients tactfully, showing respect and doing the very best for them. This was her duty, happiness and pride. Her detractors said she would die in a hospital after begging on the street because she was getting old. She was old, but she loved Sasha and was loved in return.[15]

In the story, every indication was given that Sasha would become a prostitute in order to support her aunt. Prostitution offered comfort and a good wage and was, in certain respects, to be preferred over factory, shop, and perhaps, home.

Olga, Sasha and Claudia were poor, but they had love and each other's support. Not so for the boy Vanka, an apprentice to a shoemaker, in Chekhov's story, "Vanka." This nine-year old orphan boy wrote a letter to his grandfather back in the village describing his life in the city and begging to return. His letter showed the stark contrast between the lovely memories of life on the estate where his beloved grandfather was the watchman, and the horror of the city.[16]

The young apprentice told of how he was abused by the master and his wife. He had to work all day and suffer the abuse of the older boys and workmen. When he did not please the master, he was beaten. The day before writing his letter, he was knocked unconscious by the master. At night, he had to rock the master's baby in its cradle if it cried. A few nights before, he had been beaten because he fell asleep while rocking the cradle.[17]

Vanka was always hungry and tired. He was fed only what was left at the table and the master and his wife ate all the cabbage soup and drank all of the tea. He got only bread for breakfast, porridge for lunch, and then bread in the evening again. He slept in the entry so he could rock the baby. If the baby awakened, he got no sleep at all. The only reason he did not run away was that he had no boots and feared the frost. He suffered from loneliness, depression, fits of crying and would do anything to return to the village.[18]

If Chekhov's grandfather were in the city, he might not have fared any better than the boy. Chekhov in his story, "Heartache," dealt with being old and alone in the city. In "Heartache," an old cabby lamented the fact that his son had died before him. He was then alone with no one to take care of him and with no one to learn from him. He was completely alone, abused by people, with no one to help him bear his grief. He earned enough to feed his horse and not much else. He slept on a bench in a large room with the other cabbies. One wonders how long he would last with hunger, cold, and loneliness on his old, tired heels.[19]

In Russian cities factories were becoming increasingly important as sources of employment. Chekhov has given us a clear picture of the factory through several of his stories, such as: "Three Years;" "A Woman's Kingdom;" "A Case History;" and "Lovely Woman: From a Doctor's Notes." The people who worked in the factories shared problems with the other non-factory, urban workers as outlined by Chekhov in his stories on factory and non-factory workers. They had poor wages, poor working conditions, poor food, poor housing and little hope for better.[20]

Some people who worked in a factory lived in rooms they rented and others lived in factory barracks. Chekhov described the condition in one of these tenements in "A Woman's Kingdom." As one approached the tenement, it appeared dark, deep-set, and it stunk. There was the sound of men coughing by the walls. Everywhere in the halls was the foul stench that had met one at the gate. The staircases were narrow and dirty with high steps. The landings were cluttered with rags, bins and pots of excrement. When a person entered a flat, one could tell the occupation of the worker by the distinctive smell of either varnish, tar, leather, or smoke, depending on their job. This particular apartment had a rather acrid stench, for the occupant was a clerk. He had a pregnant, consumptive wife and five children. The eldest child was fifteen and the youngest was three years old. The children all slept in one small room on two beds. The family also took in a boarder to help pay the rent.[21]

The workers' barracks were consistent with their humble station. An old house which was literally falling down and an outbuilding served as a barracks for the workers. They slept four to a room. The place smelled from stove fumes and food odors. The men and boys slept and sat on their beds. They ate out of a common bowl even though they had individual plates.[22]

Even a professional, like a plant accountant, had difficulty. He lived in a one-story structure attached to a large shed. It was dark, cramped, damp, and shabby inside. The accountant who lived alone ate at cheap cafes. He was poorly nourished and exhausted from overwork. But there was little else he could do on his wage of forty rubles a month.[23] This story illustrates the common problem of poor pay, poor housing, and poor food which in many cases could lead to poor health. Their work place, the factory, was no better than their living space.

To Chekhov, the factories were grim, gloomy, and dust-covered conglomerations of mill-sheds, sometimes with smokestacks, surrounded by smaller sheds and workers' barracks, with a factory yard that was partially paved, dirty, and always depressing. This entire mass was surrounded by a fence and gate. Chekhov sensed a mindless monster waiting to consume all within.[24]

Inside the buildings there was the naked power of the machines and the heat of the furnaces. The heat and the noise was almost unbearable. At times, the machines broke loose and injured the men as in "A Woman's Kingdom," when a gear hit a man and opened his skull, exposing his brain. He was back at work though, with just a bit of a stutter as evidence of the accident. Another man lost his sight because he worked all day in the heat by the furnaces.[25]

Poor working conditions grew out of the rise of industrial capitalism. Chekhov concerned himself with the evil effects of the factory system and capitalism in many of his stories. In "A Case History," he explained how several thousand men worked unceasingly in unhealthy conditions to make cheap printed cotton. The workers lived on the edge of starvation. The only way to rid oneself of the nightmare was to get drunk. One hundred people supervised the operation. They spent their time keeping track of and abusing the others.[26]

Only two or three bosses benefited from all of this suffering. The factory was a monster – a devil who ruled everyone; the bosses and workers alike. That devil deceived everyone. The young factory owner in "A Woman's Kingdom" did not know how the whole thing worked and felt strange about making so much from something she did not even understand. Chekhov referred to the process as a mindless, primitive force from which no one really benefited.[27]

Given the choices open to the lower-class of Russia, people looked for any alternative. Some women chose, or were compelled, into prostitution. Chekhov has left the impression that Sasha, in "The Peasants," might choose that alternative.

In "An Attack of Nerves," Chekhov took the reader through the red light district of "S" Street. He initially presented, through a young student, the liberal view of prostitution, which was that immoral women, who, under the pressure of fatal circumstances, environment, bad education, poverty, and so on, were forced to sell their honor for money. Their families wept for them as though they were dead. They had no true love, no children or civil rights. Science treats them as evil, and men address them with contemptuous familiarity. They were, however, made in the image and likeness of God, and if they acknowledged their sin, they could hope for salvation. People would never forgive them their past, but God loved Mary Magdalene as much as anyone.

A student on his way to a red-light district for the first time felt he could tell a prostitute by her dress and manner, as he had seen in the humor magazines. She would be the figure out of a tragic story. The women would be in the dark, secretive places, wearing white bed jackets with their hair down; they would be afraid of the light.[28] This was his view before he went.

When the student finally reached the red-light district, there was music flowing from each house and bright light shone from windows and wide-open doors. Cabs were lined up waiting for patrons, and people walked by as on any other street. He thought there was this kind of excitement at the slave markets in ancient times, also.

When he went into a house and met the whores, he found that none met his preconceived ideas. The girls were all dressed in bright dresses, most with bows of some sort. They were generally young and of different varieties. The madame was stout and congenial like everyone. A blonde, attractive girl asked him to buy her a drink and he did. He learned later that the madame made a large profit from the drinks (the drink cost six rubles). The girls were told to ask for a drink.[29]

The thing that struck the student most was that there was nothing novel or interesting about the place. It was just a blend of the dresses, a cheap gilt mirror, the piano and the indifferent faces. Everything was ordinary, prosaic and uninteresting. The only thing striking was the bad taste: an almost conscious style. Gaudy dresses, long trains, bows, and purplish rouge on the cheeks: these were all parts of the general "S" Street style which could not be changed. He thought how poorly these people sold themselves. They did not seem to realize that sin was only interesting when it was beautiful and wore a mask of virtue. He concluded that it was all very dull.[30]

The student struck up a conversation with one of the women. He learned that she was seventeen years old, her parents had sold soap and candles, and that she had gotten into the business because her first beau was a salesman who spent fifty rubles on underwear for her.[31] She liked nice things and got them in her business.

Another girl he spoke with informed him that the madame kept her girls very well. They were awakened at two or three in the afternoon for coffee, and ate dinner, which included beefsteak and dessert, at six in the evening. He came to realize, as she spoke, that she was not the fallen woman he had conceived in his daydreams. She was the inhabitant of a different world, a world which he did not understand.[32]

He spoke to a brunette and told her begging was preferable to prostitution. She asked him to get her a drink with a sleepy-eyed expression. She and the others were not of his world. The musicians were not threadbare and hungry, but sleek and very well dressed. The lackeys were well fed and looked comfortable. He did not know how to act. The other patrons, two army officers, several young men other than his friends, all looked comfortable. And the whores were doing what they chose because they liked the comforts. They did not feel shame or guilt.[33]

The young student came to the realization that if prostitution was something evil and needed to be stopped, it would not be by going after the women. The people who had to be helped were the men, like his friends, that supported it and collectively, slowly killed the girls. It was they who were exploiting hunger, ignorance, and stupidity. Individual men had to stop it by rejecting the indifference of society to the problem and its causes.[34]

Leroy-Beaulieu identifies the following under one important group of wage workers, the *meshchane*: the poorer townspeople; the mechanics; the members of the trades; and finally, the "miscellany" that do not fit into class (raznochintsy). They usually earned their livelihood from small business or manual trade. Many did not have a specific means of survival. They could not own above a certain level of goods or property. Although legally townsmen, they would go to the country to earn money when they could. These were the most typical inhabitants of the town and the lowest of them.

The peasants and the poor townspeople frequently exchanged residences and competed with each other in manual labor and retail trade on the smallest scale, in factories or at fairs. The townsmen drifted with crafts to the country, and the rural men drifted to the town with their tools and labor.[35]

The peasant, at least, had his cabin and lot, as well as his share of the common land. Not so with the townspeople. They lived by their wits, hand to mouth. Some may have achieved wealth but most led a precarious existence. Most rented rooms. Only about ten percent owned houses. It was this group that bore the tax burden along with the peasants. These people, along with the former household serfs, "court people" who were freed outside the commune, provided Russia with a ready-made landless proletariat.

Leroy-Beaulieu points out that there was mobility for them if they made money. The transition was easy since they held similar values. If they made enough money, they could be classified as merchants. If they lost money, they would drop back down again. These people, along with the peasant workers, were the people of the cities and towns of Russia.[36]

The factory had its roots as far back as Peter the Great. The tradition of using a rural labor supply in manufacturing went hand-in-hand with the factory. The need for a supply of free labor to keep pace with industrialization was one of the reasons for the emancipation of the serfs. In fact, since the end of the eighteenth century, serfs had been working in factories as free labor to pay their owners, the obrok. After the liberation of the serfs, some rural labor trickled into the cities.[37] The crown had wanted a labor force structured so that it would not become a landless urban proletariat. Thus, the crown kept the peasant tied to the commune and the rural area. After 1890, when the industrial boom began and agricultural prices dropped, the flow of workers to the city accelerated. Wages were higher in industry and the towns. In the wake of this expansion, the number of new workers in the urban industries increased by 184,500 per year for 1891 to 1900, triple the average from 1861 to 1870.[38]

T. Von Laue asserts that most Russian Factory workers were also peasants during the period from 1892 to 1903.[39] Liashchenko maintains that nine-tenths of all Russian urban workers were classified in the estate of the peasantry.[40] Reginald Zelnik indicates that thirty percent of the population of the city of St. Petersburg were peasants there for temporary jobs. They were very fluid and had strong ties to the countryside. They moved back and forth frequently.[41] This view is supported by L. Haimson who believed the ties to the country were very strong. In fact, many peasants had to get the commune's permission to renew their passport to remain in the city.[42]

Many urban workers had strong psychological and economic ties to the countryside. They owned land in the country which was farmed by relatives. They were in the city only under the pressure of poverty to supplement their agricultural earnings. Some with families came alone and hated the factories and would return to the country for protracted periods of time. While in the city, they sent money home regularly.

Not all city workers had ties to the land. Those who had no land or home in the country, especially the unmarried ones, came and stayed. These became the urban proletariat that the government had feared but industry needed.[43]

The government tried not to permit the integration of the peasant worker into the town and did little or nothing to improve conditions. When the rush of the 1890's came, conditions deteriorated. During this period, St. Petersburg experienced the factory system at its worst. The more industrialization progressed, the worse things became.[44] Yet in the cities, there was great physical contrast between the large industries, like cotton and metal, and small primitive workshops. They existed side by side in the city. Both employed the peasant worker with the same resultant distress to the workers.[45]

S. N. Prokopovich, in his study of peasants in post-reform manufacturing, says the conditions in European Russia for workers were not good and virtually precluded a normal family life. According to the 1897 census, about sixty percent of the workers in European Russia lived alone, and the average worker's family consisted of only 1.98 persons although an average family in the population as a whole consisted of 5.63 persons.[46] K. A. Pazhitnov writes that in the employer-owned barracks, life was wretched. All that could be expected was one corner of a room for a worker. These conditions demonstrate the plight of the urban workers.[47] Wages were also a problem for the workers. Drawing on a survey made between 1908 and 1910, Gliksman indicated that there was a direct relationship between wages and the size of a family. The average wage of a worker between 1908 and 1910 was 290 rubles per year. Only workers making over 400 rubles a year could have a normal family life. That level would be for skilled and semi-skilled laborers. Those who made less than 300 rubles per year could not afford a wife. Another survey done in St. Petersburg, where the average was high at 472 rubles, showed that nine-tenths of those making less than 400 rubles lived alone. Only those with wages above 600 rubles tended to have families with children. The higher the father's wage, the greater the number of children.[48]

Children were an economic burden to a working couple, especially to the mother. Unwanted children were often aborted or sold after birth, and sometimes abandoned or killed.[49] The babies were sold to groups of women known as "angel factories." These women brought "baskets full of dead and half-dead infants, choking in their own excrement" to collect the fee of two rubles per head at the official shelters. According to Bernice Madison, the mortality rate among these children was 75 percent.[50] There were virtually no child-care facilities. Working women entrusted their children to old women or incompetent older children.[51] Chekhov reflected this problem of child supervision in his stories "Sleepy" and "Vanka."

D. M. Wallace writes that the Russian upper-classes and many intellectuals were reluctant to see capitalism grow in Russia. One should not confuse industry with capitalism. By "capitalism," they meant the social organization in which the two main factors are a small "body of rich capitalists and an enormous pauper proletariat living hand to mouth," at the mercy of heartless employers. He believes that Russia was following in the footsteps of the wealthy countries. Wallace writes that "if . . . she continues to do so, she will inevitably be saddled with the same disastrous results" as the West experienced, "plutocracy, pauperism, unrestrained competition in all spheres of activity, and a greatly intensified struggle for life, in which the weaker will necessarily go to the wall."[52]

Wallace noted that the concern over competition creating social inequity, plutocracy, and pauperism was a favorite topic for Russian theorists. Wallace indicates that there was reason for discussion because Count Witte was deliberately trying to create a landless proletariat "in order to increase the amount of cheap labour for the benefit of the Capitalists."[53]

Karpovich maintains that, because of the backwardness of the country, the conditions during Russian industrialization were probably ". . . worse in Russia than they had been anywhere else." As a general rule, workers "were overworked, underpaid, and badly fed and lodged." They were subjected to "ruthless exploitation" by capitalists.[54]

William Blackwell believes that miners suffered the greatest privations, while the oil workers of Baku were exploited like colonial natives. In central Russia, the lives of women and children were blighted in the textile factories by long working hours at low wages.[55] It was not until the 1880's that some very limited reforms were made for women and children, and, in 1897, the work day was reduced to eleven and one-half hours. Factory inspection was established but was unable to overcome the opposition of employers.[56]

The peasant women did what they could to avoid the poverty of the countryside and the equally dismal life of working for wages in town or in the city. Some went into the convent. Nuns in Russia increased from 7,000 in 1885 to 47,000 in 1911. Some women took up seasonal work. Others began to make annual tours of the towns in the area as prostitutes.[57]

It is generally recognized that poverty caused much of the prostitution in late nineteenth-century Russia. Richard Stites notes that the influx of peasant women from the countryside increased prostitution.[58] S. S. Shashkov, in his study on Russian women, indicates that the prostitutes in St. Petersburg came almost equally from three groups: meshchanstvo, or petit bourgeoisie; soldier's wives and daughters; and peasants. Only a small number came from the gentry and a few were foreigners, primarily Germans. The ages ranged widely from very young to old. In Moscow, some were registered as young as eleven, twelve, and thirteen years old.[59]

Prostitutes either joined a brothel or worked the streets alone. There were 150 houses in St. Petersburg with varying qualities of accommodations and human merchandise. The upper-quality establishments catered to the gentry, officials, and the rich. They employed the most attractive women. As the prostitute deteriorated, she descended the ladder of houses until she was old and out on the street. Conditions in the lowest of the houses were very bad. One of them, a Moscow tavern, was called 'The Crimea.' It had a basement whorehouse known on the streets as "Hell." Here, patrons took their delights "under bestial conditions." Loners who chose to remain independent walked the streets of the Empire: Nevsky in St. Petersburg; the Kreshchatik in Kiev; or the Odessa waterfront. The "Loners" (odinochki) were better able to control their incomes. However, many ended as "aged, painted streetwalkers, doing their business in courtyards and staircases and under bridges . . ." for a handful of coins.[60]

Urbanization, industrialization, and rigid divorce laws increased the number of clients and prostitutes. In St. Petersburg, the estimate of the number of prostitutes, registered and unregistered, was between 30,000 and 50,000 out of a population of 1,400,000. Other centers were Moscow and its satellite factory towns, the Baltic, the mining regions of the Ukraine, and the maritime cities on the Black Sea. The newcomers were mostly peasant migrants. Young recruiters for the brothels would meet the trains and offer the young rural girls good jobs and lodging at nearby "hotels." The young women who joined were trying to avoid the poverty they had fled from in the country. Servants and women workers could only receive, at maximum, 15 to 20 rubles a month. While the lowest paid whore could earn 40 rubles, an attractive woman could earn as much as 500 to 700 rubles.[61]

Child prostitution caused the greatest furor. In 1906 a report titled "Children of the Streets," described the whole problem in great detail. Child seduction fed the white slavery rings. These highly-organized rings would recruit in towns, drawing in girls from shops, inns, factories, and railroad stations. Once recruited, they were registered and given a yellow passport by the State. According to Stites, girls were recruited from all over Russia. The Pale was drained of children. Jews and Gentiles alike were recruited and sent all over Russia and the world.[62]

Ironically, the commonality of the peasant, the peasant-worker, the urban worker and the town worker, as well as the small artisan (meshchanstvo) was revealed in their common problems: poverty and abuse. This eventually led some of the women of this group to prostitution as a positive alternative to their situation. Chekhov was correct in his perceptions and those perceptions are supported by scholarly opinion.

Middle Class

A Western-type middle-class was in the process of evolving in Russia. For the purpose of this study, those with moderate wealth from merchant or manufacturing enterprises or those with status because of professional background are grouped as the middle-class. The gentry, regardless of wealth or profession, are grouped separately.

In "My Life" the young housepainter says the whole town looked on the rich as foreigners. They had nothing in common with them.[63] In "A Dreary Story" people above and below the middle-class on the social scale resented their solid way of eating and their solid jokes but most of all their attempts at speaking French.[64]

Some of the middle-class were unable to shake their fear of losing their wealth and sliding back into a lower position. For example, in "A Marriageable Girl" 'Gran', a very stout, ugly, bushy-browed, bewhiskered old woman prays to be spared from bankruptcy. She owns rows of stalls in the market and a grand house with columns.[65] Gran's family had nothing to worry about, but her daughter who ran the house, had her four servants sleeping on the bare floor in the kitchen. They had no beds or blankets, only rags, stink and vermin. The daughter spoke French and acted in private theatricals. She was obviously quality. Neither she nor the old lady did anything all day. No one in the family worked anymore. All the old lady did was worry about bankruptcy. When they finally changed things in response to protests the servants were given one room in the filthy basement of the grand house. The story warns that the time will come when the house will vanish without a trace.[66]

The attitude of many of the middle-class is seen in the story "A Commercial Venture." Andrew Siderov inherited some money and decided to open a bookstore. The town, which was stagnating in ignorance and prejudice, needed one. What the town needed was ideas. He rented a shop and went to Moscow to buy books, brought them back to the valley, and arranged them on the shelves. But some people asked for other items and the books did not sell. He moved some books and replaced them with other items. Gradually his ideas changed and so did his stock. He became one of the town's leading shopkeepers. He dealt in crockery, tobacco, tar, soap, rolls, dressmaking material, haberdashery, chandlery, guns, leatherware and ham. He expanded and owned a wine cellar in the market and a bathhouse. His precious books lost their value to him and he sold them off at three rubles per hundredweight. He sneered at his former friends who spoke of literature, progress and lofty ideas. He called them "Americans." He had more substantial concerns.[67]

In "Three Years," Chekhov showed the development of two members of this middle group in society. Both Nina and Laptev spent their childhood in Moscow. Nina's family was in business and she had a long, boring childhood. Her strict father and invalid mother had given her little joy and more than one birch rod beating. The servants in the house had been dirty, coarse, and hypocritical. Priests and monks came to drink and eat but they were as coarse and hypocritical as the servants. They made a fuss over the father because he gave them food and drink even though they disliked him. Her brothers received an education, but she received none. She escaped by marrying into a landowning family. Her father disliked her husband but she dearly loved him. The father thought he was a nobody because he did nothing of substance.[68]

Laptev's family were also in business in Moscow. He remembered his father began teaching him by beating him before he was five years old. He was forbidden to play and awoke each day wondering if he would be beaten that day. Religion was beaten into him so he feared it as an adult. When he was eight he started work at the warehouse as an office boy, where he was beaten almost daily.

Laptev finally broke away from his father's house when he went to the university. After completing his studies he became part owner of a wholesale haberdashery business with a turnover of two million a year. Only the father, a secretive old-time merchant, knew exactly how much they made each year.

Laptev's brother, Alexis, was a pompous fool. He believed that they were from an illustrious house. They were both Orthodox and considered themselves superior to Jews and Germans. Laptev did not agree with Alexis. His was no illustrious house; his Grandfather beat his father, his father beat him. He hoped the family would end with his generation. He spent his whole life afraid because of his boyhood.[69]

The old man ran the business like a black art. He knew everything about everything. Laptev knew nothing of the intricacies of business and when he tried to reform the business he realized the problems. However, he did stop them from beating the boys who worked there.

He did not relate to his pompous, profit-making brother or his mysterious old merchant father. Nor did he like the lifestyle of the aristocracy. The aristocracy realized he was rich but did not like him because he walked like a shop assistant. He was in the middle. His brother and father represented the old system that had made the money; Laptev would spend it.[70] His brother would have taken advantage of anything to make a profit; even the death of a friend.[71]

Others made their money through manufacturing. Anne, in "A Woman's Kingdom," did not understand the factory, but her father and uncle did. Her father was a dreamer, but a hard worker. Her uncle was as hard as nails. He was an old believer and was inflexible in religion and politics. He lived an austere and rigid life. He excluded his brother from control of the business. Only three years before he died did he soften toward his brother, his only heir. That was how, ultimately, the business fell intact to Anne. She did not understand it, and had advisors run things. They, of course, cheated her, which she knew but tolerated because that was the system. Anne felt guilty making money from something she did not understand, but she realized her parents would not have felt that way. She also realized that, although rich and educated, she was not really upper-class. She decided that when she married it would be to a mechanic.[72]

The professional middle-class were best represented in Chekhov as physicians. Their attitudes vary, but, in general, the position they held in society was related to their profession and then to the wealth they acquired.

The first case in point was the doctor in "His Wife." He was the son of a village priest brought up in a church school. He was a plain man; a surgeon by profession. His problem was that he married a woman with the tastes of the gentry. She spoke French and lived the gay life of high society. Her husband, in turn, earned ten thousand rubles a year but had nothing in his pocket. He could not even send money to his mother. He was in debt for fifteen thousand rubles. He was a slave to his wife's social life. She wanted the gentry life and he did not share her values.[73]

In "Three Years," Chekhov sketched a doctor who was trying to solve his money problems by becoming wealthy through real estate deals. He did not have any cash because he either gambled it away or put it into buying houses. He bought houses and rented them. He even mortgaged his own home to finance the building of another home which he planned to mortgage also. He was expanding and becoming a real land magnate. When one saw his house and the outbuildings he rented to workers, one realized that he did nothing to improve the living conditions of his renters.[74]

In this story the professional men of the province are viewed as living in the midst of people who were barbarous, mean, and who lived in squalor. Chekhov indicates there were twenty-eight doctors in the town and they had all made their fortunes. They all bought their own houses while the rest of the people lived in wretched conditions. One of the persons in the story was in need of surgery and none of the local doctors would do it. A surgeon had to be brought in to operate because the local doctors were not keeping up their skills. They were too busy making money, mostly in fields other than medicine.[75]

These physicians form a stark contrast to the dedication of the Zemstvo doctors, who labored at low wages. They were even rather pale when compared with Chekhov's own efforts. These professionals were well on their way to being bourgeois in the negative Russian point of view.

The middle-class, as indicated previously, was in the process of evolving. The classification, *kuptsy*, for merchants, was only part of the middle-class as it evolved. As Leroy-Beaulieu points out, the merchants could never be considered a closed class. All that was necessary to be awarded that title was to own a certain capital and pay a license fee. The peasant, the poor townsmen, even the nobleman who engaged in commerce could add his name to the rolls of merchants. He just had to have the means. On the other hand, a merchant who lost his money could drop down into the *meshchane*.[76]

After emancipation the barriers between classes were not so much legal as they were barriers of wealth, education, and culture. The barriers existed between those whom wealth has "not yet lifted over the threshold of culture." In the past in the large cities there were always two clubs; one for nobility, the other for merchants. A Russian merchant usually was a man with a long beard, in a kaftan and high leather boots. He remained as faithful as the peasant to the traditions and dress of old Russia.

The two did not mix socially. But this was changing rapidly. The nobility and the emerging bourgeoisie were meeting in public assemblies in the towns and provinces and were being drawn together in manners, tastes, and culture. The gentry was becoming more national and the middle-class was becoming more European.[77]

In the 1880's the long beard and kaftan were gone but the old-time merchant was now the faithful guardian of old customs. He was sometimes the owner of a large fortune. He could be orthodox or a dissenter, but he was like the common people, only distinguished by his wealth. He was a faithful observer of fasts and holidays. He was characterized by superstition and slyness, plain living and vastness of commercial operations. On the other hand, there was the modern merchant, often the son or grandson of the old-style merchant, clean-shaven and anxious to give up ancestral customs. He would imitate the nobility and take on the French fashions. This type increased daily. They had palatial houses with "drawing rooms furnished luxuriously if not always tastefully," and all the trappings of the West.[78]

The sons and daughters of this new group learned French and travelled abroad. Many led a life indistinguishable from the nobility in Paris. When they returned home they conspired to be admitted into the social circle of the nobility.[79]

In addition to these persons, progress in education led to the birth of a professional wing within this middle-class. Lawyers, physicians, engineers, writers, and professors are all included in this new group. Leroy-Beaulieu believed that this group, the new middle-class, would become the directing group.

Many Russians feared the idea of a bourgeois element in society. They held a view consistent with that held by French urban workers – the view of the bourgeoisie as exploiter. They did not see the role of the bourgeoisie as filling the gap between lower and upper classes.[80]

A classic example of the truly wealthy middle-class' evolution can be seen in Valentine Bill's work *The Forgotten Class*. This work focuses on three generations of the Morozov family. The Grandfather, Savva Morozov, worked his way out of serfdom and built a textile business. His son, Timothy, had great technical expertise and single-mindedness leading to ruthlessness. He had the tortured conscience of an Old Believer because he had sinned against his workers by exploiting them. Timothy's son, Savva Morozov, was educated. He possessed a social conscience and a desire to reform the conditions in the family's factories. His mother, reflecting his father's rigid spirit, had him removed from his leadership position in the family's enterprises. Shortly afterward, Savva shot himself, perhaps because of his inability to continue his work toward needed reform.[81]

An important middle-class attitude which was revealed by Valentine Bill was that some of the wealthy middle-class were not interested in becoming nobles. Bill writes that the young Savva Morozov believed that the entrepreneurs had arrived at the summit of Russia's social structure. They held "vast powers and responsibilities" and they preempted "the role and importance of the nobility."[82] As Radion Denissovich Rydlov indicated he did not want to be admitted to the nobility because, "we are the cream of society, no one is able to outshine us any longer."[83] He believed "Everything revolves at present around capital." Savva Morozov indicated that the merchant should focus on only one thing which was his own element, reckoning profit and loss.

Valentine Bill believed that the Morozov's were exceptional in many ways but they were also typical of the Russian bourgeoisie. They were typical in their peasant origin. Also typical was their affiliation with Old Belief. The Morozov's were representative of the Russian bourgeoisie in the painful efforts of the first generation to remove themselves from serfdom. As with the other Russian bourgeoisie the second generation was cold-blooded and uncompromisingly tyrannical. The third generation was interested in cultural and artistic achievements. They were also forced to respond to the rising tide of revolution. Valentine Bill believes "These are all among the salient factors marking the road of the Russian bourgeoisie."[84] Chekhov indicated these factors and captured the spirit of the generations of the Morozov's in his stories.

Gentry - Landowners

In Russia the landowners had traditionally been the leading class. They were first by tradition and then by law. As the Russian political and social system evolved, the landowning class evolved into an aristocracy which thought itself superior to other Russians. Chekhov reveals the folly of their supposed superiority in several stories.[85]

In the story "At a Country House," Chekhov gives the reader an insight into the way the reactionary gentry saw themselves. A landowner speaks to his guest, who is an acting coroner. He holds forth about equality. He asserts that the swineherd is equal to Goethe or Frederick the Great. That is all well and good, but breeding will out. He pompously demands that his guest, a lawyer, take the "scientific view." His scientific view is a perversion of Darwin.[86]

The landowner would have liked someone like this lawyer to be his son-in-law so that he would be free from the worry of the estate and the arrears he owed on it. These thoughts flashed through his mind as he spoke about breeding.

He maintained that bravery and nobility were transmitted by heredity, along with the bumps on one's head. This nobility was preserved thanks to "sexual selection." The noble families instinctively shunned unions beneath their station, therefore, the mentally superior have been preserved by shunning the common herd. He felt it was not the working class who gave Russia her literature, learning, arts, law, and concepts of honor and duty. Humanity owed all that to the uppercrust and he was going to preserve the purity of his class. He would not even shake hands with the common man. The lowest backwoods squire was of more value than the finest businessman.[87]

The landowner was certain that all the trouble Russian society was experiencing came from admitting the lower orders to fields previously closed to them. High society, academia, literature, local government, the courts, all are worse for their presence in them. Such scum, he felt, made no contribution to society. He lamented the fact that some even tried to pass as decent men even though an intellectual would steal one's wallet while one was talking to him.[88]

While he spoke he was interrupted by his son and daughter who spoke French to each other and unconsciously slighted their father and the lawyer by speaking Russian to them. They were complaining of boredom caused by being forced to live in the country. They would prefer to live in the city. The children were in effect treating their father and the lawyer as creatures of a lower order who only spoke Russian and lived in the country away from the truly civilized French-speaking city dwellers. The children's father, the landlord, then commenced to again lament the effects of treating the lower orders equally.

He called on the guest, hopefully his future son-in-law, to join him, and like Richard the Lion-hearted they would smite the scum. His guest, the lawyer, then replied, "I can't do that . . . because I'm working-class myself . . . My father was a working man . . . and I see nothing wrong in that." He left quickly, but with a clear parting shot that he was working-class and proud of it![89]

The incident confused the landowner. He was a former university man, an idealist. What was wrong. But he had not been anywhere outside the county in twenty years nor had he read a book in that time. Was there an evil spirit inside of him spreading hate against his will?[90]

Chekhov exposed the reactionary view of the role of the gentry in "A Country House." He also revealed a condition in the society which made the reactionary's position more difficult. The outward signs of the upper-class were wealth, culture, education, attire and the French language. The middle-class had access to these so it was now more difficult to discriminate. Perhaps this made the upper-class more uncertain of itself and therefore even more protective of itself.

The use of French as a symbol of the upper-class is noted many times by Chekhov. In "The Duel" the woman wanted to dance and speak French, both of which stimulated her. In the story "Home" Chekhov notes the language's use as a means of exclusion. A young gentry girl was speaking to a young soldier. Her mother, seeing this, told the daughter, in French, to stop and go home. She then spoke sharply to the soldier in Russian, the language of the lower classes.[91]

Education and birth were key factors in Russian society. Manners were one of the outward signs of these. The young tutor, when he introduced himself to "The Privy Councilor," called himself a pedagogue who was formerly a student at the veterinary institute and was a nobleman by birth.[92]

Orlov in "An Anonymous Story" looks at both classes and chooses his class, the upper-class, as preferable. He sees the peasants as sunk in drink, sloth, thieving and degeneracy. He was aware of the evils of upper-class society and upper-class marriages. He found both classes repugnant, but in taste he chose the upper-class. "At least we of the upper-class speak decent French and read a book now and then. The kaftan brigade are only interested in pleasing their customers." Orlov was not even satisfied that the peasants and the tradesmen fed them. He felt it reflected negatively on both upper and lower-class.[93]

Many people were attracted to the gentry. Even "Ariadne" was impressed by titles. She found them delightful and mysterious. Others were attracted by the lifestyle of healthy, good-looking, well-nourished people who did nothing all day long. They were aimless and unoccupied as in "The Artist's Story." Perhaps, they might busy themselves with amateur theatricals as they wintered in town, as the Azhogins in "My Life."[94] It was the little touches that counted. Chekhov noted in "The Duel" that upper-class families dressed for lunch and dinner. In "An Anonymous Story" Chekhov indicates that a formal dress would cost 400 rubles when a charwoman earned only 20 kopeks per day.[95]

In "The Name Day Party" Chekhov brought the reader into the lives of a gentry couple. The wife was from the gentry of the highest circle. She had been to the university and was very wealthy. Her husband was from a lower station on the social ladder and owed his position and money to her. The wife felt her husband resented her because he owed everything to her. He, on the other hand, was resented by the others of the upper circle because of his lower birth and his overbearing manner. They called him a "Junker."

The society in which they traveled was very superficial. They argued about things which they really did not care about. The best conversations were the most superficial ones. The husband, feeling inferior to his wife, mocked her for her university education.

Her priorities were also questionable. When she was pregnant, in order to continue looking beautiful in her superficial world, she wore a corset. The corset cost her the baby. She realized she could never make her husband upper-class, and he could not understand why she needed to look beautiful for society and lose their baby. They were of two different worlds.[96]

In "The Black Monk" Chekhov sketches a picture of the beautiful life the gentry led. In this story he described Pesotsky's house and garden. Pesotsky was a landowner and a horticulturalist. His house was a *period piece* with columns and plaster lions. His greatest treasure was his beautiful English garden. People asked why his park existed. He said it was essential to the state. The garden was a symbol of the leadership role in agriculture that the gentry was supposed to perform but did not. In most cases the gentry no longer cared to keep up the garden. The key to the beauty and success of his garden was his love and work. He worked in the garden from dawn till dusk. It is clear that the garden was a symbol of the land held by the gentry of Russia. If it was to bloom it would require work and love. Pesotsky's great concern is that he is old and if the garden is to survive someone would have to take care of it. He said that it would be taken care of by his "under gardeners," who clearly are the lower-class farmers. Pesotsky believed that the worst enemies of the land were men whose hearts were not in it. The implication for the state and the gentry is clear. The gentry would lose its leadership role and the state would lose its principal supporters.[97]

The problem Chekhov alluded to in "The Black Monk"' is specifically stated in "A Marriageable Girl" when a young member of the gentry proclaims that Russia is supporting many useless loafers. He, and those like him, do nothing while others and Russia try to carry them.[98]

The opposite of the idler, who knew he was a drain on society was the man who thought he was productive. In "The Artist's Story" the landowner talked about how much work there was in running a model farm. In actual fact, his farm was anything but a model. He was lazy and stupid as opposed to his own image of himself as intelligent and efficient.[99]

Chekhov gives the reader an insight into the lives of two landowners in "Ariadne." Chekhov also gives clear indication of two types of gentry estates. One is operated by its owners who work hard to make it grow; the other, unchanged since emancipation, is going bankrupt through senseless luxury. The owners would borrow and drag others under with them.[100] The reader gets the sense of one segment, the upper portion of the gentry, dragging the lower hardworking rural gentry down with them.

A young gentry farmer falls in love with a beautiful but vain and shallow woman. Her father owns a large property which has fallen to ruin because of their self-indulgence. The young man and his father run a smaller productive estate. They worked hard and it pays off. However, they could not afford the self-indulgence which Ariadne engaged in. Perhaps Chekhov intended Ariadne as a symbol of the upper-class. She is a vain, shallow, wasteful, and unfeeling beauty. The young man, became infatuated with her and squandered his money, putting his father in bankruptcy for her. When he finally realizes what she is, he still feels honor bound to keep her, perhaps as Russia kept the gentry. The young landowner had felt guilty about spending money, not working, and ruining the estate chasing Ariadne. He returned and started to rebuild. He would ultimately make up for his mistake. Those others like Ariadne would continue to squander their resources.[101]

A similar contrast was presented by Chekhov in "The Privy Councilor." A gentry woman living in the provinces receives a visit, for the first time in over a decade, from her brother who is a privy councilor from St. Petersburg. He has ostensibly come to visit in the rural setting of his sister's home in a provincial town.[102]

Chekhov utilized the visit to show the reader the contrast between the gentry senior chinovnik and the rural life of the landowner. The woman even sends her child away so that the Privy Councilor's valet can have his room. The valet was better dressed and better spoken than the gentry family. Everything was done to please him but nothing succeeded.

One of the high points of the story came when his meaningless courtly chatter was taken seriously by one of the common people. The Councilor flattered a gypsy girl in a way which infuriated her husband and almost got the courtier killed. The gypsies were hardworking and honest. They meant what they said and thought the councilor had meant what he said. Two different worlds collided; reality and the court.[103]

The Privy Councilor receives word that the governor of the province is coming to visit. He will, of course, have to be fed. This throws the house into a turmoil. They slaughter all kinds of fowl including some not intended for eating. They exhaust themselves preparing the meal. The Privy Councilor's only response is to rage at them for the poor-quality food and their primitive manners.

What finally emerges is that the Privy Councilor hated the country. He wanted to be abroad but was flat broke. He borrowed the money to go abroad from his sister. To go abroad he borrowed money from the very people he criticized. Once again Chekhov shows how the artificial upper portion of the gentry stayed alive by drawing from the resources of the lower rural gentry.[104]

The list of deteriorating estates is a long one in Chekhov's works. In "Neighbors" the twenty-seven-year-old landlord reminds the reader of *Oblomov*. He was fat, unmarried, and a university graduate. He does nothing but eat and talk of abstractions. In "Three Years" Panaurov, another landowner, lives the grand life and squanders his wife's money for a few years.[105] In "The Savage" the old Cossack estate owner was just too poor and ignorant to make a go of it.[106] The same tragic story can be seen in "All Friends Together." Sergey marries into an estate and squanders its resources in six years. He said he was an idealist. Actually he was a frivolous idle person who was too inept and lazy to manage property.[107]

In the long run these estates will be sold as General Cheprakov's was in "My Life." The family was poor so they sold the estate to live. The son took a job as a stationmaster. Two other gentry lads took jobs as clerks. The rich middle class were buying up the estates as investments. In "Home," the country gentry lost their estates for factory sites owned by professional people of the middle class like

Dr. Neshchapov. Even the estates that are kept up are mortgaged.[108]   In pre-Reform Russia, inhabited land could be owned only by the gentry. Land ownership became a symbol of privilege and security in post-reform Russia. A land hunger developed in Russia among the non-gentry.

Chekhov gives an example of the non-gentry fixation with buying land in "Gooseberries." In this story a clerk named Nikolas virtually starves himself and his wife so he can buy three hundred acres of land in the country. He begins to take on the airs of the gentry. He forgets that his grandfather was a laborer and his father an army private. He feels he is above the common herd. He is a landowner.[109]

Chekhov, in his story, "Concerning Love," points out a root problem for the rural landowner. If a person actually worked the land himself he would be exhausted at the end of a day. He would be too tired to be reading philosophy and too dirty for fine furniture. This was particularly true in the summer during hay time when he slept in the barn because he was too tired to go to bed. Here, as in Ariadne, the hard-working gentry farmer can make it, but only at the price of eliminating the artificial and wasteful leisure life of times past.[110]

The upper class attitude toward the ordinary man can be seen in many of Chekhov's stories. In "The Princess," the princess treated her workers as subhuman, squeezing the last little bit of work out of each of them.[111]   In "Heartache," young men from the gentry class beat the cab driver to make him go faster. He was an old pest to them. The servile attitude demanded by the gentry can be seen in "The Name Day Party" when the peasants bow to the land owner's carriage as it passes. They cannot see him but they bow anyway. In "The Privy Councilor" the workmen carrying the councilor's trunks were so impressed with their quality they bow to the trunks. Bowing was the habit. They had learned this in order to survive.[112]

Chekhov perceived that the gentry's attitude toward servants was mixed and often negative. In his continuation of the story "The Peasants," he notes that decent folk talk of freedom, of loving their neighbor, and of helping the poor, but they keep servants. They are just like the serf owners – they cannot get along without servants whom they humiliate everyday.[113]

Probably the most congenial servant-master relationship described by Chekhov was in "My Life." A former serf owner and his former serfs continue on as they had before emancipation. The old peasants would not leave. They were leftovers from an age now past.[114]   This is a stark contrast to life under the Princess on her estate. The atmosphere on the estate was based on loathing. This was the atmosphere Chekhov saw on all large country estates: sleek footmen standing in every hallway to keep out improperly dressed people; all the strong and fit men and women standing about in view of the Princess; the old and ugly do the work out of sight.[115]

Perhaps an even worse condition existed in "Home." The estate was not farmed but all the servants were exhausted. They spent all their time fetching things for the mistress and her lazy family. She does not have the peasants flogged anymore, but the manager of the estate sometimes beats them. Even her grandfather occasionally hits one with his cane for old times sake.[116] The mistress of the estate exhausts the servants making cherry jam. She presides over the jam-making like a high priestess yet does none of the work. The servants slave away but they receive none of the jam they have made.[117]

Perhaps the most degrading experience for the servant was his status as a non-person. In "An Anonymous Story" Orlov wants to tell a young gentry woman she was being used. He tried to tell her but she would not believe a servant. It was only when he unmasked himself as a spy of gentry birth that she would believe him. He was a person not just a servant.[118]

Professionals did not fare much better at the hands of the gentry snobs. They were treated as servants by people like the Princess. They were paid more than servants but were still humiliated. Dr. Sable was constantly ignored by the gentry landowner in "My Wife."[119]

Even in their charity, the gentry could be patronizing. In "My Wife" a gentry woman found her whole reason for being in acting charitably.[120] The princess gratifies her ego by being loved as lady bountiful in her old ladies' home. The home, like the Princess' charity, was a sham. Her attempt at running a school fails because the children can sense her real nature.[121]

Chekhov clearly indicated the options for the gentry. They must give up the life of waste and inactivity. If they wish to own land they must make it work through their own labor and interest. Chekhov also rejected the literary view of the superfluous man. In his story "The Duel" he destroys the respectability of claiming that the gentry's inactivity can be excused as being due to the age. The intellectual must get up and get to work by studying science and improving his lot through hard work and science. When seeking truth there is no easy way. You take two steps forward to one step back. Nothing is easy in this world. There is pain, but willpower must drive one on. If the intellectuals want to do something they should harmonize the humanities with the sciences to seek truth, and then, live those truths.[122]

G. T. Robinson writes that in spite of the amount of control the gentry had over emancipation, they did not emerge from the emancipation era in a strong position. Many of the gentry pushed for emancipation because they were desperate for money. Many of them needed money to pay off existing debts. Nearly half the money paid for redemption was returned to the Treasury to pay gentry obligations. In many instances they saw no incentive to take their money and use it to modernize their farms.

When the price of grain dropped, this also hurt the gentry and diminished their interest in farming. They were forced into competition with Western Europe, Siberia, and America. Another element was that the personal traditions and habits of the nobility did not fit them for the new life. This weighed heavily in the balance of success or failure.[123] The emancipation, the new markets and new techniques were very different from the easygoing lifestyle of the serf owner. Often they lacked the desire or the ability to meet this new demand.

Several alternatives were attempted between the poles of selling the land and capitalist farming. One option was renting the land to peasants in return for their labor on plots which would provide for the landlord's consumption. The peasant would use his horses and tools sometimes and in other areas they would use the landlord's. Finally the landlord could rent all or part of his land.[124]

Most significant as an alternative was the sale of the land. The nobles sold land at an ever-increasing rate as Russia approached the turn of the century. The nobles were losing control of the land and were in rapid economic decline. The state tried to prop them up with the Nobles Land Bank. By 1904, one third of the nobles had mortgaged their property to the Nobles Land Bank and even more were indebted to private lenders. Almost 14,000,000 rubles were owed to the Nobles Land Bank in arrears. As their economic power declined the state moved to shore up the gentry's political position. However, the sale of land continued.[125]

Among those buying land were some townsmen, individual peasants, peasants' associations, and merchants. For a time merchants speculated in land. However, the speculation declined as did the relative amount of land the merchants held in relation to other groups. The peasantry was gaining upon the townsmen in the competition to acquire private land. Between 1877 and 1905, the merchants bought an ever increasing amount of small holdings in land. Through this the interest of gentry, bourgeois and richer peasants saw their interests drifting together.[126]

Working against landowner's cooperation was the class system. The *dvorianstvo* has been called the hereditary cultured class. Leroy-Beaulieu saw right to the core of the Russian nobility when he calls it a serving nobility. He quotes one Russian as saying the nobles are all those "who are not peasants, priests, or merchants-tradesmen or shopkeeper . . ." Included are all those of a certain cultural level in the towns or country. In this respect, "In Russia, the nobility is everybody."[127]

Beyond this there was a select group of families, the *znat*. These were the select of the society. Their position was not linked to owning land so they retained their unique aura after emancipation. The other group of nobles were the *kniazia*, the hereditary princes from ancient Russia.[128]

With the end of serfdom, the principal privilege unique to the gentry, the ownership of inhabited land, came to an end. The upper class then fell back on their role as the educated and cultural class. But as educational opportunities expanded to include non-gentry, the drawing room society of the gentry set up invisible social barriers. The symbols of this were education, manners and most especially the ability to speak fluent French. French became a sign of class and a barrier to separate the lower orders from the social elite. The upper class became more and more isolated from the Russian-speaking mass of society. Although this was their goal, it was also their greatest weakness.[129]

With regard to the gentry's treatment of servants, Richard Stites provides a significant insight from the Princess Dolgorukaya. She confessed that the gentry rewarded their servants' loyalty with abuse, long hours and low wages. The servants were paid three to four rubles per month. They were given food and a corner in which to sleep.[130] As for the workers on the estates in general, John Maynard quotes an Official Commission Report of 1897, to the effect that "nowhere are the relations between employer and employed so strained as in agriculture."[131]

Chekhov's perceptions as to the decline of the gentry, and their general relation with the people of Russia are supported by scholarly opinion.[132]

Chekhov's perceptions and concepts about the lower classes of Russian society have been proven to be true as are his observations about the other groups of that society. This was the truth he used to smash Russian society's popular image of itself.

NOTES

1   "The Savage," in *Oxford Chekhov*, 8:229-30.

2   "My Life," in *Ibid.*, 8:181.

3   "My Life," in *Ibid.*, 8:121, 134.

4   "My Life," in *Ibid.*, 8:134, 141.

5   "My Life," in *Ibid.*, 8:142.

6   "My Life," in *Ibid.*, 8:142.

7   "My Life," in *Ibid.*, 8:136.

8   "My Life," in *Ibid.*, 8:149-150.

9   "My Life," in *Ibid.*, 8:149-50.

10   "Murder," in *Ibid.*, 8:47.

11   "Murder," in *Ibid.*, 8:46.

12   "Peasants," in *Ibid.*, 8:266.

13   "Peasants," in *Ibid.*, 8:265.

14   "Peasants," in *Ibid.*, 8:267, 268.

15   "Peasants," in *Ibid.*, 8:265-67.

16   "Vanka," in *Portable Chekhov*, p. 34.

17   "Vanka," in *Ibid.*, p. 36.

18   "Vanka," in *Ibid.*, pp. 36, 38.

19   "Vanka," in *Portable Chekhov*, p. 34; Chekhov's story, "Sleepy," is clearly an early version of "Vanka." The young, abused child, driven mad by lack of sleep, strangled a crying baby so she could sleep herself.

20   "A Woman's Kingdom," in *Oxford Chekhov*, 7:61.

21   "A Woman's Kingdom," in *Ibid.*, 7:61-63.

22   "Three Years," in *Ibid.*, 7:175, 219.

23   "Lovely Woman: From a Doctor's Notes," in *Ibid.*, 8:262-63.

24   "Lovely Woman: From a Doctor's Notes," in *Ibid.*, 8:262-63; "A Case History," in *Ibid.*, 9:74, 69-70; "A Woman's Kingdom," in *Ibid.*, 7:59.

25   "A Woman's Kingdom," in *Ibid.*, 7:71.

26   "A Case History," in *Ibid.*, 9:74.

27   "A Woman's Kingdom," in *Ibid.*, 7:59; "A Case History," *Ibid.*, 9:74-75.

28   "An Attack of Nerves," in *Portable Chekhov*, pp. 222-23, 225.

29   "An Attack of Nerves," in *Ibid.*, pp. 226-28.

30   "An Attack of Nerves," in *Ibid.*, pp. 228-30.

31   "An Attack of Nerves," in *Ibid.*, p. 233.

32   "An Attack of Nerves," in *Ibid.*, p. 232.

33   "An Attack of Nerves," in *Ibid.*, pp. 233-36.

34   "An Attack of Nerves," in *Ibid.*, 239-44, 250-51.

35   Leroy-Beaulieu, *The Empire of the Tsars and the Russians*, 1:334-35.

36   *Ibid.*, 1:336-37.

37   Terence Emmons, "The Peasant and Emancipation," in *The Peasant in Nineteenth-Century Russia*, pp. 43-44.

38   P. I. Lyashchenko, *History of the National Economy of Russia to the 1917 Revolution*, (New York: The Macmillan Co., 1949), pp. 486-87, 526-32 passism.

39   Zelnik, "The Peasant and the Factor," in *The Peasant of Nineteenth Century Russia*, p. 158.

40   Lyashchenko, *History of the National Economy of Russia to the 1917 Revolution*, p. 504.

41   Zelnik, "The Peasant and the Factory," in *The Peasant in Nineteenth Century Russia*, pp. 187,159.

42   M. Tugan-Baranovsky, *Russkaia fabrika v proshlom i* nastoiashchem (St. Petersburg, 1898), I, 416-417, quoted in Gliksman, "The Russian Urban Worker," in *The Transformation of Russian Society*, p. 313.

43   Gliksman, "The Russian Urban Worker," in *The Transformation of Russian Society*, pp. 313-14.

44   Zelnik, "The Peasant and the Factory," in *The Peasant in Nineteenth Century Russia*, pp. 185-86.

45   *Ibid.*, pp. 186-87.

46 S. M. Prokopovich, "Krest'ianstvo i poreformennaia fabrika," *Velikaia reforma* 6 vols. (Moscow, 1911), 1:269; cited in Gliksman, "The Russian Urban Worker," in *The Transformation of Russian Society*, p. 314.

47 K. A. Pazhitnov, *Poloyhenie rabochago klassa v Rossi* (n.p., 1906), pp. 47-55, 125-139. Cited in *Ibid.*, p. 314.

48 Pazhitnov, *Poloyheni rabochago klassa v Rossi*, p. 139. Cited in *Ibid.*, p. 314.

49 Richard Stites, *The Women's Liberation Movement in Russia*, p. 165.

50 Bernice Madison, "Russia's Illegitimate Children Before and After the Revolution," cited in: *Ibid.*, p. 179

51 *Ibid.*, p. 165.

52 D. M. Wallace, *Russia*, p. 587.

53 *Ibid.*, pp. 587-88.

54 Michael Karpovich, *Imperial Russia, 1801-1917*, p. 58.

55 William Blackwell, *The Industrialization of Russia: An Historical Perspective* (New York: Thomas Crowell Co., 1970), p. 45.

56 *Ibid.*, p. 45 Karpovich, *Imperial Russia, 1801-1917*, p. 58.

57 Stites, *The Women's Liberation Movement in Russia*, p. 161.

58 *Ibid.*, p. 18.

59 S. S. Shashkov, *Ocherk istorii russkoi zhenshchiny*, re. ed., (SBP, 1872), pp. 245-275, 258-267, 271. Quoted in Stites, *The Women's Liberation Movement in Russia*, p. 61.

60 *Ibid.*

61 Stites, *The Women's Liberation Movement in Russia*, pp. 182-183.

62 *Ibid.*, p. 184.

63 "My Life," in *Oxford Chekhov*, 8:154.

64 "A Dreary Story," in *Ibid.*, 5:56.

65 "A Marriageable Girl," in *Ibid.*, 9:209.

66 "A Marriageable Girl," in *Ibid.*, 9:208, 222.

67 "A Commercial Venture," in *Ibid.*, 6:257-59.

68 "Three Years," in *Ibid.*, 7:154.

69 "Three Years," in *Ibid.*, 7:215, 179, 177.

70 "Three Years," in *Ibid.*, 7:221-22.

71 "Three Years," in *Ibid.*, 7:187.

72 "A Woman's Kingdom," *Ibid.*, 7:78-79.

73 "His Wife," in *Ibid.*, 8:16-17.

74 "Three Years," in *Ibid.*, 7:160-61.

75 "Three Years," in *Ibid.*, 7:157.

76 Leroy-Beaulieu, *The Empire of the Tsars and The Russians*, 1:338.

77 *Ibid.*, 1:340-341.

78 *Ibid.*, 1:341.

79 *Ibid.*, 1:341.

80 *Ibid.*, 1:343-345.

81 Valentine Bill, *The Forgotten Class* (New York: Frederick Praeger, 1959), pp. 14-18, 24, 31, 32.

82 *Ibid.*, p. 27.

83 *Ibid.*, pp. 27, 33, 31.

84 *Ibid.*, pp. 34-35.

85 For the purpose of this study the gentry will be considered the pomeshchiks and dvorianin who were the traditional land holders in Moscovite society. It should also be noted that not all dvoriane were pomeshchinki but all pomeshchiki were dvoriane; they were not mutually exclusive terms.

86 "At A Country House," in *Oxford Chekhov*, 7:133.

87 "At A Country House," in *Ibid.*, 7:136-37.

88 "At A Country House," in *Ibid.*, 7:138-39.

89 "At A Country House," in *Ibid.*, 7:136-37.

90 "At A Country House," in *Ibid.*, 7:138-39.

91 "Home," in *Ibid.*, 5:155; "The Duel," in *Ibid.*, 8:245.

92 "The Privy Councilor," in *Portable Chekhov*, p. 46

93 "An Anonymous Story," in *Oxford Chekhov*, 6:193-94, 219.

94 "Ariadne," in *Ibid.*, 8:77; "The Artist's Story, in *Ibid.*, 8:102; "My Life," in *Ibid.*, 8:121.

95 "The Duel," in *Ibid.*, 5:157; "An Anonymous Story," in *Ibid.*, 6:212.

96 "The Name-Day Party," in *Portable Chekhov*, pp. 181, 194, 199, 196-97.

97 "The Black Monk," in *Oxford Chekhov*, 7:27-28, 34-35.

98 "A Marriageable Girl," in *Oxford Chekhov*, 9:215.

99 "The Artist's Story," in *Ibid.*, 8:100, 97.

100 "Ariadne," in *Ibid.*, 8:85, 84, 83, 76, 75, 74.

101 "Ariadne," in *Ibid.*, 8:77, 92, 91, 87, 85.

102 "The Privy Councilor," in *Portable Chekhov*, p. 40.

103   "The Privy Councilor," in *Ibid.*, pp. 40-45, 50-51, 56, 59-60.

104   "The Privy Councilor," in *Ibid.*, pp. 59-60.

105   "Neighbors," in *Oxford Chekhov*, 6:102; "Three Years," in *Oxford Chekhov*, 7:155, 158, 170.

106   "The Savage," in *Ibid.*, 8:231, 233.

107   "All Friends Together," in *Ibid.*, 9:227-28, 234, 238-40.

108   "My Life," in *Ibid.*, 8:129-31; "Home," in *Ibid.*, 8:239, 245.

109   "Gooseberries," in *Ibid.*, 9:32-36.

110   "Concerning Love," in *Ibid.*, 9:42-43.

111   "The Princess," in *Ibid.*, 5:23-24.

112   "The Privy Councilor," in *Portable Chekhov*, pp. 122, 208-43.

113   "The Peasants," in *Oxford Chekhov*, 8:306.

114   "My Wife," in *Ibid* 6:55.

115   "The Princess," in *Ibid.*, 5:22-23.

116   "Home," in *Ibid.*, 8:241, 238, 239.

117   "Home," in *Ibid.*, 8:245.

118   "An Anonymous Story," in *Ibid.*, 6:212, 231-32.

119   "My Wife," in *Ibid.*, 6:33; "The Princess," in *Ibid.*, 5:23.

120   "My Wife," in *Ibid.*, 6:58.

121   "The Princess," in *Ibid.*, 5:24-25, 29.

122   "The Duel," in *Ibid.*, 5:140-224.

123   G. T. Robinson, *Rural Russia Under the Old Regime*, pp. 129-130.

124   *Ibid.*, p. 130.

125   *Ibid.*, pp. 131-132.

126   *Ibid.*, pp. 132-134.

127   Leroy-Beaulieu, *The Empire of the Tsars and the Russian*,1:347-350.

128   *Ibid.*, 351-355.

129   *Ibid.*, 381-392.

130   Richard Stites, *The Woman's Liberation Movement in Russia*, p. 162.

131   John Maynard, *The Russian Peasant and Other Studies*, p. 69.

132   For additional information see: D. M. Wallace, *Russia*, pp. 283-324.

CHAPTER X

CONCLUSION

*"Chekhov ranged through all the classes of Russia
in his portrayals and gently sketched the
weaknesses of all"*

S. Harcave

This study has demonstrated that Anton Pavlovich Chekhov was an agent for change and an iconoclast. This view stands as a revision to many popularly held views of Chekhov. It has shown that Chekhov carefully chose what he wrote about; that he exploded stereotypes and that he clearly stated the problems of Russian society in his stories. He felt that his readers would be moved to bring about change through individual initiative if they saw clearly what Russian problems really were.

Despite this, Chekhov did not support any ideology or party program which advocated revolution. The effectiveness of Chekhov's work can be seen in the way that he destroyed an important Russian myth. In 1897 Anton Chekhov exploded the century old myth of the Russian peasant and clarified the peasant question with the publication of his "The Peasants." Chekhov's perception of the problems, attitudes and the details of peasant life have been proved to be true. The publication of his views provoked immediate government censorship but it helped open the eyes of the Russian public and undoubtedly contributed to the spontaneous, broad-based revolution from below against the Tsar in 1905.

Influences on Chekhov in the Formulation of His Method

It has been demonstrated that Chekhov's medical education opened his mind and imprinted it with the scientific method. It is also clear that he was always fascinated by the experimental role of the discoverers who broke new paths. He was especially interested in Darwin, who provided one of the main planks in Chekhov's philosophy. Chekhov himself stated, "... There is no doubt in my mind that my study of medicine has had a serious impact on my literary activities." This

157

scientific background led him to refuse to enter areas he did not understand. The effect of Chekhov's acceptance of the scientific method was widely recognized by his critics and contemporaries.

This study has shown that Chekhov's crisp precise writing style reflected some aspects of his medical training. The writing of laboratory reports, papers, and case studies leave a mark on any student. This tendency toward bare-bones facts and clear, concise brevity is evident in Chekhov's style of writing. Because Chekhov was a physician, he was able to draw upon a wealth of material unavailable to another writer living in the same place and time.

The second major influence on Chekhov was his "mistress," literature. His literary studies and contributed greatly to the development of his personal method.

As this study indicated, Chekhov began his writing career writing short tales on a daily basis for humor magazines. Since he was allowed no more than 100 lines his style became extremely compressed. After graduating from medical school he began to take his writing more seriously. He came to the attention of some of the giants of the time and fell briefly under the influence of Tolstoi.

It has been seen that Chekhov took particular pleasure in and learned, from Tolstoi, Maupassant, Flaubert and Zola. Chekhov was, for a time (1886-87), under the influence of Tolstoi and his doctrine of non-resistance to evil which he abandoned as his own style and philosophy matured. Maupassant reinforced Chekhov's realistic representation of everyday life with an emphasis on details to show the various aspects of that life. Chekhov was so attracted to Flaubert's style as a short story writer that it influenced Chekhov's own short stories. On the other hand, Chekhov gravitated to Zola because of content and method, not style or structure as with Flaubert. Zola stressed scientific method, precise methods of observation and the reporting of the infinitesimal facts of reality. Flaubert aided Chekhov in his developing short story form and Zola reinforced Chekhov's own belief in the scientific method and a detailed representation of life. Zola stimulated Chekhov to write "The Peasants" and "In the Hollow" which reflect Zola's and Chekhov's common method.

Method

Having established these dominant influences on the formulation of Chekhov's method, this study examined that method in some detail. It was shown how by May 1886, Chekhov had become serious about his literary work and developed a method which he described to his brother, Aleksandr in the following terms: 1. an absence of lengthy verbiage of political, social, or economic nature; 2. total objectivity; 3. truthful descriptions of persons and objects; 4. extreme brevity; 5. audacity and originality: avoidance of stereotypes; 6. and finally compassion.

This author added to the above list Chekhov's formulation of images and his statement of problems. This investigation has revealed that Chekhov believed that there was much more to the act of writing than just a transfer from eye to paper, a mindless photographic exchange.

How Did Chekhov Choose His Topics and How Did He Formulate
His Impressions?

As a physician, Chekhov observed dispassionately the process of literary creation. He saw that it began with the posing of some questions or the stirring of some particular interest. As he said, "The artist observes, selects, guesses and synthesizes." Artistic creation is the result of quiet premeditation and purpose it does not come from "unthinking emotionality" as some populist critics had posited.

It has been learned that Chekhov could not conceive of being what one populist had called him, a "mindless giant" without a purpose. When the author "observes, selects, guesses and synthesizes," he does so with a question and purpose in mind.

This investigation of Chekhov has pointed out that he wrote only from memory, never "directly from observed life." "What I need is to have the subject filtered through memory, and that there should remain on it, as on a filter, only what is important or typical." In the process of responding to his initial question, the author filtered out what is typical; that is why Chekhov did not base his writing on one instance in life.

Because of the nature of this filtering process, Chekhov insisted that "It is bad for the artist to take on something he doesn't understand." The author ". . . must pass judgment only on what he understands . . ." In sum, the author must formulate his question, observe, and filter out the typical; but this is to be done only in areas where he has knowledge which will permit him to make informed judgments.

Method In "The Lesser Russian Tradition"

It has been established that Chekhov's method and motive was substantially different from the method and motive of the Populists, Reductionists and Orthodox Soviet authors. It has been noted that Chekhov, Nobakov and Pushkin followed the beat of a different drummer which came from the "biological sciences." These men were from "the lesser Russian tradition" that drew its method from the biological sciences. That tradition stressed "objective and independent literary art, not subservient to ideology, nationalism or religion." Chekhov said he did not write of "what can be" or "should be." He wrote "first of what exists."

Specific Points Of Method According To Chekhov: No Polemics

It has been established that Chekhov would not include a particular political point of view in his work. He said that he would ". . . have to limit" himself ". . . to descriptions of how" his ". . . heroes love, marry, give birth, die, and how they speak." "Us/We describe life as it is and stop dead right there . . ." Chekhov formulated clear statements of the problems. The reader was to supply the solutions.

Objectivity and Truth

It has been shown that Chekhov would not let the social canons of Victorian society color his work any more than he would let politics. For Chekhov, literature was an art because it portrayed life as it actually was. "Its aim is the truth, unconditional and honest." The author is not a cosmetician or entertainer. "He is a man bound by contract to his sense of duty and to his conscience," The author is duty bound, once he starts the job, to carry it through no matter how horrified he may be. He must overcome his squeamishness and soil his imagination with the grime of life. "He is just like any ordinary reporter." Just like the reporter, he cannot limit his topics to "high-minded ladies" and "honest men." "To a chemist, there is nothing impure on earth. The writer should be just as objective as the chemist; he should liberate himself from everyday subjectivity . . ." Chekhov clearly stressed objectivity and truth at the expense of any polemical tendency as a key element in his method. This belief in objectivity had its origin in the scientific and literary influences that molded him.

Brevity

This study explains that Chekhov's objectivity and lack of excess was reinforced by his extreme brevity. Chekhov felt that "Brevity is the sister of talent" and "the art of writing is the art of contracting." He exhorted people "to write well, i.e., briefly" while he characterized his skill as knowing ". . . how to talk briefly about big things." Chekhov combined something of his scientific approach with the writing style that he acquired during his humor magazine days. In order to be factual and brief, Chekhov virtually eliminated the beginning and middle of his stories and focused on the ending.

Audacity and Originality

This study maintains that Chekhov did not fit the realistic literary mold of the age; he was an impressionist. He belonged to the tradition of Realism, but he progressed beyond it. Gorkii said in a letter to Chekhov in 1900: "Do you know what you are doing? You are killing Realism and you will soon finish it off . . . This form has outlived its time – that is a fact?" Initially, Chekhov was moving back toward Pushkin who stressed rationality, objectivity and classical restraint. Chekhov's originality was immediately noticed by Tolstoi. "Chekhov created new forms of writing, completely new, in my opinion, to the entire world, the like of which I have encountered nowhere . . . . Chekhov has his own special form, like the impressionists." Tolstoi believed Chekhov worked as though he were a man daubing on canvas, using whatever paint was around, seemingly without selection. It seemed that none of it was related to the rest. However, if you stepped back a distance from the canvas and viewed it again, you would get an overall impression, an unchangeable picture of real life. Chekhov's portrayal of persons and events are the patches of color and individual strokes that make up the impressionist portrait. It is at this point that his choice of what to write about is critical. It is here that he chooses to create impressions of what he cares about.

Detail and Truth

This work has established that Chekhov's impressionism did not interfere with his objectivity or the truth of his representations of life. On the contrary, it focused his attention specifically on the individual details which made up these patches and lines. Following his own warnings, Chekhov tended to use patches and lines which he knew and understood. These patches united to give an impression of the entire society based on fact. If it were not for his focus, he might have been tempted to tamper with incidentals because details could be viewed as window dressing. These details are essential details to be developed truthfully, but in a literary style which makes this appear to have been casually, perhaps even "mindlessly," chosen.

This study demonstrated that details were critical to Chekhov and he followed his own model by truthfully representing people and objects. Chekhov's critics focused on his apparent fixation with minutiae and ignored the great social issues of the day. Only the Soviets recognized the importance of detail. This author is in agreement with them on this point and on their view of Chekhov as a positive force.

If there is one continuity in Chekhov, from his earliest stories through to his last, it may be in the truth of his detail. This is one of the great values of Chekhov. This author maintains that it was possible for Chekhov to incorporate both subjectivity and objectivity through the use of his impressionistic approach and his religious attention to detail.

Compassion

Chekhov's final point in his model was compassion. On the surface, cold and objective, one might not think of Chekhov as caring about people. This study maintains that compassion for Chekhov was his concern about the problems and condition of people in the society. Chekhov's compassion led him to choose the things he wrote about. He was also careful to focus on what he understood through experience, thus guaranteeing for Chekhov the truth of his portrayal. He would not color the truth of the facts to achieve his goal. He would not be subjective in that sense. Chekhov said "subjectivity is a terrible thing." Things ". . . must be examined like objects, like symptoms, with perfect objectivity . . ." Chekhov was objective in that he would not permit influences to force him to change the facts or details he portrayed. He wanted only the truth.

Choosing Problems To Write About Out Of Compassion (Concern)

One of the most significant points this study has been that Chekhov would not be subjective in the sense of advocating a specific ideology or party to solve problems, but he did accept demands that, "an artist approach his work con-sciously . . ." However, he warned about confusing two concepts: "the solution of a problem and the correct formulation of a problem." Only the second was required of the author. "Not a single problem is resolved . . ." by Tolstoi's great works, but because the problems in them are formulated correctly, they satisfy you completely. "The judge is required to formulate the questions correctly, but the decision is left to the jurors, each according to his own task." Chekhov might have concluded by saying "I rely entirely on the reader to add for himself the subjective elements which are lacking in the story." It has been shown that Chekhov would only write on things he knew about. Chekhov had to be knowledgeable about the topics he chose. He chose to write about the problems in society out of a sense of compassion. Chekhov believed that by painting a true impression, using his objective details, he would show the problems of Russian life for what they were. Once this was successfully accomplished, the readers could provide their own subjective contribution as to political, economic or social solutions through whatever means they deemed appropriate.

This author maintains that Chekhov's choice of topics was made with the purpose of provoking change in mind, yet he was objective in his detail and general impression. The patches of paint and the impression when one stepped back were all correct and objective. The face to be represented was, however, Chekhov's own choice, and this choice was influenced by his personal concerns.

What Were the Things Chekhov Cared About Which Led Him To the Topics He Examined in His Stories?

An analysis of his letters and all of his stories indicate he was concerned with: religion; political, artistic, and spiritual freedom; equality for all races and creeds; special devotion to equality for the peasantry, Jews and women; and personal action to achieve public good. He was particularly concerned about prejudice and ignorance, education, medical care, poverty, the quality of life of all classes and the establishment of a society, free from tyranny, under law. Because Chekhov was so deeply committed to these concerns he was impelled to write about them.

Chekhov's Views on Individuals Changing Things

Darwin and Zola had helped bring about change through changing the consciousness of individuals. This study has proved Chekhov intended to do the same. Chekhov's belief in individual initiative was strongly connected to his understanding that "Russia was rich in good people." Chekhov viewed Russia's salvation emerging from the actions of individuals such as peasants, intellectuals, and people drawn from all groups throughout the country. In Chekhov's vision, although such individuals were few in number and widely dispersed, they nevertheless played an inconspicuous, but important, role in society. "They do not dominate," he wrote, "yet their work is visible."

It has been shown that Chekhov saw the combined efforts of individuals creating a science which was moving inexorably forward. As a result, individuals' social consciousness was increasing and moral issues were coming to the fore. All this was being accomplished without the "intelligentsia en masse" and in spite of the other pressures of Russian society. The march of progress through the efforts of a broad base of individual acts would ultimately triumph rather than through the isolated acts of the revered intelligentsia.

Chekhov's Experience

In order to write effectively and accurately about a topic, an author must be thoroughly familiar with the subject matter. There is no doubt that Chekhov was thoroughly familiar with Russian life and society. Chekhov's knowledge came from others' experiences and his own experiences both at home and in his travels. Using Chekhov's letters this study presented a profile of Chekhov's travels which revealed the extent of his direct knowledge of Russia and the world. He knew Moscow and its surrounding provinces, he traveled through the Ukraine, the heart of old Russia, the cradle of Russian civilization and the heart of the black earth region. He traveled to St. Petersburg, the symbol of the Imperial era and hub of the Western-oriented intelligentsia. He journeyed to the south, to the Crimea and even through the mysterious Caucasus. He traveled through Siberia, the hope-filled frontier region of Russia and Sakhalin. He even briefly contacted Chinese civilization and the civilization of Ceylon. He had also traveled widely in key areas of Western civilization. Chekhov's experience and knowledge was at its greatest when dealing with Moscow and the country south through the Ukraine. It is in these regions that Chekhov casts most of his stories. All told the knowledge which Chekhov had at his disposal, through his experience, was very impressive and added depth and balance to his work.

Chekhov's Philosophy

A study of Chekhov's letters revealed Chekhov's personal philosophy on religion and politics. It is this author's view that Chekhov was a humanist who valued religion as a source of ethics and solace for the people. He rejected all political labels but his views were very similar to those of a Zemstvo liberal. Chekhov was also an individualist who believed in personal action to achieve good. He wanted freedom of the press, religion, thought, and assembly. He loved justice and supported trial by jury. He rejected racism, sexism and religious bigotry. These views caused him to subjectively choose to write about subjects which he, as a liberal, humanist, physician and writer, felt should be exposed objectively to public review.

Exploding the Myth of the Peasants

The problems of the peasant had weighed heavily on Russia but this study indicates nineteenth century Russian literature tended not to address the problem properly. Instead, the dominant image in literature was a romanticized view of the peasant as a Rousseauian noble savage. Tolstoi and Dostoevskii raised the image to the fullest in their novels. The image of the peasant was used to give a directionless intelligentsia a truth to guide them. This study proves that when

Chekhov's view of the peasants was published in 1897 it exploded the Tolstoian myth. The story "The Peasants" is a classic statement of one of Russia's problems, "the peasant problem." To educated Russia, this story as an "apparently innocent sketch, produced something of the effect of the child who pointed out that the Emperor had no clothes on."

Chekhov the Iconoclast

This study outlines Chekhov's two general descriptions of the peasantry. One is from the "inside" in "The Peasants" through the eyes of Olga, a tragically widowed peasant woman. The other is from the "outside" in "My Life," where a wealthy girl and her lover live a Tolstoian existence working the land on a country estate. The picture Chekhov painted was utterly human and as this study proved it was true. It did not owe its form to the 19th century folk myth that dominated literature until Chekhov shattered it.

This study juxtaposed Chekhov's views with scholarly analysis. Scholars generally support Chekhov's perceptions and this authors view of Chekhov's effect. Professor Donald Fanger of Harvard University believes that it is only with the appearance of Chekhov's "The Peasants" in 1897 that the myth of the peasant was broken. For Chekhov the peasants were not Rousseauian noble savages or Tolstoi's Christian examples, they were just people living in grinding poverty. A contemporary critic noted, "As the author presents the matter, not only learning from the people, but even teaching them appears almost impossible . . ." he continues by saying, "all these characters are represented as somehow rudely possessed by a life that gives neither time for reflection nor freedom for demonstrating anything except purely instinctive urges with unusually faint glimmerings of human reason."

It has been noted that Professor Fanger feels Tolstoi had painted the peasant existence for the sake of Christian examples, whereas Chekhov wrote as an expression of what is and nothing else. Chekhov killed the myth of the peasant with "The Peasants."

The response to Chekhov's exploding the century-long myth was immediate. In fact, it began before publication. On the strength of a report by a deputy censor, S. Sokolov, the entire censorship committee voted to cut the core of the ending out of "the Peasants." If Chekhov refused, the entire printing was to be confiscated. The full story appeared only later when it was published as part of a collection.

When it was published even in a censored form, Tolstoi was shocked and called the story "a sin against the common people." Chekhov "does not know his peasants." "The Peasants" shook the intelligentsia because many had idealized the peasants as something special for the same reasons as had the writers of the nineteenth century. In spite of the outrage by government and dissenting intellectuals alike, Chekhov's perceptions about the peasants and the other classes and institutions of Russian society were correct.

Even the censor's report on "The Peasants" did not claim Chekhov's perceptions were false. The censor felt Chekhov deserved special attention and he was censored because the picture he painted was too gloomy. For this reason, the Moscow Censorship Committee decided on April 3, 1897, to eliminate the summation at the end of "The Peasants." Even the censors could not deny Chekhov's truth. They could only suppress it.

The Facts of Peasant Life

The final stage of this study has established the objectivity and accuracy of Chekhov's perception of Russian life at the end of the nineteenth century. This was achieved by the direct comparison of the views of contemporary observers and scholarly opinion with Chekhov's perceptions of the conditions of life for the peasants, the wage workers, the new middle class, and the gentry. Chekhov's perceptions of the peasant villages south of Moscow and the general condition of life of the peasants were found to be correct. His description of the situation of the condition of women and Jews in Russian society was consistent with scholarly opinion. Chekhov's representation of the role of religion and the army in the people's lives proved to be true, as did his statement of the deteriorating conditions in agriculture at the turn of the century.

Chekhov's view of the poor urban workers and even of prostitutes proved to be consistent with scholarly opinion. His presentations on the middle class and the gentry proved to be equally correct. On the basis of this investigation it is correct to say that the stories of Anton Chekhov present an objective and accurate picture of Russian life in the late nineteenth century.

The social historian who wishes to portray the daily lives of turn of the century Russians, their social relations, and show the general quality of their lives would do well to draw on the work of Anton Chekhov. Chekhov does not give statistics on literacy rates, average class size, average age at death, or infant mortality rates. He does give a clear picture of the facts of peasant attitudes toward education and the quality and availability of education in villages. In health care he clearly outlines the problems of disease and the health care system, especially in the villages south of Moscow. One can gain an indelible picture of infant mortality and the relative size of the problem from his descriptions. Chekhov also gives an invaluable insight into lower-class attitudes. The social historian who wanted to show his students what Russian life was actually like would not err in using Chekhov's proven perceptions as a source. Above all, Chekhov smashed the myths and stereotypes of his own time.

BIBLIOGRAPHY

Works of Chekhov

Chekhov, Anton Pavlovich. *Anton Chekhov's Short Stories: Texts of the Stories, Backgrounds, Criticism.* Selected and edited by Ralph E. Matlaw. New York: W. W. Norton and Co., 1979.

——————————. *The Chorus girl and Other Stories.* Trans. Constance Garnett. London: Chatto and Windus, 1927.

——————————. *The Darling and Other Stories.* Trans. Constance Garnett. London: Chatto and Windus, 1921.

——————————. *The Duel and Other Stories.* Trans. Constance Garnett. London: Chatto and Windus, 1916.

——————————. *Letters of Anton Chekhov.* Trans. by Michael Henry Heim in collaboration with Simon Karlinsky. Selection, commentary and introduction by Simon Karlinsky. New York: Harper and Row, Publishers, 1973.

——————————. *Letters on the Short Story and Other Literary Topics by Anton Chekhov.* Ed. by Louis S. Friedland. New York: Dover Publications, Inc., 1966.

——————————. *Letters of Anton Chekhov.* Ed. Avrahm Yarmolinsky. Trans. Bernard Guilbert Guerney and Lynn Solotaroff. New York: Viking Press, 1973.

——————————. *Literaturnoe Nasledstvo.* V. V. Vinogradov et al eds. Vol. 68, Moscow, ISV. Akademiia Nauk U.S.S.R., 1960.

——————————. *The Oxford Chekhov.* Trans. and ed. Ronald Hingley. Oxford: Oxford University Press, 1978. 9 vols.

——————————. *The Party and Other Stories.* Trans. Constance Garnett. London: Chatto and Windus, 1925.

——————————. *Polnoe sobranie sochinenii i pisem A. P. Chekhova.* Under the general editorship of S. D. Balukhatyi, V. P. Potemkin, and N. S. Tikhanov. Moscow, Goslitizdat 1944- 1951. 20 vols.

——————————. *The Portable Chekhov.* Ed. Avrahm Yarmolinsky. New York: Viking Press, 1968.

——————————. "Protokol sudebño-meditsinskigo vskrytiia" (studentcheskaia rabota Chekhov): in *Sbornik dokumentov i materialov.* Edited by Abrahm B. Derman. Moscow, 1947.

——————————. *The Schoolmaster and Other Stories.* Trans. Constance Garnett. London: Chatto and Windus, 1921.

——————————. *Select Tales of Tchehov.* Trans. Constance Garnett. London: Chatto and Windus, 1967. 2 vols.

——————————. *Selected Stories.* Trans. Ann Dunningham. With a Foreword by Ernest J. Simmons. New York: The New American Library, 1960.

——————————. *Selected Works.* Vol. 1: Stories. Moscow: Progress Publishers, 1973.

——————————. *The Wife and Other Stories.* Trans. Constance Garnett. London: Chatto and Windus, 1918.

Sources Consulted

Adams, Arthur E.   "Robedonostev and the Rule of Firmness," *The Slavonic and East European Review* 32 (December, 1953): 132-139.

Berlin, Isaiah.   Introduction to *Roots of the Revolution,* by Franco Vernturi. New York: Alfred A. Knopf, 1960.

Bialyi, G. A.   "Iumoristicheski rasskazy A. P. Chekhov," in *Isv. Akademiia Nauk U. S. S. R.* Otd. lit. i iaz. Vol. 13, Vyp. 4, (1954): 305-316.

Bill, Valentine.   *The Forgotten Class: the Russian Bourgeoisie from the Earliest Beginnings to 1900.* New York: Frederick A. Praeger, Publishers, 1959.

Black, Cyril E.   "The Nature of Imperial Russian Society," *Slavic Review* 20 (December, 1961): 574-582.

Black, Cyril E., ed.   *The Transformation of Russian Society: Aspects of Social Change since 1861.* Cambridge, Mass.: Harvard University Press, 1960.

Blackwell, William L.   *The Industrialization of Russia: An Historical Perspective.* New York: Thomas Y. Crowell Co., 1970.

Blum, Jerome.   *Lord and Peasant in Russia from the Ninth to the Nineteenth Century.* New York: Atheneum, 1964.

Bruford, W. H.   *Chekhov and His Russia: A Sociological Study.* Hamden, Conn.: Archon Books, 1971.

Chizhevsky, Dimitri.   "Chekhov in the Development of Russian Literature," in *Chekhov: A Collection of Critical Essays,* pp. 49-61. Edited by Robert Louis Jackson. Englewood Cliffs: Prentice-Hall, 1967.

Chlenov, M. A. "A. P. Chekhov i meditsina," in *Russkie vedomosti*, (1906), no. 1.

Chudakov, A. P. *Poetika Chekhova*. Moscow, 1971.

Chukovskii, Kornei. *Chekhov, the Man*. Translated by Pauline Rose. London: Hutchinson, 1945.

——————————. *O. Chekhove*. Moscow, 1967.

Curtiss, John S, "The Peasant and the Army," in *The Peasant in Nineteenth-Century Russia*, pp. 108-132. Edited by Wayne Vucinich. Stanford: Stanford University Press, 1968.

Davie, D., ed. *Russian Literature and Modern English Fiction*. Chicago: The University of Chicago Press, 1965.

Derman, A. B. *O Masterstve Chekhov*. Moscow, 1959.

Dmytryshyn, Basil, ed. *Imperial Russia: A Source Book, 1700-1917*. New York: Holt, Rinehart and Winston, Inc., 1967.

Dunham, Vera S. "The Strong-Woman Motif" in *The Transformation of Russian Society: Aspects of Social Change since 1861*. Edited by Cyril E. Black. Cambridge, Mass.: Harvard University Press, 1960.

Eekman, T., ed. *Anton Chekhov, 1860-1960: Some Essays*. Leiden: E. J. Brill, 1960.

Ehrenburg, Ilya. *Chekhov, Stendahl, and Other Essays*. Edited by Harrison E. Salisbury. New York: Alfred A. Knopf, 1963.

Eichenbaum, Boris. "Chekhov at Large," in *Chekhov: A Collection of Critical Essays*, pp. 21-31. Edited by Robert Louis Jackson. Englewood Cliffs: Prentice-Hall, Inc., 1967.

——————————. "O Chekhove" in *Zvezda* 5-6 (1944): 75-79.

Fanger, Donald. "The Peasant in Literature" in *The Peasant in Nineteenth-Century Russia*, pp. 231-262. Edited by Wayne Vucinich. Stanford: Stanford University Press, 1968.

Field, Daniel. *Rebels in the Name of the Tsar*. Boston: Houghton Mifflin Co., 1976.

Fischer, George. "The Intelligentsia and Russia" in *The Transformation of Russian Society*, pp. 253-273. edited by Cyril E. Black. Cambridge, Mass.: Harvard University Press, 1960.

——————————. *Russian Liberalism*. Cambridge, Mass.: Harvard University Press, 1958.

Gerschenkron, Alexander. "Agrarian Policies and Industrialization, Russia, 1861-1917" in *Cambridge Economic History of Europe*, Vol. 6, pt. 2: 712-713.

——————————. "Problems and Patterns of Russian Economic Development," in *The Transformation of Russian Society: Aspects of Social Change since 1861*, pp. 42-71. Edited by Cyril E. Black. Cambridge, Mass.: Harvard University Press, 1960.

Gilles, Daniel. *Chekhov: Observer without Illusion.* Translated by Charles Lam Markmann. New York: Funk and Wagnalls, 1968.

Gitovich, N. I. *Letopis Zhizni i tvorchestva A. P. Chekhova.* Moscow, 1955.

Glickman, Rose and Stites, Richard, eds. *Women in Nineteenth- Century Russia.*

Gliksman, Jerry. "The Russian Urban Worker" in *The Transformation of Russian Society: Aspects of Social Change since 1861,* pp. 311-322. Edited by Cyril E. Black. Cambridge, Mass.: Harvard University Press, 1960.

Gorky, Maxim. "Fragments from Reminiscences" from *On Literature,* pp. 32-42 in *Chekhov: A Collection of Critical Essays,* pp. 125-205. Edited by Robert Louis Jackson. Englewood Cliffs: Prentice-Hall, Inc., 1967.

——————————. *On Literature* in *Anton Chekhov's Short Stories.* Edited by Ralph E. Matlaw. New York: W. W. Norton and Co., 1979.

Grossman, Leonid. "The Naturalism of Chekhov," in *Chekhov: A Collection of Critical Essays,* pp. 32-48. Edited by Robert Louis Jackson. Englewood Cliffs: Prentice-Hall, Inc., 1967.

Haimson, Leopold H. "The Parties and the State: the Evolution of Political Attitudes" in *The Transformation of Russian Society: Aspects of Social Change since 1861,* pp. 110-144. Edited by Cyril E. Black. Cambridge, Mass.: Harvard University Press, 1960.

Harcave, Sidney, ed. *Readings in Russian History,* vol. 2. New York: Thomas Y. Crowell Co., 1962.

——————————. *Russia: A History.* 6th edition. Philadelphia: J. B. Lippincott, 1968.

Haxthausen, Baron von. *The Russian Empire: Its People, Institutions, and Resources.* Translated by Robert Faire. London: Chapman and Hall, 1856. 2 vols.

Hingley, Ronald. *Chekhov: A Biographical and Critical Study.* New York: Barnes and Noble, Inc., 1966.

——————————. *Russian Writers and Society, 1825-1904.* New York: McGraw-Hill Book Co., 1967.

Jackson, Robert Louis, ed. *Chekhov: A Collection of Critical Essays.* Englewood Cliffs: Prentice-Hall, Inc., 1967.

——————————. "Introduction: Perspectives on Chekhov" in *Chekhov: A Collection of Critical Essays,* pp. 1-20. Edited by Robert Louis Jackson. Englewood Cliffs: Prentice-Hall, Inc., 1967.

Johnson, William H. E. *Russia's Educational Heritage.* New Brunswick, 1950.

Karlinsky, Simon. "Nabokov and Chekhov: the Lesser Russian Tradition." *Tri-Quarterly* (Winter, 1970): 7-16.

Karpovich, Michael. *Imperial Russia, 1801-1917.* New York: Holt, Rinehart and Winston, 1960.

——————————. "Two Types of Russian Liberalism: Maklahov and Miliukov," in *Readings in Russian History*, vol. 2, pp. 91-104. Edited by Sidney Harcave. New York: Thomas Y. Crowell Co., 1962.

Katsell, Jerome H. *The Potential for Growth and Change: Chekhov's Mature Prose, 1881-1903*. Ph. D. Dissertation, University of California at Los Angeles, 1972; Ann Arbor, University Microfilms, International, 1972.

Kramer, Karl D. *The Chameleon and the Dream: the Image of Reality in Cekhov's Stories*. The Hague: Mouton, 1970.

LeRoy-Beaulieu, Anatole. *The Empire of the Tsars and the Russians*. Translated from the third French edition by Zenaide A. Ragozin. New York: G. P. Putnam's Sons, 1893- 1903. 3 vols.

Lindsey, Byron T. *Early Chekhov: Development of Character and Meaning in the Short Stories, 1880-1887*. Ph. D. dissertation, Cornell University, 1975: Ann Arbor, Xerox University Microfilms, 1975.

Lyaschensko, P. *History of the National Economy of Russia to the 1917 Revolution*. New York. 1949.

Maiakovskii, Vladimir. "Dva Chekhova," in *Polno Sobranie Sochienenii*, Vol. 50, pp. 294-300. Moscow, 1955.

Matlaw, Ralph A. "Chekhov and the Novel," in *Anton Chekhov, 1860-1960: Some Essays*, pp. 148-167. Edited by T. Eekman. Leiden, E. J. Brill, 1960.

Matossian, Mary. "The Peasant Way of Life," in *The Peasant in Nineteenth-Century Russia*, pp. 1-40. Edited by Wayne Vucinich. Stanford: Stanford University Press, 1968.

Maynard, John, *Russia in Flux*. New York: Collier Books, 1964.

——————————. *The Russian Peasant and Other Studies*. With a Foreword by Ernest Barker. New York: Collier Books, 1962.

Mehnert, Klaus. "Changing Attitudes of Russian Youth" in *The Transformation of Russian Society: Aspects of Social Change since 1861*, pp. 496-514. Edited by Cyril E. Black. Cambridge, Mass.: Harvard University Press, 1960.

Meve, E. V. *Meditsina v tvorchestve i zhini A. P. Chekhova*. Kiev: GMIz, 1961.

Miller, Wright. *The Russians as People*. New York, 1961.

Mirsky, D. D. "Chekhov and the English" in *Russian Literature and Modern English Fiction*. Edited by D. Davie. Chicago: The University of Chicago Press, 1965.

——————————. *A History of Russia*. New York: Alfred A. Knopf, 1949. 2 vols.

Myshkovskaia, L. *Chekhov i iumoristicheskie zhurnaly 80-Kh godov*. Moscow, 1929.

Pavlovsky, G. *Agricultural Russia on the Eve of the Revolution.* London, 1930.

Pushkarev, Sergei. *The Emergence of Modern Russia, 1801-1917.* Translated by Robert H. McNeal and Tova Yedlin. New York: Holt, Rinehart and Winston, 1963.

Rappoport, A. S. *Home Life in Russia.* New York: The Macmillan Co., 1913.

Rayfield, Donald. *Chekhov: The Evolution of His Art.* New York: Barnes and Noble, 1975.

Redfield, Robert. *The Little community and Peasant Society and Culture.* Chicago: The University of Chicago Press, 1960.

Reshetar, John S. "Russian Ethnic Values" in *The Transformation of Russian Society: Aspects of Social Change since 1861,* pp. 559-573. Edited by Cyril E. Black. Cambridge, Mass.: Harvard University Press, 1960.

Riasanovsky, Nicholas V. *A History of Russia.* 2nd edition. New York: Oxford University Press, 1969.

Robinson, G. T. *Rural Russia under the Old Regime.* Berkeley: University of California Press, 1969.

Roskin, A. "Notes on Chekhov's Realism," in *Literaturny i kritik,* no. 7 (1939): 58-77.

Shestov, Leon. *Chekhov and Other Essays.* New introduction by Sidney Monas. Ann Arbor, The University of Michigan Press, 1966.

Simmons, Ernest J. *Chekhov: A Biography.* Boston: Little, Brown and Co., 1962; Chicago: University of Chicago Press, 1970.

—————————, ed. *Continuity and Change in Russian and Soviet Thought.* With an introduction by Ernest J. Simmons. Cambridge, Mass.: Harvard University Press, 1955.

—————————. *Introduction to Russian Realism.* Bloomington: Indiana University Press, 1965.

—————————, ed. *Through the Glass of Soviet Literature: Views of Russian Society.* With an Introduction by Ernest J. Simmons. New York: Columbia University Press, 1961.

Skabichevskii, A. M. *Sochineniia,* pp. 933-936. St. Petersburg, 1903. Quoted in Byron T. Lindsey, *Early Chekhov: Development of Character and Meaning in the Short Stories, 1880-1887.* Ph. D. dissertation, Cornell University, 1975. Ann Arbor, Xerox University Microfilms, 1975.

Skerpan, Alfred A. "The Russian National Economy and Emancipation" in *Essays in Russian History: A Collection Dedicated to George Vernadsky,* pp. 161-230. Edited by Alan D. Ferguson and Alfred Levin. Hamden, Conn.: Archon Books, 1964.

Slonim, Marc. *An Outline of Russian Literature.* New York: Oxford University Press, 1958.

Stites, Richard. *The Women's Liberation Movement in Russia: Feminism, Nihilism, and Bolshevism, 1860-1930.* Princeton, Princeton University Press, 1978.

Toumanova, Nina A. *Anton Chekhov, the Voice of Twilight Russia.* Ph. D. dissertation. New York: Columbia University, 1937.

Treadgold, Donald W. *The Great Siberian Migration.* Princeton: Princeton University Press, 1957.

———————————. "The Peasant and Religion" in *The Peasant in Nineteenth-Century Russia*, pp. 72-107. Edited by Wayne Vucinich. Stanford: Stanford University Press, 1968.

Vakar, Nicholas. *The Taproot of Soviet Society.* New York, Harper and Row, 1961.

Volin, Lazar. "The Russian Peasant: From Emancipation to Kolkhoz" in *The Transformation of Russian Society: Aspects of Social Change since 1861*, pp. 292-310. Edited by Cyril E. Black. Cambridge, Mass.: Harvard University Press, 1960.

Von Laue, Theodore H. "A Secret Memorandum of Sergei Witte on the Industrialization of Imperial Russia," *The Journal of Modern History* 26 (March, 1954): 60-74.

———————————. *Sergei Witte and the Industrialization of Russia.* New York: Columbia University Press, 1963; Atheneum, 1969.

Vucinich, Alexander. "The State and the Local Community" in *The Transformation of Russian Society: Aspects of Social Change since 1861*, pp. 191-208. Ed. Cyril E. Black. Cambridge, Mass.: Harvard University Press, 1960.

Wallace, Sir Donald MacKenzie. *Russia.* New York: Henry Holt and Co., 1905.

Watters, Francis M. "The Peasant and the Village Commune" in *The Peasants in Nineteenth-Century Russia*, pp. 133-157. Ed. by Wayne Vucinich. Stanford: Stanford University Press, 1968.

Williams, R. H. *Russia of the Russians.* London: Charles Scribner's Sons, 1917.

Wolf, Eric. *Peasants.* Englewood Cliffs: Prentice-Hall, Inc., 1966.
　　Yermilov, Vladimir. *Anton Pavlovich Chekhov.* Translated by Ivy Litvinov. Moscow: Foreign Language Publishing House, n.d.

Zelnik, Reginald E. "The Peasant and the Factory" in *The Peasant in Nineteenth-Century Russia*, pp. 158-190. Ed. Wayne Vucinich. Stanford: Stanford University Press, 1968.